THE PROMISE OF
Peace

ELLEN G. WHITE

Design Copyright © 2018 by Typo Fire

First printing, 2018

Sunset and tree cover design by Ariel Warren
Mountains and lake cover design by Robert Koorenny
Layout Design by Ariel Warren
Copy edited by Arlene Clark

Type set: 10.75 pt. Minion Pro

All images used are not restricted by licensing and no attribution is required.

Published by Typo Fire, www.typofire.com
Printed in the U.S.A.

White, Ellen G., 1827-1915
    The Promise of Peace

ISBN 13: 978-0-9851702-2-6

Contents

1. Why Was Sin Permitted 4

2. The Creation 10

3. The Temptation and Fall 14

4. The Plan of Redemption 21

5. Satan's Enmity Against the Law 25

6. The Tabernacle and Its Services 31

7. God With Us 38

8. As A Child 44

9. The Baptism 49

10. The Temptation 51

11. The Victory 56

12. At the Marriage Feast 59

13. The Sermon On the Mount 64

14. The Sabbath 72

15. The Feast At Simon's House 77

16. Let Not Your Heart Be Troubled 83

17. Gethsemane 92

18. Before Annas and the Court of Caiaphas 97

19. In Pilate's Judgment Hall 105

20. Calvary 114

21. It Is Finished 124

22. In Joseph's Tomb 128

23. The Lord Is Risen 134

24. To My Father, and Your Father 140

Why Was Sin Permitted?

. . . .

"God is love." 1 John 4:16. His nature, His law, is love. It ever has been; it ever will be. "The high and lofty One that inhabiteth eternity," whose "ways are everlasting," changeth not. With Him "is no variableness, neither shadow of turning." Isaiah 57:15; Habakkuk 3:6; James 1:17.

Every manifestation of creative power is an expression of infinite love. The sovereignty of God involves fullness of blessing to all created beings. The psalmist says:

> "Strong is Thy hand, and high is Thy right hand.
> Righteousness and judgment are
> the foundation of Thy throne:
> Mercy and truth go before Thy face.
> Blessed is the people that
> know the joyful sound:
> They walk, O Lord, in the light
> of Thy countenance.
> In Thy name do they rejoice all the day:
> And in Thy righteousness are they exalted.
> For Thou art the glory of their strength: …
> For our shield belongeth unto Jehovah,
> And our king to the Holy One."
>   Psalm 89:13–18, RV.*

The history of the great conflict between good and evil, from the time it first began in heaven to the final overthrow of rebellion and the total eradication of sin, is also a demonstration of God's unchanging love.

---

* In this text and in some other Bible quotations used in this book the word "Jehovah" is employed instead of "Lord," as rendered in the American Supplement to the Revised Version.

The Sovereign of the universe was not alone in His work of beneficence. He had an associate—a co-worker who could appreciate His purposes, and could share His joy in giving happiness to created beings. "In the beginning was the Word, and the Word was with God, and the Word was God. The same was in the beginning with God." John 1:1, 2. Christ, the Word, the only begotten of God, was one with the eternal Father—one in nature, in character, in purpose—the only being that could enter into all the counsels and purposes of God. "His name shall be called Wonderful, Counselor, The mighty God, The everlasting Father, The Prince of Peace." Isaiah 9:6. His "goings forth have been from of old, from everlasting." Micah 5:2. And the Son of God declares concerning Himself: "The Lord possessed Me in the beginning of His way, before His works of old. I was set up from everlasting. …When He appointed the foundations of the earth: then I was by Him, as one brought up with Him: and I was daily His delight, rejoicing always before Him." Proverbs 8:22–30.

The Father wrought by His Son in the creation of all heavenly beings. "By Him were all things created, … whether they be thrones, or dominions, or principalities, or powers: all things were created by Him, and for Him." Colossians 1:16. Angels are God's ministers, radiant with the light ever flowing from His presence and speeding on rapid wing to execute His will. But the Son, the anointed of God, the "express image of His person," "the brightness of His glory," "upholding all things by the word of His power," holds supremacy over them all. Hebrews 1:3. "A glorious high throne from the beginning," was the place of His sanctuary (Jeremiah 17:12); "a scepter of righteousness," the scepter of His kingdom (Hebrews 1:8). "Honor and majesty are before Him: strength and beauty are in His sanctuary." Psalm 96:6. Mercy and truth go before His face (Psalm 89:14).

The law of love being the foundation of the government of God, the happiness of all intelligent beings depends upon their perfect accord with its great principles of righteousness. God desires from all His creatures the service of love—service that springs from an appreciation of His character. He takes no pleasure in a forced obedience; and to all He grants freedom of will, that they may render Him voluntary service.

So long as all created beings acknowledged the allegiance of love, there was perfect harmony throughout the universe of God. It was the joy of the heavenly host to fulfill the purpose of their Creator. They delighted in reflecting His glory and showing forth His praise. And while love to God was supreme, love for one another was confiding and unselfish. There was no note of discord to mar the celestial harmonies. But a change came over this happy state. There was one who perverted the freedom that God had granted to His creatures. Sin originated with him who, next to Christ, had been most honored of God and was highest in power and glory among the inhabitants of heaven. Lucifer, "son of the morning," was first of the covering cherubs, holy and undefiled. He stood in the presence of the great Creator, and the ceaseless beams of glory enshrouding the eternal God rested upon him. "Thus saith the Lord God; Thou sealest up the sum, full of wisdom, and perfect in beauty. Thou hast been in Eden the garden of God; every precious stone was thy covering. … Thou art the anointed cherub that covereth; and I have set thee so: thou wast upon the holy mountain of God; thou hast walked up and down in the midst of the stones of fire. Thou wast perfect in thy ways from the day that thou wast created, till iniquity was found in thee." Ezekiel 28:12–15.

Little by little Lucifer came to indulge the desire for self-exaltation. The Scripture says, "Thine heart was lifted up because of thy beauty, thou hast corrupted thy wisdom by reason of thy brightness." Ezekiel 28:17. "Thou hast said in thine heart, … I will exalt my throne above the stars of God. … I will be like the Most High." Isaiah 14:13, 14. Though all his glory was from God, this mighty angel came to regard it as pertaining to himself. Not content with his position, though honored above the heavenly host, he ventured to covet homage due alone to the Creator. Instead of seeking to make God supreme

Satan's rebellion was to be a lesson to the universe through all coming ages—a perpetual testimony to the nature of sin and its terrible results.

in the affections and allegiance of all created beings, it was his endeavor to secure their service and loyalty to himself. And coveting the glory with which the infinite Father had invested His Son, this prince of angels aspired to power that was the prerogative of Christ alone.

Now the perfect harmony of heaven was broken. Lucifer's disposition to serve himself instead of his Creator aroused a feeling of apprehension when observed by those who considered that the glory of God should be supreme. In heavenly council the angels pleaded with Lucifer. The Son of God presented before him the greatness, the goodness, and the justice of the Creator, and the sacred, unchanging nature of His law. God Himself had established the order of heaven; and in departing from it, Lucifer would dishonor his Maker and bring ruin upon himself. But the warning, given in infinite love and mercy, only aroused a spirit of resistance. Lucifer allowed his jealousy of Christ to prevail, and became the more determined.

To dispute the supremacy of the Son of God, thus impeaching the wisdom and love of the Creator, had become the purpose of this prince of angels. To this object he was about to bend the energies of that master mind, which, next to Christ's, was first among the hosts of God. But He who would have the will of all His creatures free, left none unguarded to the bewildering sophistry by which rebellion would seek to justify itself. Before the great contest should open, all were to have a clear presentation of His will, whose wisdom and goodness were the spring of all their joy.

The King of the universe summoned the heavenly hosts before Him, that in their presence He might set forth the true position of His Son and show the relation He sustained to all created beings. The Son of God shared the Father's throne, and the glory of the eternal, self-existent One encircled both. About the throne gathered the holy angels, a vast, unnumbered throng—"ten thousand times ten thousand, and thousands of thousands" (Revelation 5:11), the most exalted angels, as ministers and subjects, rejoicing in the light that fell upon them from the presence of the Deity. Before the assembled inhabitants of heaven the King declared that none but Christ, the Only Begotten of God, could fully enter into His purposes, and to Him it was committed to execute the mighty counsels of His will. The Son of God had wrought the Father's will in the creation of all the hosts of heaven; and to Him, as well as to God, their homage and allegiance were due. Christ was still to exercise divine power, in the creation of the earth and its inhabitants. But in all this He would not seek power or exaltation for Himself contrary to God's plan, but would exalt the Father's glory and execute His purposes of beneficence and love.

The angels joyfully acknowledged the supremacy of Christ, and prostrating themselves before Him, poured out their love and adoration. Lucifer bowed with them, but in his heart there was a strange, fierce conflict. Truth, justice, and loyalty were struggling against envy and jealousy. The influence of the holy angels seemed for a time to carry him with them. As songs of praise ascended in melodious strains, swelled by thousands of glad voices, the spirit of evil seemed vanquished; unutterable love thrilled his entire being; his soul went out, in harmony with the sinless worshippers, in love to the Father and the Son. But again he was filled with pride in his own glory. His desire for supremacy returned, and envy of Christ was once more indulged. The high honors conferred upon Lucifer were not appreciated as God's special gift, and therefore, called forth no gratitude to his Creator. He gloried in his brightness and exaltation and aspired to be equal with God. He was beloved and reverenced by the heavenly host, angels delighted to execute his commands, and he was clothed with wisdom and glory above them all. Yet the Son of God was exalted above him, as one in power and authority with the Father. He shared the Father's counsels, while Lucifer did not thus enter into the purposes of God. "Why," questioned this mighty angel, "should Christ have the supremacy? Why is He honored above Lucifer?"

Leaving his place in the immediate presence of the Father, Lucifer went forth to diffuse the spirit of discontent among the angels. He worked with mysterious secrecy, and for a time concealed his real purpose under an appearance of reverence for God. He began to insinuate doubts concerning the laws that governed heavenly beings, intimating that though laws might be necessary for the inhabitants of the worlds, angels, being more exalted, needed no such restraint, for their own wisdom was a sufficient guide. They were not beings that could bring dishonor to God; all their thoughts were holy; it was no more possible for them than for God Himself to err. The exaltation of the Son of God as equal with the Father was represented as an injustice to Lucifer, who, it was claimed, was also entitled to reverence and honor. If this prince of angels could but attain to his true, exalted position, great good would accrue to the entire host of heaven; for it was his object to secure freedom for all. But now even the liberty which they had hitherto enjoyed was at an end; for an absolute Ruler had been appointed them, and to His authority all must pay homage. Such were the subtle deceptions that through the wiles of Lucifer were fast obtaining in the heavenly courts.

There had been no change in the position or authority of Christ. Lucifer's envy and misrepresentation and his claims to equality with Christ had made necessary a statement of the true position of the Son of God; but this had been the same from the beginning. Many of the angels were, however, blinded by Lucifer's deceptions.

Taking advantage of the loving, loyal trust reposed in him by the holy beings under his command, he had so artfully instilled into their minds his own distrust and discontent that his agency was not discerned. Lucifer had presented the purposes of God in a false light—misconstruing and distorting them to excite dissent and dissatisfaction. He cunningly drew his hearers on to give utterance to their feelings; then these expressions were repeated by him when it would serve his purpose, as evidence that the angels were not fully in harmony with the government of God. While claiming for himself perfect loyalty to God, he urged that changes in the order and laws of heaven were necessary for the stability of the divine government. Thus while working to excite opposition to the law of God and to instill his own discontent into the minds of the angels under him, he was ostensibly seeking to remove dissatisfaction and to reconcile disaffected angels to the order of heaven. While secretly fomenting discord and rebellion, he with consummate craft caused it to appear as his sole purpose to promote loyalty and to preserve harmony and peace.

The spirit of dissatisfaction thus kindled was doing its baleful work. While there was no open outbreak, division of feeling imperceptibly grew up among the angels. There were some who looked with favor upon Lucifer's insinuations against the government of God. Although they had heretofore been in perfect harmony with the order which God had established, they were now discontented and unhappy because they could not penetrate His unsearchable counsels; they were dissatisfied with His purpose in exalting Christ. These stood ready to second Lucifer's demand for equal authority with the Son of God. But angels who were loyal and true maintained the wisdom and justice of the divine decree and endeavored to reconcile this disaffected being to the will of God. Christ was the Son of God; He had been one with Him before the angels were called into existence. He had ever stood at the right hand of the Father; His supremacy, so full of blessing to all who came under its benignant control, had not heretofore been questioned. The harmony of heaven had never been interrupted; wherefore should there now be discord? The loyal angels could see only terrible consequences from this dissension, and with earnest entreaty they counseled the disaffected ones to renounce their purpose and prove themselves loyal to God by fidelity to His government.

In great mercy, according to His divine character, God bore long with Lucifer. The spirit of discontent and disaffection had never before been known in heaven. It was a new element, strange, mysterious, unaccountable. Lucifer himself had not at first been acquainted with the real nature of his feelings; for a time he had feared to express the workings and imaginings of his mind; yet he did not dismiss them. He did not see whither he was drifting. But such efforts as infinite love and wisdom only could devise, were made to convince him of his error. His disaffection was proved to be without cause, and he was made to see what would be the result of persisting in revolt. Lucifer was convinced that he was in the wrong. He saw that "the Lord is righteous in all His ways, and holy in all His works" (Psalm 145:17); that the divine statutes are just, and that he ought to acknowledge them as such before all heaven. Had he done this, he might have saved himself and many angels. He had not at that time fully cast off his allegiance to God. Though he had left his position as covering cherub, yet if he had been willing to return to God, acknowledging the Creator's wisdom, and satisfied to fill the place appointed him in God's great plan, he would have been reinstated in his office. The time had come for a final decision; he must fully yield to the divine sovereignty or place himself in open rebellion. He nearly reached the decision to return, but pride forbade him. It was too great a sacrifice for one who had been so highly honored to confess that he had been in error, that his imaginings were false, and to yield to the authority which he had been working to prove unjust.

A compassionate Creator, in yearning pity for Lucifer and his followers, was seeking to draw them back from the abyss of ruin into which they were about to plunge. But His mercy was misinterpreted. Lucifer pointed to the long-suffering of God as an evidence of his own superiority, an indication that the King of the universe would yet accede to his terms. If the angels would stand firmly with him, he declared, they could yet gain all that they desired. He persistently defended his own course, and fully committed himself to the great controversy against his Maker. Thus it was that Lucifer, "the light bearer," the sharer of God's glory, the attendant of His throne, by transgression became Satan, "the adversary" of God and holy beings and the destroyer of those whom heaven had committed to his guidance and guardianship.

Rejecting with disdain the arguments and entreaties of the loyal angels, he denounced them as deluded slaves. The preference shown to Christ he declared an act of injustice both to himself and to all the heavenly host, and announced that he would no longer submit to this invasion of his rights and theirs. He would never again acknowledge the supremacy of Christ. He had determined to claim the honor which should have been given him, and take command of all who would become his followers; and he promised those who would enter his ranks a new and better government, under which all would enjoy freedom. Great numbers of the angels signified their purpose to accept him as their leader. Flattered by the favor with which his advances were received, he hoped to win all the angels to his side, to become equal with God Himself, and to be obeyed by the entire host of heaven.

Still the loyal angels urged him and his sympathizers to submit to God; and they set before them the inevitable result should they refuse: He who had created them could overthrow their power and signally punish their rebellious daring. No angel could successfully oppose the law of God,

> *A compassionate Creator, in yearning pity for Lucifer and his followers, was seeking to draw them back from the abyss of ruin into which they were about to plunge.*

which was as sacred as Himself. They warned all to close their ears against Lucifer's deceptive reasoning, and urged him and his followers to seek the presence of God without delay and confess the error of questioning His wisdom and authority.

Many were disposed to heed this counsel, to repent of their disaffection, and seek to be again received into favor with the Father and His Son. But Lucifer had another deception ready. The mighty revolter now declared that the angels who had united with him had gone too far to return; that he was acquainted with the divine law, and knew that God would not forgive. He declared that all who should submit to the authority of heaven would be stripped of their honor, degraded from their position. For himself, he was determined never again to acknowledge the authority of Christ. The only course remaining for him and his followers, he said, was to assert their liberty, and gain by force the rights which had not been willingly accorded them.

So far as Satan himself was concerned, it was true that he had now gone too far to return. But not so with those who had been blinded by his deceptions. To them the counsel and entreaties of the loyal angels opened a door of hope;

*I*t was necessary
for his plans to be
fully developed, that
their true nature
and tendency might
be seen by all.

and had they heeded the warning, they might have broken away from the snare of Satan. But pride, love for their leader, and the desire for unrestricted freedom were permitted to bear sway, and the pleadings of divine love and mercy were finally rejected.

God permitted Satan to carry forward his work until the spirit of disaffection ripened into active revolt. It was necessary for his plans to be fully developed, that their true nature and tendency might be seen by all. Lucifer, as the anointed cherub, had been highly exalted; he was greatly loved by the heavenly beings, and his influence over them was strong. God's government included not only the inhabitants of heaven, but of all the worlds that He had created; and Lucifer had concluded that if he could carry the angels of heaven with him in rebellion, he could carry also all the worlds. He had artfully presented his side of the question, employing sophistry and fraud to secure his objects. His power to deceive was very great. By disguising himself in a cloak of falsehood, he had gained an advantage. All his acts were so clothed with mystery that it was difficult to disclose to the angels the true nature of his work. Until fully developed, it could not be made to appear the evil thing it was; his disaffection would not be seen to be rebellion. Even the loyal angels could not fully discern his character or see to what his work was leading.

Lucifer had at first so conducted his temptations that he himself stood uncommitted. The angels whom he could not bring fully to his side, he accused of indifference to the interests of heavenly beings. The very work which he himself was doing, he charged upon the loyal angels. It was his policy to perplex with subtle arguments concerning the purposes of God. Everything that was simple he shrouded in mystery, and by artful perversion cast doubt upon the plainest statements of Jehovah. And his high position, so closely connected with the divine government, gave greater force to his representations.

God could employ only such means as were consistent with truth and righteousness. Satan could use what God could not—flattery and deceit. He had sought to falsify the word of God and had misrepresented His plan of government, claiming that God was not just in imposing laws upon the angels; that in requiring submission and obedience from His creatures, He was seeking merely the exaltation of Himself. It was therefore necessary to demonstrate before the inhabitants of heaven, and of all the worlds, that God's government is just, His law perfect. Satan had made it appear that he himself was seeking to promote the good of the universe. The true character of the usurper and his real object must be understood by all. He must have time to manifest himself by his wicked works.

The discord which his own course had caused in heaven, Satan charged upon the government of God. All evil he declared to be the result of the divine administration. He claimed that it was his own object to improve upon the statutes of Jehovah. Therefore God permitted him to demonstrate the nature of his claims, to show the working out of his proposed changes in the divine law. His own work must condemn him. Satan had claimed from the first that he was not in rebellion. The whole universe must see the deceiver unmasked.

Even when he was cast out of heaven, Infinite Wisdom did not destroy Satan. Since only the service of love can be acceptable to God, the allegiance of His creatures must rest upon a conviction of His justice and benevolence. The inhabitants of heaven and of the worlds, being unprepared to comprehend the nature or consequences of sin, could not then have seen the justice of God in the destruction of Satan. Had he been immediately blotted out of existence, some would have served God from fear rather than from love. The influence of the deceiver would not have been fully destroyed, nor would the spirit of rebellion have been utterly eradicated. For the good of the entire universe through ceaseless ages, he must more fully develop his principles, that his charges against the divine government might be seen in their true light by all created beings, and that the justice and mercy of God and the immutability of His law might be forever placed beyond all question.

Satan's rebellion was to be a lesson to the universe through all coming ages—a perpetual testimony to the nature of sin and its terrible results. The working out of Satan's rule, its effects upon both men and angels, would show what must be the fruit of setting aside the divine authority. It would testify that with the existence of God's government is bound up the well-being of all the creatures He has made. Thus the history of this terrible experiment of rebellion was to be a perpetual safeguard to all holy beings, to prevent them from being deceived as to the nature of transgression, to save them from committing sin, and suffering its penalty.

He that ruleth in the heavens is the one who sees the end from the beginning—the one before whom the mysteries of the past and the future are alike outspread, and who, beyond the woe and darkness and ruin that sin has wrought, beholds the accomplishment of His own purposes of love and blessing. Though "clouds and darkness are round about Him: righteousness and judgment are the foundation of His throne." Psalm 97:2, RV. And this the inhabitants of the universe, both loyal and disloyal, will one day understand. "His work is perfect: for all His ways are judgment: a God of truth and without iniquity, just and right is He." Deuteronomy 32:4.

The Creation

This chapter is based on Genesis 1 and 2.

....

"By the word of the Lord were the heavens made; and all the host of them by the breath of His mouth." "For He spake, and it was;" "He commanded, and it stood fast." Psalm 33:6,9. He "laid the foundations of the earth, that it should not be removed forever." Psalm 104:5.

As the earth came forth from the hand of its Maker, it was exceedingly beautiful. Its surface was diversified with mountains, hills, and plains, interspersed with noble rivers and lovely lakes; but the hills and mountains were not abrupt and rugged, abounding in terrific steeps and frightful chasms, as they now do; the sharp, ragged edges of earth's rocky framework were buried beneath the fruitful soil, which everywhere produced a luxuriant growth of verdure. There were no loathsome swamps or barren deserts. Graceful shrubs and delicate flowers greeted the eye at every turn. The heights were crowned with trees more majestic than any that now exist. The air, untainted by foul miasma, was clear and healthful. The entire landscape outvied in beauty the decorated grounds of the proudest palace. The angelic host viewed the scene with delight, and rejoiced at the wonderful works of God.

After the earth with its teeming animal and vegetable life had been called into existence, man, the crowning work of the Creator, and the one for whom the beautiful earth had been fitted up, was brought upon the stage of action. To him was given dominion over all that his eye could behold; for "God said, Let Us make man in Our image, after Our likeness: and let them have dominion over ... all the earth. ... So God created man in His own image; ... male and female created He them." Here is clearly set forth the origin of the human race; and the divine record is so plainly stated that there is no occasion for erroneous conclusions. God created man in His own image. Here is no mystery. There is no ground for the supposition that man was evolved by slow degrees of development from the lower forms of animal or vegetable life. Such teaching lowers the great work of the Creator to the level of man's narrow, earthly conceptions. Men are so intent upon excluding God from the sovereignty of the universe that they degrade man and defraud him of the dignity of his origin. He who set the starry worlds on high and tinted with delicate skill the flowers of the field, who filled the earth and the heavens with the wonders of His power, when He came to crown His glorious work, to place one in the midst to stand as ruler of the fair earth, did not fail to create a being worthy of the hand that gave him life. The genealogy of our race, as given by inspiration, traces back its origin, not to a line of developing germs, mollusks, and quadrupeds, but to the great Creator. Though formed from the dust, Adam was "the son of God."

He was placed, as God's representative, over the lower orders of being. They cannot understand or acknowledge the sovereignty of God, yet they were made capable of loving and serving man. The psalmist says, "Thou madest him to have dominion over the works of Thy hands; Thou hast put all things under his feet: ... the beasts of the field; the fowl of the air, ... and whatsoever passeth through the paths of the seas." Psalm 8:6–8.

Man was to bear God's image, both in outward resemblance and in character. Christ alone is "the express image" of the Father (Hebrews 1:3); but man was formed in the likeness of God. His nature was in harmony with the will of God. His mind was capable of comprehending divine things. His affections were pure; his appetites and passions were under the control of reason. He was holy and happy in bearing the image of God and in perfect obedience to His will.

As man came forth from the hand of his Creator, he was of lofty stature and perfect symmetry. His countenance bore the ruddy tint of health and glowed with the light of life and joy. Adam's height was much greater than that of men who now inhabit the earth. Eve was somewhat less in stature; yet her form was noble and full of beauty. The sinless pair wore no artificial garments; they were clothed with a covering of light and glory, such as the angels wear. So long as they lived in obedience to God, this robe of light continued to enshroud them.

Among all the creatures that God had made on the earth, there was not one equal to man.

After the creation of Adam every living creature was brought before him to receive its name; he saw that to each had been given a companion, but among them "there was not found an help meet for him" Genesis 2:20. Among all the creatures that God had made on the earth, there was not one equal to man. And God said, "It is not good that the man should be alone; I will make him an help meet for him" Genesis 2:18. Man was not made to dwell in solitude; he was to be a social being. Without companionship the beautiful scenes and delightful employments of Eden would have failed to yield perfect happiness. Even communion with angels could not have satisfied his desire for sympathy and companionship. There was none of the same nature to love and to be loved.

God Himself gave Adam a companion. He provided "an help meet for him"—a helper corresponding to him—one who was fitted to be his companion, and who could be one with him in love and sympathy. Eve was created from a rib taken from the side of Adam, signifying that she was not to control him as the head, nor to be trampled under his feet as an inferior, but to stand by his side as an equal, to be loved and protected by him. A part of man, bone of his bone, and flesh of his flesh, she was his second self, showing the close union and the affectionate attachment that should exist in this relation. "For no man ever yet hated his own flesh; but nourisheth and cherisheth it." Ephesians 5:29. "Therefore shall a man leave his father and his mother, and shall cleave unto his wife; and they shall be one" Genesis 2:24.

God celebrated the first marriage. Thus the institution has for its originator the Creator of the universe. "Marriage is honorable" (Hebrews 13:4); it was one of the first gifts of God to man, and it is one of the two institutions that, after the Fall, Adam brought with him beyond the gates of Paradise. When the divine principles are recognized and obeyed in this relation, marriage is a blessing; it guards the purity and happiness of the race, it provides for man's social needs, it elevates the physical, the intellectual, and the moral nature.

"And the Lord God planted a garden eastward in Eden; and there He put the man whom He had formed." Genesis 2:8 Everything that God had made was the perfection of beauty, and nothing seemed wanting that could contribute to the happiness of the holy pair; yet the Creator gave them still another token of His love, by preparing a garden especially for their home. In this garden were trees of every variety, many of them laden with fragrant and delicious fruit. There were lovely vines, growing upright, yet presenting a most graceful appearance, with their branches drooping under their load of tempting fruit of the richest and most varied hues. It was the work of Adam and Eve to train the branches of the vine to form bowers, thus making for themselves a dwelling from living trees covered with foliage and fruit. There were fragrant flowers of every hue in rich profusion. In the midst of the garden stood the tree of life, surpassing in glory all other trees. Its fruit appeared like apples of gold and silver, and had the power to perpetuate life.

The creation was now complete. "The heavens and the earth were finished, and all the host of them." "And God saw everything that He had made, and, behold, it was very good." Genesis 1:31. Eden bloomed on earth. Adam and Eve had free access to the tree of life. No taint of sin or shadow of death marred the fair creation. "The morning stars sang together, and all the sons of God shouted for joy." Job 38:7.

The great Jehovah had laid the foundations of the earth; He had dressed the whole world in the garb of beauty and had filled it with things useful to man; He had created all the wonders of the land and of the sea. In six days the great work of creation had been accomplished. And God "rested on the seventh day from all His work which He had made. And God blessed the seventh day, and sanctified it: because that in it He had rested from all His work which God created and made" Genesis 2:2,3. God looked with satisfaction upon the work of His hands. All was perfect, worthy of its divine Author, and He rested, not as one weary, but as well pleased with the fruits of His wisdom and goodness and the manifestations of His glory.

After resting upon the seventh day, God sanctified it, or set it apart, as a day of rest for man. Following the example of the Creator, man was to rest upon this sacred day, that as he should look upon the heavens and the earth, he might reflect upon God's great work of creation; and that as he should behold the evidences of God's wisdom and goodness, his heart might be filled with love and reverence for his Maker.

In Eden, God set up the memorial of His work of creation, in placing His blessing upon the seventh day. The Sabbath was committed to Adam, the father and representative of the whole human family. Its observance was to be an act of grateful acknowledgment, on the part of all who should dwell upon the earth, that God was their Creator and their rightful Sovereign; that they were the work of His hands and the subjects of His authority. Thus the institution was wholly commemorative, and given to all mankind. There was nothing in it shadowy or of restricted application to any people. God saw that a Sabbath was essential for man, even in Paradise. He needed to lay aside his own interests and pursuits for one day of the seven, that he might more fully contemplate the works of God and meditate upon His power and goodness. He needed a Sabbath to remind him more vividly of God and to awaken gratitude because all that he enjoyed and possessed came from the beneficent hand of the Creator.

God designs that the Sabbath shall direct the minds of men to the contemplation of His created works. Nature speaks to their senses, declaring that there is a living God, the Creator, the Supreme Ruler of all. "The heavens declare the glory of God; and the firmament showeth His handiwork. Day unto day uttereth speech, and night unto night showeth knowledge." Psalm 19:1, 2. The beauty that clothes the earth is token of God's love. We may behold it in the everlasting hills, in the lofty trees, in the opening buds and the delicate flowers. All speak to us of God. The Sabbath, ever pointing to Him who made them all, bids men open the great book of nature and trace therein the wisdom, the power, and the love of the Creator.

The Sabbath, ever pointing to Him who made them all, bids men open the great book of nature and trace therein the wisdom, the power, and the love of the Creator.

Our first parents, though created innocent and holy, were not placed beyond the possibility of wrongdoing. God made them free moral agents, capable of appreciating the wisdom and benevolence of His character and the justice of His requirements, and with full liberty to yield or to withhold obedience. They were to enjoy communion with God and with holy angels; but before they could be rendered eternally secure, their loyalty must be tested. At the very beginning of man's existence a check was placed upon the desire for self-indulgence, the fatal passion that lay at the foundation of Satan's fall. The tree of knowledge, which stood near the tree of life in the midst of the garden, was to be a test of the obedience, faith, and love of our parents. While permitted to eat freely of every other tree, they were forbidden to taste of this, on pain of death. They were also to be exposed to the temptations of Satan; but if they endured the trial, they would finally be placed beyond his power, to enjoy perpetual favor with God.

God placed man under law, as an indispensable condition of his very existence. He was a subject of the divine government, and there can be no government without law. God might have created man without the power to transgress His law; He might have withheld the hand of Adam from touching the forbidden fruit; but in that case man would have been, not a free moral agent, but a mere automaton. Without freedom of choice, his obedience would not have been voluntary, but forced. There could have been no development of character. Such a course would have been contrary to God's plan in dealing with the inhabitants of other worlds. It would have been unworthy of man as an intelligent being, and would have sustained Satan's charge of God's arbitrary rule.

God made man upright; He gave him noble traits of character, with no bias toward evil. He endowed him with high intellectual powers, and presented before him the strongest possible inducements to be true to his allegiance. Obedience, perfect and perpetual, was the condition of eternal happiness. On this condition he was to have access to the tree of life.

The home of our first parents was to be a pattern for other homes as their children should go forth to occupy the earth. That home, beautified by the hand of God Himself, was not a gorgeous palace. Men, in their pride, delight in magnificent and costly edifices and glory in the works of their own hands; but God placed Adam in a garden. This was his dwelling. The blue heavens were its dome; the earth, with its delicate flowers and carpet of living green, was its floor; and the leafy branches of the goodly trees were its canopy. Its walls were hung with the most magnificent adornings—the handiwork of the great Master Artist. In the surroundings of the holy pair was a lesson for all time—that true happiness is found, not in the indulgence of pride and luxury, but in communion with God through His created works. If men would give less attention to the artificial, and would cultivate greater simplicity, they would come far nearer to answering the purpose of God in their creation. Pride and ambition are never satisfied, but those who are truly wise will find substantial and elevating pleasure in the sources of enjoyment that God has placed within the reach of all.

To the dwellers in Eden was committed the care of the garden, "to dress it and to keep it." Their occupation was not wearisome, but pleasant and invigorating. God appointed labor as a blessing to man, to occupy his mind, to strengthen his body, and to develop his faculties. In mental and physical activity Adam found one of the highest pleasures of his holy existence. And when, as a result of his disobedience, he was driven from his beautiful home, and forced to struggle with a stubborn soil to gain his daily bread, that very labor, although widely different from his pleasant occupation in the garden, was a safeguard against temptation and a source of happiness. Those who regard work as a curse, attended though it be with weariness and pain, are cherishing an error. The rich often look down with contempt upon the working classes, but this is wholly at variance with God's purpose in creating man. What are the possessions of even the most wealthy in comparison with the heritage given to the lordly Adam? Yet Adam was not to be idle. Our Creator, who understands what is for man's happiness, appointed Adam his work. The true joy of life is found only by the working men and women. The angels are diligent workers; they are the ministers of God to the children of men. The Creator has prepared no place for the stagnating practice of indolence.

While they remained true to God, Adam and his companion were to bear rule over the earth. Unlimited control was given them over every living thing. The lion and the lamb sported peacefully around them or lay down together at their feet. The happy birds flitted about them without fear; and as their glad songs ascended to the praise of their Creator, Adam and Eve united with them in thanksgiving to the Father and the Son.

The holy pair were not only children under the fatherly care of God but students receiving instruction from the all-wise Creator. They were visited by angels, and were granted communion with their Maker, with no obscuring veil between. They were full of the vigor imparted by the tree of life, and their intellectual power was but little less than that of the angels. The mysteries of the visible universe—"the wondrous works of Him which is perfect in knowledge" (Job 37:16)—afforded them an exhaustless source of instruction and delight. The laws and operations of nature, which have engaged men's study for six thousand years, were opened to their minds by the infinite Framer and Upholder of all. They held converse with leaf and flower and tree, gathering from each the secrets of its life. With every living creature, from the mighty leviathan that playeth among the waters to the insect mote that floats in the sunbeam, Adam was familiar. He had given to each its name, and he was acquainted with the nature and habits of all. God's glory in the heavens, the innumerable worlds in their orderly revolutions, "the balancings of the clouds," the mysteries of light and sound, of day and night—all were open to the study of our first parents. On every leaf of the forest or stone of the mountains, in every shining star, in earth and air and sky, God's name was written. The order and harmony of creation spoke to them of infinite wisdom and power. They were ever discovering some attraction that filled their hearts with deeper love and called forth fresh expressions of gratitude.

So long as they remained loyal to the divine law, their capacity to know, to enjoy, and to love would continually increase. They would be constantly gaining new treasures of knowledge, discovering fresh springs of happiness, and obtaining clearer and yet clearer conceptions of the immeasurable, unfailing love of God.

3

The Temptation and Fall

This chapter is based on Genesis 3.

....

No longer free to stir up rebellion in heaven, Satan's enmity against God found a new field in plotting the ruin of the human race. In the happiness and peace of the holy pair in Eden he beheld a vision of the bliss that to him was forever lost. Moved by envy, he determined to incite them to disobedience, and bring upon them the guilt and penalty of sin. He would change their love to distrust and their songs of praise to reproaches against their Maker. Thus he would not only plunge these innocent beings into the same misery which he was himself enduring, but would cast dishonor upon God, and cause grief in heaven.

Our first parents were not left without a warning of the danger that threatened them. Heavenly messengers opened to them the history of Satan's fall and his plots for their destruction, unfolding more fully the nature of the divine government, which the prince of evil was trying to overthrow. It was by disobedience to the just commands of God that Satan and his host had fallen. How important, then, that Adam and Eve should honor that law by which alone it was possible for order and equity to be maintained.

The law of God is as sacred as God Himself. It is a revelation of His will, a transcript of His character, the expression of divine love and wisdom. The harmony of creation depends upon the perfect conformity of all beings, of everything, animate and inanimate, to the law of the Creator. God has ordained laws for the government, not only of living beings, but of all the operations of nature. Everything is under fixed laws, which cannot be disregarded. But while everything in nature is governed by natural laws, man alone, of all that inhabits the earth, is amenable to moral law. To man, the crowning work of creation, God has given power to understand His requirements, to comprehend the justice and beneficence of His law, and its sacred claims upon him; and of man unswerving obedience is required.

Like the angels, the dwellers in Eden had been placed upon probation; their happy estate could be retained only on condition of fidelity to the Creator's law. They could obey and

live, or disobey and perish. God had made them the recipients of rich blessings; but should they disregard His will, He who spared not the angels that sinned, could not spare them; transgression would forfeit His gifts and bring upon them misery and ruin.

The angels warned them to be on their guard against the devices of Satan, for his efforts to ensnare them would be unwearied. While they were obedient to God the evil one could not harm them; for, if need be, every angel in heaven would be sent to their help. If they steadfastly repelled his first insinuations, they would be as secure as the heavenly messengers. But should they once yield to temptation, their nature would become so depraved that in themselves they would have no power and no disposition to resist Satan.

The tree of knowledge had been made a test of their obedience and their love to God. The Lord had seen fit to lay upon them but one prohibition as to the use of all that was in the garden; but if they should disregard His will in this particular, they would incur the guilt of transgression. Satan was not to follow them with continual temptations; he could have access to them only at the forbidden tree. Should they attempt to investigate its nature, they would be exposed to his wiles. They were admonished to give careful heed to the warning which God had sent them and to be content with the instruction which He had seen fit to impart.

In order to accomplish his work unperceived, Satan chose to employ as his medium the serpent—a disguise well adapted for his purpose of deception. The serpent was then one of the wisest and most beautiful creatures on the earth. It had wings, and while flying through the air presented an appearance of dazzling brightness, having the color and brilliancy of burnished gold. Resting in the rich-laden branches of the forbidden tree and regaling itself with the delicious fruit, it was an object to arrest the attention and delight the eye of the beholder. Thus in the garden of peace lurked the destroyer, watching for his prey. The angels had cautioned Eve to beware of separating herself from her husband while occupied in their daily labor in the garden; with him she would be in less danger from temptation than if she were alone. But absorbed in her pleasing task, she unconsciously wandered from his side. On perceiving that she was alone, she felt an apprehension of danger, but dismissed her fears, deciding that she had sufficient wisdom and strength to discern evil and to withstand it. Unmindful of the angels' caution, she soon found herself gazing with mingled curiosity and admiration upon the forbidden tree. The fruit was very beautiful, and she questioned with herself why God had withheld it from them. Now was the tempter's opportunity. As if he were able to discern the workings of her mind, he addressed her: "Yea, hath God said, Ye shall not eat of every tree of the garden?" Genesis 3:1. Eve was surprised and startled as she thus seemed to hear the echo of her thoughts. But the serpent continued, in a musical voice, with subtle praise of her surpassing loveliness; and his words were not displeasing. Instead of fleeing from the spot she lingered wonderingly to hear a serpent speak. Had she been addressed by a being like the angels, her fears would have been excited; but she had no thought that the fascinating serpent could become the medium of the fallen foe.

To the tempter's ensnaring question she replied: "We may eat of the fruit of the trees of the garden: but of the fruit of the tree which is in the midst of the garden, God hath said, Ye shall not eat of it, neither shall ye touch it, lest ye die. And the serpent said unto the woman, Ye shall not surely die: for God doth know that in the day ye eat thereof, then your eyes shall be opened, and ye shall be as gods, knowing good and evil."

By partaking of this tree, he declared, they would attain to a more exalted sphere of existence and enter a broader field of knowledge. He himself had eaten of the forbidden fruit, and as a result had acquired the power of speech. And he insinuated that the Lord jealously desired to withhold it from them, lest they should be exalted to equality with Himself. It was because of its wonderful properties, imparting wisdom and power, that He had prohibited them from tasting or even touching it. The tempter intimated that the divine warning was not to be actually fulfilled; it was designed merely to intimidate them. How could it be possible for them to die? Had they not eaten of the tree of life? God had been seeking to prevent them from reaching a nobler development and finding greater happiness.

Such has been Satan's work from the days of Adam to the present, and he has pursued it with great success. He tempts men to distrust God's love and to doubt His wisdom. He is constantly seeking to excite a spirit of irreverent curiosity, a restless, inquisitive desire to penetrate the secrets of divine wisdom and power. In their efforts to search out what God has been pleased to withhold, multitudes overlook the truths which He has revealed, and which are essential to salvation. Satan tempts men to disobedience by leading them to believe they are entering a wonderful field of knowledge. But this is all a deception. Elated with their ideas of progression, they are, by trampling on God's requirements, setting their feet in the path that leads to degradation and death.

Satan represented to the holy pair that they would be gainers by breaking the law of God. Do we not today hear similar reasoning? Many talk of the narrowness of those who obey God's commandments, while they themselves claim to have broader ideas and to enjoy greater liberty. What is this but an echo of the voice from Eden, "In the day ye eat thereof"—transgress the divine requirement—"ye shall be as gods"? Satan claimed to have received great good by eating of the forbidden fruit, but he did not let it appear that by transgression he had become an outcast from heaven. Though he had found sin to result in infinite loss, he concealed his own misery in order to draw others into the same position. So now the transgressor seeks to disguise his true character; he may claim to be holy; but his exalted profession only makes him the more dangerous as a deceiver. He is on the side of Satan, trampling upon the law of God, and leading others to do the same, to their eternal ruin.

Eve really believed the words of Satan, but her belief did not save her from the penalty of sin. She disbelieved the words of God, and this was what led to her fall. In the judgment men will not be condemned because they conscientiously believed a lie, but because they did not believe the truth, because they neglected the opportunity of learning what is truth. Notwithstanding the sophistry of Satan to the contrary, it is always disastrous to disobey God. We must set our hearts to know what is truth. All the lessons which God has caused to be placed on record in His word are for our warning and instruction. They are given to save us from deception. Their neglect

> *The law of God is as sacred as God Himself. It is a revelation of His will, a transcript of His character, the expression of divine love and wisdom.*

will result in ruin to ourselves. Whatever contradicts God's word, we may be sure proceeds from Satan.

The serpent plucked the fruit of the forbidden tree and placed it in the hands of the half-reluctant Eve. Then he reminded her of her own words, that God had forbidden them to touch it, lest they die. She would receive no more harm from eating the fruit, he declared, than from touching it. Perceiving no evil results from what she had done, Eve grew bolder. When she "saw that the tree was good for food, and that it was pleasant to the eyes, and a tree to be

Whatever contradicts God's word, we may be sure proceeds from Satan.

desired to make one wise, she took of the fruit thereof, and did eat." Genesis 3:6 It was pleasant to the taste, and as she ate, she seemed to feel a vivifying power, and imagined herself entering upon a higher state of existence. Without a fear she plucked and ate. And now, having herself transgressed, she became the agent of Satan in working the ruin of her husband. In a state of strange, unnatural excitement, with her hands filled with the forbidden fruit, she sought his presence, and related all that had occurred.

An expression of sadness came over the face of Adam. He appeared astonished and alarmed. To the words of Eve he replied that this must be the foe against whom they had been warned; and by the divine sentence she must die. In answer she urged him to eat, repeating the words of the serpent, that they should not surely die. She reasoned that this must be true, for she felt no evidence of God's displeasure, but on the contrary realized a delicious, exhilarating influence, thrilling every faculty with new life, such, she imagined, as inspired the heavenly messengers.

Adam understood that his companion had transgressed the command of God, disregarded the only prohibition laid upon them as a test of their fidelity and love. There was a terrible struggle in his mind. He mourned that he had permitted Eve to wander from his side. But now the deed was done; he must be separated from her whose society had been his joy. How could he have it thus? Adam had enjoyed the companionship of God and of holy angels. He had looked upon the glory of the Creator. He understood the high destiny opened to the human race should they remain faithful to God. Yet all these blessings were lost sight of in the fear of losing that one gift which in his eyes outvalued every other. Love, gratitude, loyalty to the Creator—all were overborne by love to Eve. She was a part of himself, and he could not endure the thought of separation. He did not realize that the same Infinite Power who had from the dust of the earth created him, a living, beautiful form, and had in love given him a companion, could supply her place. He resolved to share her fate; if she must die, he would die with her. After all, he reasoned, might not the words of the wise serpent be true? Eve was before him, as beautiful and apparently as innocent as before this act of disobedience. She expressed greater love for him than before. No sign of death appeared in her, and he decided to brave the consequences. He seized the fruit and quickly ate.

After his transgression Adam at first imagined himself entering upon a higher state of existence. But soon the thought of his sin filled him with terror. The air, which had hitherto been of a mild and uniform temperature, seemed to chill the guilty pair. The love and peace which had been theirs was gone, and in its place they felt a sense of sin, a dread of the future, a nakedness of soul. The robe of light which had enshrouded them, now disappeared, and to supply its place they endeavored to fashion for themselves a covering; for they could not, while unclothed, meet the eye of God and holy angels.

They now began to see the true character of their sin. Adam reproached his companion for her folly in leaving his side and permitting herself to be deceived by the serpent; but they both flattered themselves that He who had given them so many evidences of His love, would pardon this one transgression, or that they would not be subjected to so dire a punishment as they had feared.

Satan exulted in his success. He had tempted the woman to distrust God's love, to doubt His wisdom, and to transgress His law, and through her he had caused the overthrow of Adam.

But the great Lawgiver was about to make known to Adam and Eve the consequences of their transgression. The divine presence was manifested in the garden. In their innocence and holiness they had joyfully welcomed the approach of their Creator; but now they fled in terror, and sought to hide in the deepest recesses of the garden. But "the Lord God called unto Adam, and said unto him, Where art thou? And he said, I heard Thy voice in the garden, and I was afraid, because I was naked; and I hid myself. And He said, Who told thee that thou wast naked? Hast thou eaten of the tree, whereof I commanded thee that thou shouldest not eat?" Genesis 3:9-11.

Adam could neither deny nor excuse his sin; but instead of manifesting penitence, he endeavored to cast the blame upon his wife, and thus upon God Himself: "The woman whom Thou gavest to be with me, she gave me of the tree, and I did eat." v.12. He who, from love to Eve, had deliberately chosen to forfeit the approval of God, his home in Paradise, and an eternal life of joy, could now, after his fall, endeavor to make his companion, and even the Creator Himself, responsible for the transgression. So terrible is the power of sin.

When the woman was asked, "What is this that thou hast done?" she answered, "The serpent beguiled me, and I did eat." v. 13. "Why didst Thou create the serpent? Why didst Thou suffer him to enter Eden?"—these were the questions implied in her excuse for her sin. Thus, like Adam, she charged God with the responsibility of their fall. The spirit of self-justification originated in the father of lies; it was indulged by our first parents as soon as they yielded to the influence of Satan, and has been exhibited by all the sons and daughters of Adam. Instead of humbly confessing their sins, they try to shield themselves by casting the blame upon others, upon circumstances, or upon God—making even His blessings an occasion of murmuring against Him.

The Lord then passed sentence upon the serpent: "Because thou hast done this, thou art cursed above all cattle, and above every beast of the field; upon thy belly shalt thou go, and dust shalt thou eat all the days of thy life." v. 14. Since it had been employed as Satan's medium, the serpent was to share the visitation of divine judgment. From the most beautiful and admired of the creatures of the field, it was to become the most groveling and detested of them all, feared and hated by both man and beast. The words next addressed to the serpent applied directly to Satan himself, pointing forward to his ultimate defeat and destruction: "I will put enmity between thee and the woman, and between thy seed and her seed; it shall bruise thy head, and thou shalt bruise his heel." v. 15.

Eve was told of the sorrow and pain that must henceforth be her portion. And the Lord said, "Thy desire shall be to thy husband, and he shall rule over thee." v. 16. In the creation God had made her the equal of Adam. Had they remained obedient to God—in harmony with His great law of love—they would ever have been in harmony with each other; but sin had brought discord, and now their union could be maintained and harmony preserved only by submission on the part of the one or the other. Eve had been the first in transgression; and she had fallen into temptation by separating from her companion, contrary to the divine direction. It was by her solicitation that Adam sinned, and she was now placed in subjection to her husband. Had the principles joined in the law of God been cherished by the fallen race, this sentence, though growing out of the results of sin, would have proved a blessing to them; but man's abuse of the supremacy thus given him has too often rendered the lot of woman very bitter and made her life a burden.

Eve had been perfectly happy by her husband's side in her Eden home; but, like restless modern Eves, she was flattered with the hope of entering a higher sphere than that which God had assigned her. In attempting to rise above her original position, she fell far below it. A similar result will be reached by all who are unwilling to take up cheerfully their life duties in accordance with God's plan. In their efforts to reach positions for which He has not fitted them, many are leaving vacant the place where they might be a blessing. In their desire for a higher sphere, many have sacrificed true womanly dignity and nobility of character, and have left undone the very work that heaven appointed them.

To Adam the Lord declared: "Because thou hast hearkened unto the voice of thy wife, and hast eaten of the tree, of which I commanded thee, saying, Thou shalt not eat of it: cursed is the ground for thy sake; in sorrow shalt thou eat of it all the days of thy life; thorns also and thistles shall it bring forth to thee; and thou shalt eat the herb of the field; in the sweat of thy face shalt thou eat bread, till thou return unto the ground; for out of it was thou taken: for dust thou art, and unto dust shalt thou return." vv. 17, 18.

It was not the will of God that the sinless pair should know aught of evil. He had freely given them the good, and had withheld the evil. But, contrary to His command, they had eaten of the forbidden tree, and now they would continue to eat of it—they would have the knowledge of evil—all the days of their life. From that time the race would be afflicted by Satan's temptations. Instead of the happy labor heretofore appointed them, anxiety and toil were to be their lot. They would be subject to disappointment, grief, and pain, and finally to death.

Under the curse of sin all nature was to witness to man of the character and results of rebellion against God. When God made man He made him rule over the earth and all living creatures. So long as Adam remained loyal to heaven, all nature was in subjection to him. But when he rebelled against the divine law, the inferior creatures were in rebellion against his rule. Thus the Lord, in His great mercy, would show men the sacredness of His law, and lead them, by their own experience, to see the danger of setting it aside, even in the slightest degree.

And the life of toil and care which was henceforth to be man's lot was appointed in love. It was a discipline rendered needful by his sin, to place a check upon the indulgence of appetite and passion, to develop habits of self-control. It was a part of God's great plan of man's recovery from the ruin and degradation of sin.

The warning given to our first parents—"In the day that thou eatest thereof thou shalt surely die" (Genesis 2:17)—did not imply that they were to die on the very day when they partook of the forbidden fruit. But on the day the irrevocable sentence would be pronounced. Immortality was promised them on condition of obedience; by transgression they would forfeit eternal life. That very day would be doomed to death.

In order to possess an endless existence, man must continue to partake of the tree of life. Deprived of this, his vitality would gradually diminish until life should become extinct. It was Satan's plan that Adam and Eve should by disobedience incur God's displeasure; and then, if they failed to obtain forgiveness, he hoped that they would eat of the tree of life, and thus perpetuate an existence of sin and misery. But after man's fall, holy angels were immediately commissioned to guard the tree of life. Around these angels flashed beams of light having the appearance of a glittering sword. None of the family of Adam were permitted to pass the barrier to partake of the life-giving fruit; hence there is not an immortal sinner.

The tide of woe that flowed from the transgression of our first parents is regarded by many as too awful a consequence for so small a sin, and they impeach the wisdom and justice of God in His dealings with man. But if they would look more deeply into this question, they might discern their error. God created man after His own likeness, free from sin. The earth was to be peopled with beings only a little lower than the angels; but their obedience must be tested; for God would not permit the world to be filled with those who would disregard His law. Yet, in His great mercy, He appointed Adam no severe test. And the very lightness of the prohibition made the sin exceedingly great. If Adam could not bear the smallest of tests, he could not have endured a greater trial had he been entrusted with higher responsibilities.

Had some great test been appointed Adam, then those whose hearts incline to evil would have excused themselves by saying, "This is a trivial matter, and God is not so particular about little things." And there would be continual transgression in things looked upon as small, and which pass unrebuked among men. But the Lord has made it evident that sin in any degree is offensive to Him.

To Eve it seemed a small thing to disobey God by tasting the fruit of the forbidden tree, and to tempt her husband also to transgress; but their sin opened the floodgates of woe upon the world. Who can know, in the moment of temptation, the terrible consequences that will result from one wrong step?

Many who teach that the law of God is not binding upon man, urge that it is impossible for him to obey its precepts. But if this were true, why did Adam suffer the penalty of transgression? The sin of our first parents brought guilt and sorrow upon the world, and had it not been for the goodness and mercy of God, would have plunged the race into hopeless despair. Let none deceive themselves. "The wages of sin is death." Romans 6:23. The law of God can no more be transgressed with impunity now than when sentence was pronounced upon the father of mankind. After their sin Adam and Eve were no longer to dwell in Eden. They earnestly entreated that they might remain in the home of their innocence and joy. They confessed that they had forfeited all right to that happy abode, but pledged themselves for the future to yield strict obedience to God. But they were told that their nature had become depraved by sin; they had lessened their strength to resist evil and had opened the way for Satan to gain more ready access to them. In their innocence they had yielded to temptation; and now, in a state of conscious guilt, they would have less power to maintain their integrity.

In humility and unutterable sadness they bade farewell to their beautiful home and went forth to dwell upon the earth, where rested the curse of sin. The atmosphere, once so mild and uniform in temperature, was now subject to marked changes, and the Lord mercifully provided them with a garment of skins as a protection from the extremes of heat and cold.

As they witnessed in drooping flower and falling leaf the first signs of decay, Adam and his companion mourned more deeply than men now mourn over their dead.

As they witnessed in drooping flower and falling leaf the first signs of decay, Adam and his companion mourned more deeply than men now mourn over their dead. The death of the frail, delicate flowers was indeed a cause of sorrow; but when the goodly trees cast off their leaves, the scene brought vividly to mind the stern fact that death is the portion of every living thing.

The Garden of Eden remained upon the earth long after man had become an outcast from its pleasant paths. The fallen race were long permitted to gaze upon the home of innocence, their entrance barred only by the watching angels. At the cherubim-guarded gate of Paradise the divine glory was revealed. Hither came Adam and his sons to worship God. Here they renewed their vows of obedience to that law the transgression of which had banished them from Eden. When the tide of iniquity overspread the world, and the wickedness of men determined their destruction by a flood of waters, the hand that had planted Eden withdrew it from the earth. But in the final restitution, when there shall be "a new heaven and a new earth" (Revelation 21:1), it is to be restored more gloriously adorned than at the beginning.

Then they that have kept God's commandments shall breathe in immortal vigor beneath the tree of life; and through unending ages the inhabitants of sinless worlds shall behold, in that garden of delight, a sample of the perfect work of God's creation, untouched by the curse of sin—a sample of what the whole earth would have become, had man but fulfilled the Creator's glorious plan.

Since the divine law is as sacred as God Himself, only one equal with God could make atonement for its transgression. None but Christ could redeem fallen man from the curse of the law and bring him again into harmony with heaven.

The Plan of Redemption

. . . .

The fall of man filled all heaven with sorrow. The world that God had made was blighted with the curse of sin and inhabited by beings doomed to misery and death. There appeared no escape for those who had transgressed the law. Angels ceased their songs of praise. Throughout the heavenly courts there was mourning for the ruin that sin had wrought.

The Son of God, heaven's glorious Commander, was touched with pity for the fallen race. His heart was moved with infinite compassion as the woes of the lost world rose up before Him. But divine love had conceived a plan whereby man might be redeemed. The broken law of God demanded the life of the sinner. In all the universe there was but one who could, in behalf of man, satisfy its claims. Since the divine law is as sacred as God Himself, only one equal with God could make atonement for its transgression. None but Christ could redeem fallen man from the curse of the law and bring him again into harmony with heaven. Christ would take upon Himself the guilt and shame of sin   sin so offensive to a holy God that it must separate the Father and His Son. Christ would reach to the depths of misery to rescue the ruined race.

Before the Father He pleaded in the sinner's behalf, while the host of heaven awaited the result with an intensity of interest that words cannot express. Long continued was that mysterious communing—"the counsel of peace" for the fallen sons of men (Zechariah 6:13). The plan of salvation had been laid before the creation of the earth; for Christ is "the Lamb slain from the foundation of the world" (Revelation 13:8); yet it was a struggle, even with the King of the universe, to yield up His Son to die for the guilty race. But "God so loved the world, that He gave His only-begotten Son, that whosoever believeth in Him should not perish, but have everlasting life." John 3:16. Oh, the mystery of redemption! The love of God for a world that did not love Him! Who can know the depths of that love which "passeth knowledge"? Through endless ages immortal minds, seeking to comprehend the mystery of that incomprehensible love, will wonder and adore.

God was to be manifest in Christ, "reconciling the world unto Himself." 2 Corinthians 5:19. Man had become so degraded by sin that it was impossible for him, in himself, to come into harmony with Him whose nature is purity and goodness. But Christ, after having redeemed man from the condemnation of the law, could impart divine power to unite with human effort. Thus by repentance toward God and faith in Christ the fallen children of Adam might once more become "sons of God." 1 John 3:2.

The plan by which alone man's salvation could be secured, involved all heaven in its infinite sacrifice. The angels could not rejoice as Christ opened before them the plan of redemption, for they saw that man's salvation must cost their loved Commander unutterable woe. In grief and wonder they listened to His words as He told them how He must descend from heaven's purity and peace, its joy and glory and immortal life, and come in contact with the degradation of earth, to endure its sorrow, shame, and death. He was to stand between the sinner and the penalty of sin; yet few would receive Him as the Son of God. He would leave His high position as the Majesty of heaven, appear upon earth and humble Himself as a man, and by His own experience become acquainted with the sorrows and temptations which man would have to endure. All this would be necessary in order that He might be able to succor them that should be tempted (Hebrews 2:18). When His mission as a teacher should be ended, He must be delivered into the hands of wicked men and be subjected to every insult and torture that Satan could inspire them to inflict. He must die the cruelest of deaths, lifted up between the heavens and the earth as a guilty sinner. He must pass long hours of agony so terrible that angels could not look upon it, but would veil their faces from the sight. He must endure anguish of soul, the hiding of His Father's face, while the guilt of transgression—the weight of the sins of the whole world—should be upon Him.

The angels prostrated themselves at the feet of their Commander and offered to become a sacrifice for man. But an angel's life could not pay the debt; only He who created man had power to redeem him. Yet the angels were to have a part to act in the plan of redemption. Christ was to be made "a little lower than the angels for the suffering of death." Hebrews 2:9. As He should take human nature upon Him, His strength would not be equal to theirs, and they were to minister to Him, to strengthen and soothe Him under His sufferings. They were also to be ministering spirits, sent forth to minister for them who should be heirs of salvation (Hebrews 1:14). They would guard the subjects of grace from the power of evil angels and from the darkness constantly thrown around them by Satan.

When the angels should witness the agony and humiliation of their Lord, they would be filled with grief and indignation and would wish to deliver Him from His murderers; but they were not to interpose in order to prevent anything which they should behold. It was a part of the plan of redemption that Christ should suffer the scorn and abuse of wicked men, and He consented to all this when He became the Redeemer of man.

Christ assured the angels that by His death He would ransom many, and would destroy him who had the power of death. He would recover the kingdom which man had lost by transgression, and the redeemed were to inherit it with Him, and dwell therein forever. Sin and sinners would be blotted out, nevermore to disturb the peace of heaven or earth. He bade the angelic host to be in accord with the plan that His Father had accepted, and rejoice that, through His death, fallen man could be reconciled to God.

Then joy, inexpressible joy, filled heaven. The glory and blessedness of a world redeemed, outmeasured even the anguish and sacrifice of the Prince of life. Through the celestial courts echoed the first strains of that song which was to ring out above the hills of Bethlehem—"Glory to God in the highest, and on earth peace, good will toward men." Luke 2:14. With a deeper gladness now than in the rapture of the new creation, "the morning stars sang together, and all the sons of God shouted for joy." Job 38:7.

To man the first intimation of redemption was communicated in the sentence pronounced upon Satan in the garden. The Lord declared, "I will put enmity between thee and the woman, and between thy seed and her seed; it shall bruise thy head, and thou shalt bruise his heel." Genesis 3:15. This sentence, uttered in the hearing of our first parents, was to them a promise. While it foretold war between man and Satan, it declared that the power of the great adversary would finally be broken. Adam and Eve stood as criminals before the righteous Judge, awaiting the sentence which transgression

had incurred; but before they heard of the life of toil and sorrow which must be their portion, or of the decree that they must return to dust, they listened to words that could not fail to give them hope. Though they must suffer from the power of their mighty foe, they could look forward to final victory.

When Satan heard that enmity should exist between himself and the woman, and between his seed and her seed, he knew that his work of depraving human nature would be interrupted; that by some means man would be enabled to resist his power. Yet as the plan of salvation was more fully unfolded, Satan rejoiced with his angels that, having caused man's fall, he could bring down the Son of God from His exalted position. He declared that his plans had thus far been successful upon the earth, and that when Christ should take upon Himself human nature, He also might be overcome, and thus the redemption of the fallen race might be prevented.

Heavenly angels more fully opened to our first parents the plan that had been devised for their salvation. Adam and his companion were assured that notwithstanding their great sin, they were not to be abandoned to the control of Satan. The Son of God had offered to atone, with His own life, for their transgression. A period of probation would be granted them, and through repentance and faith in Christ they might again become the children of God.

The sacrifice demanded by their transgression revealed to Adam and Eve the sacred character of the law of God; and they saw, as they had never seen before, the guilt of sin and its dire results. In their remorse and anguish they pleaded that the penalty might not fall upon Him whose love had been the source of all their joy; rather let it descend upon them and their prosperity.

They were told that since the law of Jehovah is the foundation of His government in heaven as well as upon the earth, even the life of an angel could not be accepted as a sacrifice for its transgression. Not one of its precepts could be abrogated or changed to meet man in his fallen condition; but the Son of God, who had created man, could make an atonement for him. As Adam's transgression had brought wretchedness and death, so the sacrifice of Christ would bring life and immortality.

Not only man but the earth had by sin come under the power of the wicked one, and was to be restored by the plan of redemption. At his creation Adam was placed in dominion over the earth. But by yielding to temptation, he was brought under the power of Satan. "Of whom a man is overcome, of the same is he brought in bondage." 2 Peter 2:19. When man became Satan's captive, the dominion which he held, passed to his conqueror. Thus Satan became "the god of this world."

The act of Christ in dying for the salvation of man would not only make heaven accessible to men, but before all the universe it would justify God and His Son in their dealing with the rebellion of Satan. It would establish the perpetuity of the law of God and would reveal the nature and the results of sin.

2 Corinthians 4:4. He had usurped that dominion over the earth which had been originally given to Adam. But Christ, by His sacrifice paying the penalty of sin, would not only redeem man, but recover the dominion which he had forfeited. All that was lost by the first Adam will be restored by the second. Says the prophet, "O tower of the flock, the stronghold of the daughter of Zion, unto thee shall it come, even the first dominion." Micah 4:8. And the apostle Paul points forward to the "redemption of the purchased possession." Ephesians 1:14. God created the earth to be the abode of holy, happy beings. The Lord "formed the earth and made it; He hath established it, He created it not in vain, He formed it to be inhabited." Isaiah 45:18. That purpose will be fulfilled, when, renewed by the power of God, and freed from sin and sorrow, it shall become the eternal abode of the redeemed. "The righteous shall inherit the land, and dwell therein for ever." "And there shall be no more curse: but the throne of God and of the Lamb shall be in it; and His servants shall serve Him." Psalm 37:29; Revelation 22:3.

Adam, in his innocence, had enjoyed open communion with his Maker; but sin brought separation between God and man, and the atonement of Christ alone could span the abyss and make possible the communication of blessing or salvation from heaven to earth. Man was still cut off from direct approach to his Creator, but God would communicate with him through Christ and angels.

Thus were revealed to Adam important events in the history of mankind, from the time when the divine sentence was pronounced in Eden, to the Flood, and onward to the first advent of the Son of God. He was shown that while the sacrifice of Christ would be of sufficient value to save the whole world, many would choose a life of sin rather than of repentance and obedience.

Crime would increase through successive generations, and the curse of sin would rest more and more heavily upon the human race, upon the beasts, and upon the earth. The days of man would be shortened by his own course of sin; he would deteriorate in physical stature and endurance and in moral and intellectual power, until the world would be filled with misery of every type. Through the indulgence of appetite and passion men would become incapable of appreciating the great truths of the plan of redemption. Yet Christ, true to the purpose for which He left heaven, would continue His interest in men, and still invite them to hide their weakness and deficiencies in Him. He would supply the needs of all who would come unto Him in faith. And there would ever be a few who would preserve the knowledge of God and would remain unsullied amid the prevailing iniquity.

The sacrificial offerings were ordained by God to be to man a perpetual reminder and a penitential acknowledgment of his sin and a confession of his faith in the promised Redeemer. They were intended to impress upon the fallen race the solemn truth that it was sin that caused death. To Adam, the offering of the first sacrifice was a most painful ceremony. His hand must be raised to take life, which only God could give. It was the first time he had ever witnessed death, and he knew that had he been obedient to God, there would have been no death of man or beast. As he slew the innocent victim, he trembled at the thought that his sin must shed the blood of the spotless Lamb of God. This scene gave him a deeper and more vivid sense of the greatness of his transgression, which nothing but the death of God's dear Son could expiate. And he marveled at the infinite goodness that would give such a ransom to save the guilty. A star of hope illumined the dark and terrible future and relieved it of its utter desolation.

But the plan of redemption had a yet broader and deeper purpose than the salvation of man. It was not for this alone that Christ came to the earth; it was not merely that the inhabitants of this little world might regard the law of God as it should be regarded; but it was to vindicate the character of God before the universe. To this result of His great sacrifice—its influence upon the intelligences of other worlds, as well as upon man—the Saviour looked forward when just before His crucifixion He said: "Now is the judgment of this world: now shall the prince of this world be cast out. And I, if I be lifted up from the earth, will draw all unto Me." John 12:31, 32. The act of Christ in dying for the salvation of man would not only make heaven accessible to men, but before all the universe it would justify God and His Son in their dealing with the rebellion of Satan. It would establish the perpetuity of the law of God and would reveal the nature and the results of sin.

From the first the great controversy had been upon the law of God. Satan had sought to prove that God was unjust, that His law was faulty, and that the good of the universe required it to be changed. In attacking the law he aimed to overthrow the authority of its Author. In the controversy it was to be shown whether the divine statutes were defective and subject to change, or perfect and immutable.

When Satan was thrust out of heaven, he determined to make the earth his kingdom. When he tempted and overcame Adam and Eve, he thought that he had gained possession of this world; "because," said he, "they have chosen me as their ruler." He claimed that it was impossible that forgiveness should be granted to the sinner, and therefore the fallen race were his rightful subjects, and the world was his. But God gave His own dear Son—one equal with Himself—to bear the penalty of transgression, and thus He provided a way by which they might be restored to His favor, and brought back to their Eden home. Christ undertook to redeem man and to rescue the world from the grasp of Satan. The great controversy begun in heaven was to be decided in the very world, on the very same field, that Satan claimed as his.

It was the marvel of all the universe that Christ should humble Himself to save fallen man. That He who had passed from star to star, from world to world, superintending all, by His providence supplying the needs of every order of being in His vast creation—that He should consent to leave His glory and take upon Himself human nature, was a mystery which the sinless intelligences of other worlds desired to understand. When Christ came to our world in the form of humanity, all were intensely interested in following Him as He traversed, step by step, the bloodstained path from the manger to Calvary. Heaven marked the insult and mockery that He received, and knew that it was at Satan's instigation. They marked the work of counteragencies going forward; Satan constantly pressing darkness, sorrow, and suffering upon the race, and Christ counteracting it. They watched the battle between light and darkness as it waxed stronger. And as Christ in His expiring agony upon the cross cried out, "It is finished" (John 19:30), a shout of triumph rang through every world and through heaven itself. The great contest that had been so long in progress in this world was now decided, and Christ was conqueror. His death had answered the question whether the Father and the Son had sufficient love for man to exercise self-denial and a spirit of sacrifice. Satan had revealed his true character as a liar and a murderer. It was seen that the very same spirit with which he had ruled the children of men who were under his power, he would have manifested if permitted to control the intelligences of heaven. With one voice the loyal universe united in extolling the divine administration.

If the law could be changed, man might have been saved without the sacrifice of Christ; but the fact that it was necessary for Christ to give His life for the fallen race, proves that the law of God will not release the sinner from its claims upon him. It is demonstrated that the wages of sin is death. When Christ died, the destruction of Satan was made certain. But if the law was abolished at the cross, as many claim, then the agony and death of God's dear Son were endured only to give to Satan just what he asked; then the prince of evil triumphed, his charges against the divine government were sustained. The very fact that Christ bore the penalty of man's transgression is a mighty argument to all created intelligences that the law is changeless; that God is righteous, merciful, and self-denying; and that infinite justice and mercy unite in the administration of His government.

5

Satan's Enmity Against the Law

· · · · · · · · · · · ·

The very first effort of Satan to overthrow God's law—undertaken among the sinless inhabitants of heaven—seemed for a time to be crowned with success. A vast number of the angels were seduced; but Satan's apparent triumph resulted in defeat and loss, separation from God, and banishment from heaven.

When the conflict was renewed upon the earth, Satan again won a seeming advantage. By transgression, man became his captive, and man's kingdom also was betrayed into the hands of the archrebel. Now the way seemed open for Satan to establish an independent kingdom, and to defy the authority of God and His Son. But the plan of salvation made it possible for man again to be brought into harmony with God, and to render obedience to His law, and for both man and the earth to be finally redeemed from the power of the wicked one.

Again Satan was defeated, and again he resorted to deception, in the hope of converting his defeat into a victory. To stir up rebellion in the fallen race, he now represented God as unjust in having permitted man to transgress His law. "Why," said the artful tempter, "when God knew what would be the result, did He permit man to be placed on trial, to sin, and bring in misery and death?" And the children of Adam, forgetful of the long-suffering mercy that had granted man another trial, regardless of the amazing, the awful sacrifice which his rebellion had cost the King of heaven, gave ear to the tempter, and murmured against the only Being who could save them from the destructive power of Satan.

There are thousands today echoing the same rebellious complaint against God. They do not see that to deprive man of the freedom of choice would be to rob him of his prerogative as an intelligent being, and make him a mere automaton. It is not God's purpose to coerce the will. Man was created a free moral agent. Like the inhabitants of all other worlds, he must be subjected to the test of obedience; but he is never brought into such a position that yielding to evil becomes a matter of necessity. No temptation or trial is permitted to come to him which he is unable to resist. God made such ample provision that man need never have been defeated in the conflict with Satan.

As men increased upon the earth, almost the whole world joined the ranks of rebellion. Once more Satan seemed to have gained the victory. But omnipotent power again cut short the working of iniquity, and the earth was cleansed by the Flood from its moral pollution.

Says the prophet, "When Thy judgments are in the earth, the inhabitants of the world will learn righteousness. Let favor be showed to the wicked, yet will he not learn righteousness, … and will not behold the majesty of Jehovah." Isaiah 26:9, 10. Thus it was after the Flood. Released from His judgments, the inhabitants of the earth again rebelled against the Lord. Twice God's covenant and His statutes had been rejected by the world. Both the people before the Flood and the descendants of Noah cast off the divine authority. Then God entered into covenant with Abraham, and took to Himself a people to become the depositaries of His law. To seduce and destroy this people, Satan began at once to lay his snares. The children of Jacob were tempted to contract marriages with the heathen and to worship their idols. But Joseph was faithful to God, and his fidelity was a constant testimony to the true faith. It was to quench this light that Satan worked through the envy of Joseph's brothers to cause him to be sold as a slave in a heathen land. God overruled events, however, so that the knowledge of Himself should be given to the people of Egypt. Both in the house of Potiphar and in the prison Joseph received an education and training that, with the fear of God, prepared him for his high position as prime minister of the nation. From the palace of the Pharaohs his influence was felt throughout the land, and the knowledge of God spread far and wide. The Israelites in Egypt also became prosperous and wealthy, and such as were true to God exerted a widespread influence. The idolatrous priests were filled with alarm as they saw the new religion finding favor. Inspired by Satan with his own enmity toward the God of heaven, they set themselves to quench the light. To the priests was committed the education of the heir

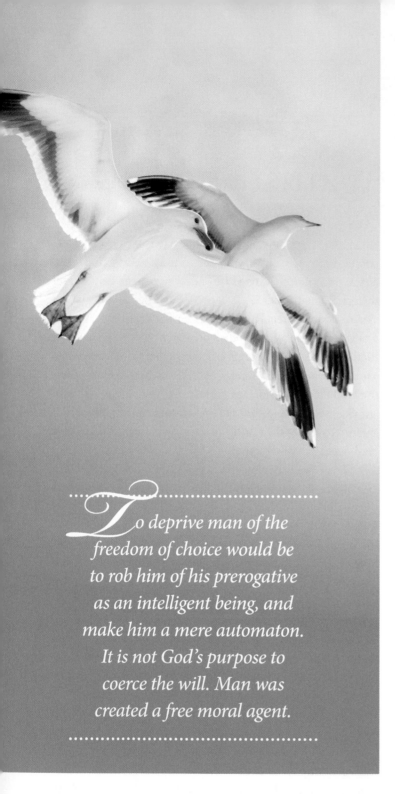

To deprive man of the freedom of choice would be to rob him of his prerogative as an intelligent being, and make him a mere automaton. It is not God's purpose to coerce the will. Man was created a free moral agent.

by Moses. When the Hebrew leader came before the king with a message from "Jehovah, God of Israel," it was not ignorance of the true God, but defiance of His power, that prompted the answer, "Who is Jehovah, that I should obey His voice? ... I know not Jehovah." Exodus 5:12. From first to last, Pharaoh's opposition to the divine command was not the result of ignorance, but of hatred and defiance.

Though the Egyptians had so long rejected the knowledge of God, the Lord still gave them opportunity for repentance. In the days of Joseph, Egypt had been an asylum for Israel; God had been honored in the kindness shown His people; and now the long-suffering One, slow to anger, and full of compassion, gave each judgment time to do its work; the Egyptians, cursed through the very objects they had worshiped, had evidence of the power of Jehovah, and all who would, might submit to God and escape His judgments. The bigotry and stubbornness of the king resulted in spreading the knowledge of God, and bringing many of the Egyptians to give themselves to His service.

It was because the Israelites were so disposed to connect themselves with the heathen and imitate their idolatry that God had permitted them to go down into Egypt, where the influence of Joseph was widely felt, and where circumstances were favorable for them to remain a distinct people. Here also the gross idolatry of the Egyptians and their cruelty and oppression during the latter part of the Hebrew sojourn should have inspired in them an abhorrence of idolatry, and should have led them to flee for refuge to the God of their fathers. This very providence Satan made a means to serve his purpose, darkening the minds of the Israelites and leading them to imitate the practices of their heathen masters. On account of the superstitious veneration in which animals were held by the Egyptians, the Hebrews were not permitted, during their bondage, to present the sacrificial offerings. Thus their minds were not directed by this service to the great Sacrifice, and their faith was weakened. When the time came for Israel's deliverance, Satan set himself to resist the purposes of God. It was his determination that that great people, numbering more than two million souls, should be held in ignorance and superstition. The people whom God had promised to bless and multiply, to make a power in the earth, and through whom he was to reveal the knowledge of His will—the people whom He was to make the keepers of His law—this very people Satan was seeking to keep in obscurity and bondage, that he might obliterate from their minds the remembrance of God.

When the miracles were wrought before the king, Satan was on the ground to counteract their influence and prevent

to the throne, and it was this spirit of determined opposition to God and zeal for idolatry that molded the character of the future monarch, and led to cruelty and oppression toward the Hebrews.

During the forty years after the flight of Moses from Egypt, idolatry seemed to have conquered. Year by year the hopes of the Israelites grew fainter. Both king and people exulted in their power, and mocked the God of Israel. This grew until it culminated in the Pharaoh who was confronted

Pharaoh from acknowledging the supremacy of God and obeying His mandate. Satan wrought to the utmost of his power to counterfeit the work of God and resist His will. The only result was to prepare the way for greater exhibitions of the divine power and glory, and to make more apparent, both to the Israelites and to all Egypt, the existence and sovereignty of the true and living God.

God delivered Israel with the mighty manifestations of His power, and with judgments upon all the gods of Egypt. "He brought forth his people with joy, and His chosen with gladness: … that they might observe His statutes, and keep His laws." Psalm 105:43–45. He rescued them from their servile state, that He might bring them to a good land—a land which in His providence had been prepared for them as a refuge from their enemies, where they might dwell under the shadow of His wings. He would bring them to Himself, and encircle them in His everlasting arms; and in return for all His goodness and mercy to them they were required to have no other gods before Him, the living God, and to exalt His name and make it glorious in the earth.

During the bondage in Egypt many of the Israelites had, to a great extent, lost the knowledge of God's law, and had mingled its precepts with heathen customs and traditions. God brought them to Sinai, and there with His own voice declared His law.

Satan and evil angels were on the ground. Even while God was proclaiming His law to His people, Satan was plotting to tempt them to sin. This people whom God had chosen, he would wrench away, in the very face of heaven. By leading them into idolatry, he would destroy the efficacy of all worship; for how can man be elevated by adoring what is no higher than himself and may be symbolized by his own handiwork? If men could become so blinded to the power, the majesty, and the glory of the infinite God as to represent Him by a graven image, or even by a beast or reptile; if they could so forget their own divine relationship, formed in the image of their Maker as to bow down to these revolting and senseless objects—then the way was open for foul license; the evil passions of the heart would be unrestrained, and Satan would have full sway.

At the very foot of Sinai, Satan began to execute his plans for overthrowing the law of God, thus carrying forward the same work he had begun in heaven. During the forty days while Moses was in the mount with God, Satan was busy exciting doubt, apostasy, and rebellion. While God was writing down His law, to be committed to His covenant people, the Israelites, denying their loyalty to Jehovah, were demanding gods of gold! When Moses came from the awful presence of the divine glory, with the precepts of the law which they had pledged themselves to obey, he found them, in open defiance of its commands, bowing in adoration before a golden image.

By leading Israel to this daring insult and blasphemy to Jehovah, Satan had planned to cause their ruin. Since they had proved themselves to be so utterly degraded, so lost to all sense of the privileges and blessings that God had offered them, and to their own solemn and repeated pledges of loyalty, the Lord would, he believed, divorce them from Himself and devote them to destruction. Thus would be secured the extinction of the seed of Abraham, that seed of promise that was to preserve the knowledge of the living God, and through whom He was to come—the true Seed, that was to conquer Satan. The great rebel had planned to destroy Israel, and thus thwart the purposes of God. But again he was defeated. Sinful as they were, the people of Israel were not destroyed. While those who stubbornly ranged themselves on the side of Satan were cut off, the people, humbled and repentant, were mercifully pardoned. The history of this sin was to stand as a perpetual testimony to the guilt and punishment of idolatry, and the justice and long-suffering mercy of God.

The whole universe had been witness to the scenes at Sinai. In the working out of the two administrations was seen the contrast between the government of God and that of Satan. Again the sinless inhabitants of other worlds beheld the results of Satan's apostasy, and the kind of government he would have established in heaven had he been permitted to bear sway.

By causing men to violate the second commandment, Satan aimed to degrade their conceptions of the Divine Being. By setting aside the fourth, he would cause them to forget God altogether. God's claim to reverence and worship, above the gods of the heathen, is based upon the fact that He is the Creator, and that to Him all other beings owe their existence. Thus it is presented in the Bible. Says the prophet Jeremiah: "The Lord is the true God, He is the living God, and an everlasting King. … The gods that have not made the heavens and the earth, even they shall perish from the earth, and from under these heavens. He hath made the earth by His power, He hath established the world by His wisdom, and hath stretched out the heavens by His discretion." "Every man is brutish in his knowledge: every founder is confounded by the graven image: for his molten image is falsehood, and there is no breath in them. They are vanity, and the work of errors: in the time of their visitation they shall perish. The portion of Jacob is not like them: for He is the former of all things." Jeremiah 10:10–12, 14–16. The Sabbath, as a memorial of God's creative power, points to Him as the maker of

*N*ever since man was created had there been witnessed such a manifestation of divine power as when the law was proclaimed from Sinai. "The earth shook, the heavens also dropped at the presence of God: even Sinai itself was moved at the presence of God, the God of Israel." Psalm 68:8.

the heavens and the earth. Hence it is a constant witness to His existence and a reminder of His greatness, His wisdom, and His love. Had the Sabbath always been sacredly observed, there could never have been an atheist or an idolater.

The Sabbath institution, which originated in Eden, is as old as the world itself. It was observed by all the patriarchs, from creation down. During the bondage in Egypt, the Israelites were forced by their taskmasters to violate the Sabbath, and to a great extent they lost the knowledge of its sacredness. When the law was proclaimed at Sinai the very first words of the fourth commandment were, "Remember the Sabbath day, to keep it holy"—showing that the Sabbath was not then instituted; we are pointed back for its origin to creation. In order to obliterate God from the minds of men, Satan aimed to tear down this great memorial. If men could be led to forget their Creator, they would make no effort to resist the power of evil, and Satan would be sure of his prey.

Satan's enmity against God's law had impelled him to war against every precept of the Decalogue. To the great principle of love and loyalty to God, the Father of all, the principle of filial love and obedience is closely related. Contempt for parental authority will soon lead to contempt for the authority of God. Hence Satan's efforts to lessen the obligation of the fifth commandment. Among heathen peoples the principle

enjoined in this precept was little heeded. In many nations parents were abandoned or put to death as soon as age had rendered them incapable of providing for themselves. In the family the mother was treated with little respect, and upon the death of her husband she was required to submit to the authority of her eldest son. Filial obedience was enjoined by Moses; but as the Israelites departed from the Lord, the fifth commandment, with others, came to be disregarded.

Satan was "a murderer from the beginning" (John 8:44); and as soon as he had obtained power over the human race, he not only prompted them to hate and slay one another, but, the more boldly to defy the authority of God, he made the violation of the sixth commandment a part of their religion.

By perverted conceptions of divine attributes, heathen nations were led to believe human sacrifices necessary to secure the favor of their deities; and the most horrible cruelties have been perpetrated under the various forms of idolatry. Among these was the practice of causing their children to pass through the fire before their idols. When one of them came through this ordeal unharmed, the people believed that their offerings were accepted; the one thus delivered was regarded as specially favored by the gods, was loaded with benefits, and ever afterward held in high esteem; and however aggravated his crimes, he was never punished. But should one be burned in passing through the fire, his fate was sealed; it was believed that the anger of the gods could be appeased only by taking the life of the victim, and he was accordingly offered as a sacrifice. In times of great apostasy these abominations prevailed, to some extent, among the Israelites.

The violation of the seventh commandment also was early practiced in the name of religion. The most licentious and abominable rites were made a part of the heathen worship. The gods themselves were represented as impure, and their worshipers gave the rein to the baser passions. Unnatural vices prevailed and the religious festivals were characterized by universal and open impurity.

Polygamy was practiced at an early date. It was one of the sins that brought the wrath of God upon the antediluvian world. Yet after the Flood it again became widespread. It was Satan's studied effort to pervert the marriage institution, to weaken its obligations and lessen its sacredness; for in no surer way could he deface the image of God in man and open the door to misery and vice.

From the opening of the great controversy it has been Satan's purpose to misrepresent God's character and to excite rebellion against His law, and this work appears to be crowned with success. The multitudes give ear to Satan's deceptions and set themselves against God. But amid the working of evil, God's purposes move steadily forward to their accomplishment; to all created intelligences He is making manifest His justice and benevolence. Through Satan's temptations the whole human race have become transgressors of God's law, but by the sacrifice of His Son a way is opened whereby they may return to God. Through the grace of Christ they may be enabled to render obedience to the Father's law. Thus in every age, from the midst of apostasy and rebellion, God gathers out a people that are true to Him—a people "in whose heart is [His] law." Isaiah 51:7.

It was by deception that Satan seduced angels; thus he has in all ages carried forward his work among men, and he will continue this policy to the last. Should he openly profess to be warring against God and His law, men would beware; but he disguises himself, and mixes truth with error. The most dangerous falsehoods are those that are mingled with truth. It is thus that errors are received that captivate and ruin the soul. By this means Satan carries the world with him. But a day is coming when his triumph will be forever ended.

God's dealings with rebellion will result in fully unmasking the work that has so long been carried on under cover. The results of Satan's rule, the fruits of setting aside the divine statutes, will be laid open to the view of all created intelligences. The law of God will stand fully vindicated. It will be seen that all the dealings of God have been conducted with reference to the eternal good of His people, and the good of all the worlds that He has created. Satan himself, in the presence of the witnessing universe, will confess the justice of God's government and the righteousness of His law.

The time is not far distant when God will arise to vindicate His insulted authority. "The Lord cometh out of His place to punish the inhabitants of the earth for their iniquity." Isaiah 26:21. "But who may abide the day of His coming? and who shall stand when He appeareth?" Malachi 3:2. The people of Israel, because of their sinfulness, were forbidden to approach the mount when God was about to descend upon it to proclaim His law, lest they should be consumed by the burning glory of His presence. If such manifestations of His power marked the place chosen for the proclamation of God's law, how terrible must be His tribunal when He comes for the execution of these sacred statutes. How will those who have trampled upon His authority endure His glory in the great day of final retribution? The terrors of Sinai were to represent to the people the scenes of the judgment. The sound of a trumpet summoned Israel to meet with God. The voice of the Archangel and the trump of God shall summon, from the whole earth, both the living and the dead to the presence of their Judge. The Father and the Son, attended by a multitude of angels, were present upon the mount. At the great judgment day Christ will come "in the glory of His Father with His angels." Matthew 16:27. He shall then sit upon the throne of His glory, and before Him shall be gathered all nations.

When the divine Presence was manifested upon Sinai, the glory of the Lord was like devouring fire in the sight of all Israel. But when Christ shall come in glory with His holy angels the whole earth shall be ablaze with the terrible light of His presence. "Our God shall come, and shall not keep silence: a fire shall devour before Him, and it shall be very tempestuous round about Him. He shall call to the heavens from above, and to the earth, that He may judge His people." Psalm 50:3, 4. A fiery stream shall issue and come forth from before Him, which shall cause the elements to melt with fervent heat, the earth also, and the works that are therein shall be burned up. "The Lord Jesus shall be revealed from heaven with His mighty angels, in flaming fire taking vengeance on them that know not God, and that obey not the gospel." 2 Thessalonians 1:7, 8.

Never since man was created had there been witnessed such a manifestation of divine power as when the law was proclaimed from Sinai. "The earth shook, the heavens also dropped at the presence of God: even Sinai itself was moved at the presence of God, the God of Israel." Psalm 68:8. Amid the most terrific convulsions of nature the voice of God, like a trumpet, was heard from the cloud. The mountain was shaken from base to summit, and the hosts of Israel, pale and trembling with terror, lay upon their faces upon the earth. He whose voice then shook the earth has declared, "Yet once more I shake not the earth only, but also heaven." Hebrews 12:26. Says the Scripture, "The Lord shall roar from on high, and utter His voice from His holy habitation;" "and the heavens and the earth shall shake." Jeremiah 25:30; Joel 3:16. In that great coming day, the heaven itself shall depart "as a scroll when it is rolled together." Revelation 6:14. And every mountain and island shall be moved out of its place. "The earth shall reel to and fro like a drunkard, and shall be removed like a cottage; and the transgression thereof shall be heavy upon it; and it shall fall, and not rise again." Isaiah 24:20.

"Therefore shall all hands be faint," all faces shall be "turned into paleness," "and every man's heart shall melt. And they shall be afraid: pangs and sorrows shall take hold of them." "And I will punish the world for their evil," saith the Lord, "and I will cause the arrogancy of the proud to cease, and will lay low the haughtiness of the terrible." Isaiah 13:7, 8, 11; Jeremiah 30:6.

When Moses came from the divine Presence in the mount, where he had received the tables of the testimony, guilty Israel could not endure the light that glorified his countenance. How much less can transgressors look upon the Son of God when He shall appear in the glory of His Father, surrounded by all the heavenly host, to execute judgment upon the transgressors of His law and the rejecters of His atonement. Those who have disregarded the law of God and trodden under foot the blood of Christ, "the kings of the earth, and the great men, and the rich men, and the chief captains, and the mighty men," shall hide themselves "in the dens and in the rocks of the mountains," and they shall say to the mountains and rocks, "Fall on us, and hide us from the face of Him that sitteth on the throne, and from the wrath of the Lamb: for the great day of His wrath is come; and who shall be able to stand?" Revelation 6:15-17. "In that day a man shall cast his idols of silver, and his idols of gold, … to the moles and to the bats; to go into the clefts of the rocks, and into the tops of the ragged rocks, for fear of the Lord, and for the glory of His majesty, when He ariseth to shake terribly the earth." Isaiah 2:20, 21.

Then it will be seen that Satan's rebellion against God has resulted in ruin to himself and to all that chose to become his subjects. He has represented that great good would result from transgression; but it will be seen that "the wages of sin is death." "For, behold, the day cometh, that shall burn as an oven; and all the proud, yea, and all that do wickedly, shall be stubble: and the day that cometh shall burn them up, saith the Lord of hosts, that it shall leave them neither root nor branch." Romans 6:23; Malachi 4:1. Satan, the root of every sin, and all evil workers, who are his branches, shall be utterly cut off. An end will be made of sin, with all the woe and ruin that have resulted from it. Says the psalmist, "Thou hast destroyed the wicked, thou hast put out their name forever and ever. O thou enemy, destructions are come to a perpetual end." Psalm 9:5, 6.

But amid the tempest of divine judgment the children of God will have no cause for fear. "The Lord will be the hope of His people, and the strength of the children of Israel." Joel 3:16. The day that brings terror and destruction to the transgressors of God's law will bring to the obedient "joy unspeakable and full of glory" "Gather My saints together unto Me," saith the Lord, "those that have made a covenant with Me by sacrifice. And the heavens shall declare His righteousness: for God is Judge Himself." 1 Peter 1:8; Psalm 50:5, 6.

"Then shall ye return, and discern between the righteous and the wicked, between him that serveth God and him that serveth Him not." Malachi 3:18. "Hearken unto Me, ye that know righteousness, the people in whose heart is My law." "Behold, I have taken out of thine hand the cup of trembling, … thou shalt no more drink it again." "I, even I, am He that comforteth you." Isaiah 51:7, 22, 12. "For the mountains shall depart, and the hills be removed; but My kindness shall not depart from thee, neither shall the covenant of My peace be removed, saith the Lord that hath mercy on thee." Isaiah 54:10.

The great plan of redemption results in fully bringing back the world into God's favor. All that was lost by sin is restored. Not only man but the earth is redeemed, to be the eternal abode of the obedient. For six thousand years Satan has struggled to maintain possession of the earth. Now God's original purpose in its creation is accomplished. "The saints of the Most High shall take the kingdom, and possess the kingdom forever, even forever and ever." Daniel 7:18.

"From the rising of the sun unto the going down of the same the Lord's name is to be praised." Psalm 113:3. "In that day shall there be one Lord, and His name one." "And Jehovah shall be king over all the earth." Zechariah 14:9. Says the Scripture, "Forever, O Lord, Thy word is settled in heaven." "All His commandments are sure. They stand fast forever and ever." Psalms 119:89; 111:7, 8. The sacred statutes which Satan has hated and sought to destroy, will be honored throughout a sinless universe. And "as the earth bringeth forth her bud, and as the garden causeth the things that are sown in it to spring forth; so the Lord God will cause righteousness and praise to spring forth before all nations." Isaiah 61:11.

6

The Tabernacle and Its Services

This chapter is based on Exodus 25 to 40; Leviticus 4 and 16.

. . . .

The command was communicated to Moses while in the mount with God, "Let them make Me a sanctuary; that I may dwell among them;" and full directions were given for the construction of the tabernacle (Exodus 25:8). By their apostasy the Israelites forfeited the blessing of the divine Presence, and for the time rendered impossible the erection of a sanctuary for God among them. But after they were again taken into favor with heaven, the great leader proceeded to execute the divine command.

Chosen men were especially endowed by God with skill and wisdom for the construction of the sacred building. God Himself gave to Moses the plan of that structure, with particular directions as to its size and form, the materials to be employed, and every article of furniture which it was to contain. The holy places made with hands were to be "figures of the true," "patterns of things in the heavens" (Hebrews 9:24, 23)—a miniature representation of the heavenly temple where Christ, our great High Priest, after offering His life as a sacrifice, was to minister in the sinner's behalf. God presented before Moses in the mount a view of the heavenly sanctuary, and commanded him to make all things according to the pattern shown him. All these directions were carefully recorded by Moses, who communicated them to the leaders of the people.

For the building of the sanctuary great and expensive preparations were necessary; a large amount of the most precious and costly material was required; yet the Lord accepted only freewill offerings. "Of every man that giveth it willingly with his heart ye shall take My offering" was the divine command repeated by Moses to the congregation. Devotion to God and a spirit of sacrifice were the first requisites in preparing a dwelling place for the Most High.

All the people responded with one accord. "They came, every one whose heart stirred him up, and every one whom his spirit made willing, and they brought the Lord's offering to the work of the tabernacle of the congregation, and for all His service, and for the holy garments. And they came, both men and women, as many as were willinghearted, and brought bracelets, and earrings, and rings, and tablets, all jewels of gold: and every man that offered, offered an offering of gold unto the Lord." Exodus 35:21, 22.

"And every man with whom was found blue, and purple, and scarlet, and fine linen, and goats' hair, and rams' skins dyed red, and sealskins, brought them. Everyone that did offer an offering of silver and brass brought the Lord's offering: and every man, with whom was found acacia wood for any work of the service, brought it.

"And all the women that were wisehearted did spin with their hands, and brought that which they had spun, the blue, and the purple, the scarlet, and the fine linen. And all the women whose heart stirred them up in wisdom spun the goats' hair.

"And the rulers brought the onyx stones, and the stones to be set, for the ephod, and for the breastplate; and the spice, and the oil; for the light, and for the anointing oil, and for the sweet incense." Exodus 35:23–28, RV.

While the building of the sanctuary was in progress the people, old and young—men, women, and children—continued to bring their offerings, until those in charge of the work found that they had enough, and even more than could be used. And Moses caused to be proclaimed throughout the camp, "Let neither man nor woman make any more work for the offering of the sanctuary. So the people were restrained from bringing." Exodus 36:6. The murmurings of the Israelites and the visitations of God's judgments because of their sins are recorded as a warning to after-generations. And their devotion, their zeal and liberality, are an example worthy of imitation. All who love the worship of God and prize the blessing of His sacred presence will manifest the same spirit of sacrifice in preparing a house where He may meet with them. They will desire to bring to the Lord an offering of the very best that they possess. A house built for God should not be left in debt, for He is thereby dishonored. An amount sufficient to accomplish the work should be freely given, that the workmen may be able to say, as did the builders of the tabernacle, "Bring no more offerings."

The tabernacle was so constructed that it could be taken apart and borne with the Israelites in all their journeyings. It was therefore small, being not more than fifty-five feet in length, and eighteen in breadth and height. Yet it was a magnificent structure. The wood employed for the building and its furniture was that of the acacia tree, which was less subject to decay than any other to be obtained at Sinai. The walls consisted of upright boards, set in silver sockets, and held firm by pillars and connecting bars; and all were overlaid with gold, giving to the building the appearance of solid gold. The roof was formed of four sets of curtains, the innermost of "fine twined linen, and blue, and purple, and scarlet: with cherubim of cunning work;" the other three respectively were of goats' hair, rams' skins dyed red, and sealskins, so arranged as to afford complete protection (Exodus 26:1).

The building was divided into two apartments by a rich and beautiful curtain, or veil, suspended from gold-plated pillars; and a similar veil closed the entrance of the first apartment. These, like the inner covering, which formed the ceiling, were of the most gorgeous colors, blue, purple, and scarlet, beautifully arranged, while inwrought with threads of gold and silver were cherubim to represent the angelic host who are connected with the work of the heavenly sanctuary and who are ministering spirits to the people of God on earth.

The sacred tent was enclosed in an open space called the court, which was surrounded by hangings, or screens, of fine linen, suspended from pillars of brass. The entrance to this enclosure was at the eastern end. It was closed by curtains of costly material and beautiful workmanship, though inferior to those of the sanctuary. The hangings of the court being only about half as high as the walls of the tabernacle, the building could be plainly seen by the people without. In the court, and nearest the entrance, stood the brazen altar of burnt offering. Upon this altar were consumed all the sacrifices made by fire unto the Lord, and its horns were sprinkled with the atoning blood. Between the altar and the door of the tabernacle was the laver, which was also of brass, made from the mirrors that had been the freewill offering of the women of Israel. At the laver the priests were to wash their hands and their feet whenever they went into the sacred apartments, or approached the altar to offer a burnt offering unto the Lord.

In the first apartment, or holy place, were the table of showbread, the candlestick, or lampstand, and the altar of incense. The table of showbread stood on the north. With its ornamental crown, it was overlaid with pure gold. On this table the priests were each Sabbath to place twelve cakes, arranged in two piles, and sprinkled with frankincense. The loaves that were removed, being accounted holy, were to be eaten by the priests. On the south was the seven-branched candlestick, with its seven lamps. Its branches were ornamented with exquisitely wrought flowers, resembling lilies, and the whole was made from one solid piece of gold. There being no windows in the tabernacle, the lamps were never all extinguished at one time, but shed their light by day and by night. Just before the veil separating the holy place from the most holy and the immediate presence of God, stood the golden altar of incense. Upon this altar the priest was to burn incense every morning and evening; its horns were touched with the blood of the sin offering, and it was sprinkled with blood upon the great Day of Atonement. The fire upon this altar was kindled by God Himself and was sacredly cherished. Day and night the holy incense diffused its fragrance

The fire upon this altar was kindled by God Himself and was sacredly cherished. Day and night the holy incense diffused its fragrance throughout the sacred apartments, and without, far around the tabernacle.

throughout the sacred apartments, and without, far around the tabernacle.

Beyond the inner veil was the holy of holies, where centered the symbolic service of atonement and intercession, and which formed the connecting link between heaven and earth. In this apartment was the ark, a chest of acacia wood, overlaid within and without with gold, and having a crown of gold about the top. It was made as a depository for the tables of stone, upon which God Himself had inscribed the Ten Commandments. Hence it was called the ark of God's testament, or the ark of the covenant, since the Ten Commandments were the basis of the covenant made between God and Israel.

The cover of the sacred chest was called the mercy seat. This was wrought of one solid piece of gold, and was surmounted by golden cherubim, one standing on each end. One wing of each angel was stretched forth on high, while the other was folded over the body (see Ezekiel 1:11) in token of reverence and humility. The position of the cherubim, with their faces turned toward each other, and looking reverently downward toward the ark, represented the reverence with which the heavenly host regard the law of God and their interest in the plan of redemption.

Above the mercy seat was the Shekinah, the manifestation of the divine Presence; and from between the cherubim, God made known His will. Divine messages were sometimes communicated to the high priest by a voice from the cloud. Sometimes a light fell upon the angel at the right, to signify approval or acceptance, or a shadow or cloud rested upon the one at the left to reveal disapproval or rejection.

The law of God, enshrined within the ark, was the great rule of righteousness and judgment. That law pronounced death upon the transgressor; but above the law was the mercy seat, upon which the presence of God was revealed, and from which, by virtue of the atonement, pardon was granted to the repentant sinner. Thus in the work of Christ for our redemption, symbolized by the sanctuary service, "mercy and truth are met together; righteousness and peace have kissed each other." Psalm 85:10.

No language can describe the glory of the scene presented within the sanctuary—the gold-plated walls reflecting the light from the golden candlestick, the brilliant hues of the richly embroidered curtains with their shining angels, the table, and the altar of incense, glittering with gold; beyond the second veil the sacred ark, with its mystic cherubim, and above it the holy Shekinah, the visible manifestation of Jehovah's presence; all but a dim reflection of the glories of the temple of God in heaven, the great center of the work for man's redemption.

A period of about half a year was occupied in the building of the tabernacle. When it was completed, Moses examined all the work of the builders, comparing it with the pattern shown him in the mount and the directions he had received from God. "As the Lord had commanded, even so had they done it: and Moses blessed them." Exodus 39:43. With eager interest the multitudes of Israel crowded around to look upon the sacred structure. While they were contemplating the scene with reverent satisfaction, the pillar of cloud floated over the sanctuary and, descending, enveloped it. "And the glory of the Lord filled the tabernacle." Exodus 40:35. There was a revealing of the divine majesty, and for a time even Moses could not enter. With deep emotion the people beheld the token that the work of their hands was accepted. There were no loud demonstrations of rejoicing. A solemn awe rested upon all. But the gladness of their hearts welled up in tears of joy, and they murmured low, earnest words of gratitude that God had condescended to abide with them.

By divine direction the tribe of Levi was set apart for the service of the sanctuary. In the earliest times every man was the priest of his own household. In the days of Abraham the priesthood was regarded as the birthright of the eldest son. Now, instead of the first-born of all Israel, the Lord accepted the tribe of Levi for the work of the sanctuary. By this signal honor He manifested His approval of their fidelity, both in adhering to His service and in executing His judgments when Israel apostatized in the worship of the golden calf. The priesthood, however, was restricted to the family of Aaron. Aaron and his sons alone were permitted to minister before the Lord; the rest of the tribe were entrusted with the charge of the tabernacle and its furniture, and they were to attend upon the priests in their ministration, but they were not to sacrifice, to burn incense, or to see the holy things till they were covered.

In accordance with their office, a special dress was appointed for the priests. "Thou shalt make holy garments for Aaron thy brother, for glory and for beauty," was the divine direction to Moses (Exodus 28:2). The robe of the common priest was of white linen, and woven in one piece. It extended nearly to the feet and was confined about the waist by a white linen girdle embroidered in blue, purple, and red. A linen turban, or miter, completed his outer costume. Moses at the burning bush was directed to put off his sandals, for the ground whereon he stood was holy. So the priests were not to enter the sanctuary with shoes upon their feet. Particles of dust cleaving to them would desecrate the holy place. They were to leave their shoes in the court before entering the sanctuary, and also to wash both their hands and their feet before ministering in the tabernacle or at the altar of burnt offering. Thus was constantly taught the lesson that all defilement must be put away from those who would approach into the presence of God.

The garments of the high priest were of costly material and beautiful workmanship, befitting his exalted station. In addition to the linen dress of the common priest, he wore a robe of blue, also woven in one piece. Around the skirt it was ornamented with golden bells, and pomegranates of blue, purple, and scarlet. Outside of this was the ephod, a shorter garment of gold, blue, purple, scarlet, and white. It was confined by a girdle of the same colors, beautifully wrought. The ephod was sleeveless, and on its gold-embroidered shoulder pieces were set two onyx stones, bearing the names of the twelve tribes of Israel.

Over the ephod was the breastplate, the most sacred of the priestly vestments. This was of the same material as the ephod. It was in the form of a square, measuring a span, and was suspended from the shoulders by a cord of blue from golden rings. The border was formed of a variety of precious stones, the same that form the twelve foundations of the City of God. Within the border were twelve stones set in gold, arranged in rows of four, and, like those in the shoulder pieces, engraved with the names of the tribes. The Lord's direction was, "Aaron shall bear the names of the children of Israel in the breastplate of judgment upon his heart, when he goeth in unto the holy place, for a memorial before the Lord continually." Exodus 28:29. So Christ, the great High Priest, pleading His blood before the Father in the sinner's behalf, bears upon His heart the name of every repentant, believing soul. Says the psalmist, "I am poor and needy; yet the Lord thinketh upon me." Psalm 40:17.

At the right and left of the breastplate were two large stones of great brilliancy. These were known as the Urim and Thummim. By them the will of God was made known through the high priest. When questions were brought for decision before the Lord, a halo of light encircling the precious stone at the right was a token of the divine consent or approval, while a cloud shadowing the stone at the left was an evidence of denial or disapprobation.

The miter of the high priest consisted of the white linen turban, having attached to it by a lace of blue, a gold plate bearing the inscription, "Holiness to Jehovah." Everything connected with the apparel and deportment of the priests was to be such as to impress the beholder with a sense of the holiness of God, the sacredness of His worship, and the purity required of those who came into His presence.

Not only the sanctuary itself, but the ministration of the priests, was to "serve unto the example and shadow of heavenly things." Hebrews 8:5. Thus it was of great importance; and the Lord, through Moses, gave the most definite and explicit instruction concerning every point of this typical service. The ministration of the sanctuary consisted of two divisions, a daily and a yearly service. The daily service was performed at the altar of burnt offering in the court of the tabernacle and in the holy place; while the yearly service was in the most holy.

No mortal eye but that of the high priest was to look upon the inner apartment of the sanctuary. Only once a year could the priest enter there, and that after the most careful and solemn preparation. With trembling he went in before God, and the people in reverent silence awaited his return, their hearts uplifted in earnest prayer for the divine blessing. Before the mercy seat the high priest made the atonement for Israel; and in the cloud of glory, God met with him. His stay here beyond the accustomed time filled them with fear, lest because of their sins or his own he had been slain by the glory of the Lord.

The daily service consisted of the morning and evening burnt offering, the offering of sweet incense on the golden altar, and the special offerings for individual sins. And there were also offerings for sabbaths, new moons, and special feasts.

Every morning and evening a lamb of a year old was burned upon the altar, with its appropriate meat offering, thus symbolizing the daily consecration of the nation to Jehovah, and their constant dependence upon the atoning blood of Christ. God expressly directed that every offering presented for the service of the sanctuary should be "without blemish." Exodus 12:5. The priests were to examine all animals brought as a sacrifice, and were to reject every one in which a defect was discovered. Only an offering "without blemish" could be a symbol of His perfect purity who was to offer Himself as "a lamb without blemish and without spot." 1 Peter 1:19. The apostle Paul points to these sacrifices as an illustration of what the followers of Christ are to become. He says, "I beseech you therefore, brethren, by the mercies of God, that ye present your bodies a living sacrifice, holy, acceptable unto God, which is your reasonable service." Romans 12:1. We are to give ourselves to the service of God, and we should seek to make the offering as nearly perfect as possible. God will not be pleased with anything less than the best we can offer. Those who love Him with all the heart, will desire to give Him the best service of the life, and they will be constantly seeking to bring every power of their being into harmony with the laws that will promote their ability to do His will.

In the offering of incense the priest was brought more

directly into the presence of God than in any other act of the daily ministration. As the inner veil of the sanctuary did no extend to the top of the building, the glory of God, which was manifested above the mercy seat, was partially visible from the first apartment. When the priest offered incense before the Lord, he looked toward the ark; and as the cloud of incense arose, the divine glory descended upon the mercy seat and filled the most holy place, and often so filled both apartments that the priest was obliged to retire to the door of the tabernacle. As in that typical service the priest looked by faith to the mercy seat which he could not see, so the people of God are now to direct their prayers to Christ, their great High Priest, who, unseen by human vision, is pleading in their behalf in the sanctuary above.

The incense, ascending with the prayers of Israel, represents the merits and intercession of Christ, His perfect righteousness, which through faith is imputed to His people, and which can alone make the worship of sinful beings

Everything connected with the apparel and deportment of the priests was to be such as to impress the beholder with a sense of the holiness of God, the sacredness of His worship, and the purity required of those who came into His presence.

acceptable to God. Before the veil of the most holy place was an altar of perpetual intercession, before the holy, an altar of continual atonement. By blood and by incense God was to be approached—symbols pointing to the great Mediator, through whom sinners may approach Jehovah, and through whom alone mercy and salvation can be granted to the repentant, believing soul.

As the priests morning and evening entered the holy place at the time of incense, the daily sacrifice was ready to be offered upon the altar in the court without. This was a time of intense interest to the worshipers who assembled at the tabernacle. Before entering into the presence of God through the ministration of the priest, they were to engage in earnest searching of heart and confession of sin. They united in silent prayer, with their faces toward the holy place. Thus their petitions ascended with the cloud of incense, while faith laid hold

upon the merits of the promised Saviour prefigured by the atoning sacrifice. The hours appointed for the morning and the evening sacrifice were regarded as sacred, and they came to be observed as the set time for worship throughout the Jewish nation. And when in later times the Jews were scattered as captives in distant lands, they still at the appointed hour turned their faces toward Jerusalem and offered up their petitions to the God of Israel. In this custom Christians have an example for morning and evening prayer. While God condemns a mere round of ceremonies, without the spirit of worship, He looks with great pleasure upon those who love Him, bowing morning and evening to seek pardon for sins committed and to present their requests for needed blessings.

The showbread was kept ever before the Lord as a perpetual offering. Thus it was a part of the daily sacrifice. It was called showbread, or "bread of the presence," because it was ever before the face of the Lord. It was an acknowledgment of man's dependence upon God for both temporal and spiritual food, and that it is received only through the mediation of Christ. God had fed Israel in the wilderness with bread from heaven, and they were still dependent upon His bounty, both for temporal food and spiritual blessings. Both the manna and the showbread pointed to Christ, the living Bread, who is ever in the presence of God for us. He Himself said, "I am the living Bread which came down from heaven." John 6:48-51. Frankincense was placed upon the loaves. When the bread was removed every Sabbath, to be replaced by fresh loaves, the frankincense was burned upon the altar as a memorial before God.

The most important part of the daily ministration was the service performed in behalf of individuals. The repentant sinner brought his offering to the door of the tabernacle, and, placing his hand upon the victim's head, confessed his sins, thus in figure transferring them from himself to the innocent sacrifice. By his own hand the animal was then slain, and the blood was carried by the priest into the holy place and sprinkled before the veil, behind which was the ark containing the law that the sinner had transgressed. By this ceremony the sin was, through the blood, transferred in figure to the sanctuary. In some cases the blood was not taken into the holy place; but the flesh was then to be eaten by the priest, as Moses directed the sons of Aaron, saying, "God hath given it you to bear the iniquity of the congregation." Leviticus 10:17. Both ceremonies alike symbolized the transfer of the sin from the penitent to the sanctuary.

Such was the work that went on day by day throughout the year. The sins of Israel being thus transferred to the sanctuary, the holy places were defiled, and a special work became necessary for the removal of the sins. God commanded that an atonement be made for each of the sacred apartments, as for the altar, to "cleanse it, and hallow it from the uncleanness of the children of Israel." Leviticus 16:19.

Once a year, on the great Day of Atonement, the priest entered the most holy place for the cleansing of the sanctuary. The work there performed completed the yearly round of ministration.

On the Day of Atonement two kids of the goats were brought to the door of the tabernacle, and lots were cast upon them, "one lot for the Lord, and the other lot for the scapegoat." Leviticus 16:8 The goat upon which the first lot fell was to be slain as a sin offering for the people. And the priest was to bring his blood within the veil, and sprinkle it

upon the mercy seat. "And he shall make an atonement for the holy place, because of the uncleanness of the children of Israel, and because of their transgression in all their sins; and so shall he do for the tabernacle of the congregation, that remaineth among them in the midst of their uncleanness." Leviticus 16:16.

"And Aaron shall lay both his hands upon the head of the live goat, and confess over him all the iniquities of the children of Israel, and all their transgressions in all their sins, putting them upon the head of the goat, and shall send him away by the hand of a fit man into the wilderness: and the goat shall bear upon him all their iniquities into a land not inhabited." Leviticus 16:21, 22. Not until the goat had been thus sent away did the people regard themselves as freed from the burden of their sins. Every man was to afflict his soul while the work of atonement was going forward. All business was laid aside, and the whole congregation of Israel spent the day in solemn humiliation before God, with prayer, fasting, and deep searching of heart.

Important truths concerning the atonement were taught the people by this yearly service. In the sin offerings presented during the year, a substituted had been accepted in the sinner's stead; but the blood of the victim had not made full atonement for the sin. It had only provided a means by which the sin was transferred to the sanctuary. By the offering of blood, the sinner acknowledged the authority of the law, confessed the guilt of his transgression, and expressed his faith in Him who was to take away the sin of the world; but he was not entirely released from the condemnation of the law. On the Day of Atonement the high priest, having taken an offering for the congregation, went into the most holy place with the blood and sprinkled it upon the mercy seat, above the tables of the law. Thus the claims of the law, which demanded the life of the sinner, were satisfied. Then in his character of mediator the priest took the sins upon himself, and, leaving the sanctuary, he bore with him the burden of Israel's guilt. At the door of the tabernacle he laid his hands upon the head of the scapegoat and confessed over him "all the iniquities of the children of Israel, and all their transgressions in all their sins, putting them upon the head of the goat." Leviticus 16:21. And as the goat bearing these sins was sent away, they were, with him, regarded as forever separated

> *As Christ at His ascension appeared in the presence of God to plead His blood in behalf of penitent believers, so the priest in the daily ministration sprinkled the blood of the sacrifice in the holy place in the sinner's behalf.*

from the people. Such was the service performed "unto the example and shadow of heavenly things." Hebrews 8:5.

As has been stated, the earthly sanctuary was built by Moses according to the pattern shown him in the mount. It was "a figure for the time then present, in which were offered both gifts and sacrifices;" its two holy places were "patterns of things in the heavens;" Christ, our great High Priest, is "a minister of the sanctuary, and of the true tabernacle, which the Lord pitched, and not man." Hebrews 9:9, 23; 8:2. As in vision the apostle John was granted a view of the temple of God in heaven, he beheld there "seven lamps of fire burning before the throne." He saw an angel "having a golden censer; and there was given unto him much incense, that he should offer it with the prayers of all saints upon the golden altar which was before the throne." Revelation 4:5; 8:3. Here the prophet was permitted to behold the first apartment of the sanctuary in heaven; and he saw there the "seven lamps of fire" and the "golden altar" represented by the golden candlestick and the altar of incense in the sanctuary on earth. Again, "the temple of God was opened" (Revelation 11:19), and he looked within the inner veil, upon the holy of holies. Here he beheld "the ark of His testament" (Revelation 11:19), represented by the sacred chest constructed by Moses to contain the law of God.

Moses made the earthly sanctuary, "according to the fashion that he had seen." Paul declares that "the tabernacle, and all the vessels of the ministry," when completed, were "the patterns of things in the heavens." Acts 7:44; Hebrews 9:21, 23. And John says that he saw the sanctuary in heaven. That sanctuary, in which Jesus ministers in our behalf, is the great original, of which the sanctuary built by Moses was a copy.

The heavenly temple, the abiding place of the King of kings, where "thousand thousands ministered unto Him, and ten thousand times ten thousand stood before Him" (Daniel 7:10), that temple filled with the glory of the eternal throne, where seraphim, its shining guardians, veil their faces in adoration—no earthly structure could represent its vastness and its glory. Yet important truths concerning the heavenly sanctuary and the great work there carried forward for man's redemption were to be taught by the earthly sanctuary and its services.

After His ascension, our Saviour was to begin His work as our High Priest. Says Paul, "Christ is not entered into the holy places made with hands, which are the figures of the true; but into heaven itself, now to appear in the presence of God for us." Hebrews 9:24. As Christ's ministration was to consist of two great divisions, each occupying a period of time and having a distinctive place in the heavenly sanctuary, so the typical ministration consisted of two divisions, the daily and the yearly service, and to each a department of the tabernacle was devoted.

As Christ at His ascension appeared in the presence of God to plead His blood in behalf of penitent believers, so the priest in the daily ministration sprinkled the blood of the sacrifice in the holy place in the sinner's behalf.

The blood of Christ, while it was to release the repentant sinner from the condemnation of the law, was not to cancel the sin; it would stand on record in the sanctuary until the final atonement; so in the type the blood of the sin offering removed the sin from the penitent, but it rested in the sanctuary until the Day of Atonement.

In the great day of final award, the dead are to be "judged out of those things which were written in the books, according to their works." Revelation 20:12. Then by virtue of the atoning blood of Christ, the sins of all the truly penitent will be blotted from the books of heaven. Thus the sanctuary will be freed, or cleansed, from the record of sin. In the type, this great work of atonement, or blotting out of sins, was represented by the services of the Day of Atonement—the cleansing of the earthly sanctuary, which was accomplished by the removal, by virtue of the blood of the sin offering, of the sins by which it had been polluted.

As in the final atonement the sins of the truly penitent are to be blotted from the records of heaven, no more to be remembered or come into mind, so in the type they were borne away into the wilderness, forever separated from the congregation.

Since Satan is the originator of sin, the direct instigator of all the sins that caused the death of the Son of God, justice demands that Satan shall suffer the final punishment. Christ's work for the redemption of men and the purification of the universe from sin will be closed by the removal of sin from the heavenly sanctuary and the placing of these sins upon Satan, who will bear the final penalty. So in the typical service, the yearly round of ministration closed with the purification of the sanctuary, and the confessing of the sins on the head of the scapegoat.

Thus in the ministration of the tabernacle, and of the temple that afterward took its place, the people were taught each day the great truths relative to Christ's death and ministration, and once each year their minds were carried forward to the closing events of the great controversy between Christ and Satan, the final purification of the universe from sin and sinners.

God With Us

....

"His name shall be called Immanuel, … God with us." "The light of the knowledge of the glory of God" is seen "in the face of Jesus Christ." From the days of eternity the Lord Jesus Christ was one with the Father; He was "the image of God," the image of His greatness and majesty, "the outshining of His glory." It was to manifest this glory that He came to our world. To this sin-darkened earth He came to reveal the light of God's love,—to be "God with us." Therefore it was prophesied of Him, "His name shall be called Immanuel." Matthew 1:23; 2 Corinthians 4:6; Colossians 1:15; Hebrews 1:3; Isaiah 7:14.

By coming to dwell with us, Jesus was to reveal God both to men and to angels. He was the Word of God,— God's thought made audible. In His prayer for His disciples He says, "I have declared unto them Thy name,"—"merciful and gracious, long-suffering, and abundant in goodness and truth,"—"that the love wherewith Thou hast loved Me may be in them, and I in them." But not alone for His earthborn children was this revelation given. Our little world is the lesson book of the universe. God's wonderful purpose of grace, the mystery of redeeming love, is the theme into which "angels desire to look," and it will be their study throughout endless ages. Both the redeemed and the unfallen beings will find in the cross of Christ their science and their song. It will be seen that the glory shining in the face of Jesus is the glory of self-sacrificing love. In the light from Calvary it will be seen that the law of self-renouncing love is the law of life for earth and heaven; that the love which "seeketh not her own" has its source in the heart of God; and that in the meek and lowly One is manifested the character of Him who dwelleth in the light which no man can approach unto.

In the beginning, God was revealed in all the works of creation. It was Christ that spread the heavens, and laid the foundations of the earth. It was His hand that hung the worlds in space, and fashioned the flowers of the field. "His strength setteth fast the mountains." "The sea is His, and He made it." Psalm 65:6; 95:5. It was He that filled the earth with beauty, and the air with song. And upon all things in earth, and air, and sky, He wrote the message of the Father's love.

Now sin has marred God's perfect work, yet that handwriting remains. Even now all created things declare the glory of His excellence. There is nothing, save the selfish heart of man, that lives unto itself. No bird that cleaves the air, no animal that moves upon the ground, but ministers to some other life. There is no leaf of the forest, or lowly blade of grass, but has its ministry. Every tree and shrub and leaf pours forth that element of life without which neither man nor animal could live; and man and animal, in turn, minister to the life of tree and shrub and leaf. The flowers breathe fragrance and unfold their beauty in blessing to the world. The sun sheds its light to gladden a thousand worlds. The ocean, itself the source of all our springs and fountains, receives the streams from every land, but takes to give. The mists ascending from its bosom fall in showers to water the earth, that it may bring forth and bud.

The angels of glory find their joy in giving,—giving love and tireless watchcare to souls that are fallen and unholy. Heavenly beings woo the hearts of men; they bring to this dark world light from the courts above; by gentle and patient ministry they move upon the human spirit, to bring the lost into a fellowship with Christ which is even closer than they themselves can know.

But turning from all lesser representations, we behold God in Jesus. Looking unto Jesus we see that it is the glory of our God to give. "I do nothing of Myself," said Christ; "the living Father hath sent Me, and I live by the Father." "I seek not Mine own glory," but the glory of Him that sent Me. John 8:28; 6:57; 8:50; 7:18. In these words is set forth the great principle which is the law of life for the universe. All things Christ received from God, but He took to give. So in the heavenly courts, in His ministry for all created beings: through the beloved Son, the Father's life flows out to all; through the Son it returns, in praise and joyous service, a tide of love, to the great Source of all. And thus through

Christ the circuit of beneficence is complete, representing the character of the great Giver, the law of life.

In heaven itself this law was broken. Sin originated in self-seeking. Lucifer, the covering cherub, desired to be first in heaven. He sought to gain control of heavenly beings, to draw them away from their Creator, and to win their homage to himself. Therefore he misrepresented God, attributing to Him the desire for self-exaltation. With his own evil characteristics he sought to invest the loving Creator. Thus he deceived angels. Thus he deceived men. He led them to doubt the word of God, and to distrust His goodness. Because God is a God of justice and terrible majesty, Satan caused them to look upon Him as severe and unforgiving. Thus he drew men to join him in rebellion against God, and the night of woe settled down upon the world.

The earth was dark through misapprehension of God. That the gloomy shadows might be lightened, that the world might be brought back to God, Satan's deceptive power was to be broken. This could not be done by force. The exercise of force is contrary to the principles of God's government; He desires only the service of love; and love cannot be commanded; it cannot be won by force or authority. Only by love is love awakened. To know God is to love Him; His character must be manifested in contrast to the character of Satan. This work only one Being in all the universe could do. Only He who knew the height and depth of the love of God could make it known. Upon the world's dark night the Sun of Righteousness must rise, "with healing in His wings." Malachai 4:2.

The plan for our redemption was not an afterthought, a plan formulated after the fall of Adam. It was a revelation of "the mystery which hath been kept in silence through times eternal." Romans 16:25, RV. It was an unfolding of the principles that from eternal ages have been the foundation of God's throne. From the beginning, God and Christ knew of the apostasy of Satan, and of the fall of man through the deceptive power of the apostate. God did not ordain that sin should exist, but He foresaw its existence, and made provision to meet the terrible emergency. So great was His love for the world, that He covenanted to give His only-begotten Son, "that whosoever believeth in Him should not perish, but have everlasting life." John 3:16.

He desires only the service of love; and love cannot be commanded; it cannot be won by force or authority. Only by love is love awakened.

Lucifer had said, "I will exalt my throne above the stars of God; ... I will be like the Most High." Isaiah 14:13, 14. But Christ, "being in the form of God, counted it not a thing to be grasped to be on an equality with God, but emptied Himself, taking the form of a servant, being made in the likeness of men." Philippians 2:6, 7, RV, margin.

This was a voluntary sacrifice. Jesus might have remained at the Father's side. He might have retained the glory of heaven, and the homage of the angels. But He chose to give back the scepter into

the Father's hands, and to step down from the throne of the universe, that He might bring light to the benighted, and life to the perishing.

Nearly two thousand years ago, a voice of mysterious import was heard in heaven, from the throne of God, "Lo, I come." "Sacrifice and offering Thou wouldest not, but a body hast Thou prepared Me. ... Lo, I come (in the volume of the Book it is written of Me,) to do Thy will, O God." Hebrews 10:5–7. In these words is announced the fulfillment of the purpose that had been hidden from eternal ages. Christ was about to visit our world, and to become incarnate. He says, "A body hast Thou prepared Me." Had He appeared with the glory that was His with the Father before the world was, we could not have endured the light of His presence. That we might behold it and not be destroyed, the manifestation of His glory was shrouded. His divinity was veiled with humanity,—the invisible glory in the visible human form.

This great purpose had been shadowed forth in types and symbols. The burning bush, in which Christ appeared to Moses, revealed God. The symbol chosen for the representation of the Deity was a lowly shrub, that seemingly had no attractions. This enshrined the Infinite. The all-merciful God shrouded His glory in a most humble type, that Moses could look upon it and live. So in the pillar of cloud by day and the pillar of fire by night, God communicated with Israel, revealing to men His will, and imparting to them His grace. God's glory was subdued, and His majesty veiled, that the weak vision of finite men might behold it. So Christ was to come in "the body of our humiliation" (Philippians 3:21, RV), "in the likeness of men." In the eyes of the world He possessed no beauty that they should desire Him; yet He was the incarnate God, the light of heaven and earth. His glory was veiled, His greatness and majesty were hidden, that He might draw near to sorrowful, tempted men.

God commanded Moses for Israel, "Let them make Me a sanctuary; that I may dwell among them" (Exodus 25:8), and He abode in the sanctuary, in the midst of His people. Through all their weary wandering in the desert, the symbol of His presence was with them. So Christ set up His tabernacle in the midst of our human encampment. He pitched His tent by the side of the tents of men, that He might dwell among us, and make us familiar with His divine character and life. "The Word became flesh, and tabernacled among us (and we beheld His glory, glory as of

the Only Begotten from the Father), full of grace and truth." John 1:14, RV, margin.

Since Jesus came to dwell with us, we know that God is acquainted with our trials, and sympathizes with our griefs. Every son and daughter of Adam may understand that our Creator is the friend of sinners. For in every doctrine of grace, every promise of joy, every deed of love, every divine attraction presented in the Saviour's life on earth, we see "God with us."

Satan represents God's law of love as a law of selfishness. He declares that it is impossible for us to obey its precepts.

The fall of our first parents, with all the woe that has resulted, he charges upon the Creator, leading men to look upon God as the author of sin, and suffering, and death. Jesus was to unveil this deception. As one of us He was to give an example of obedience. For this He took upon Himself our nature, and passed through our experiences. "In all things it behooved Him to be made like unto His brethren." Hebrews 2:17. If we had to bear anything which Jesus did not endure, then upon this point Satan would represent the power of God as insufficient for us. Therefore Jesus was "in all points tempted like as we are." Hebrews 4:15. He endured every trial to which we are subject. And He exercised in His own behalf no power that is not freely offered to us. As man, He met temptation, and overcame in the strength given Him from God. He says, "I delight to do Thy will, O My God: yea, Thy law is within My heart." Psalm 40:8. As He went about doing good, and healing all who were afflicted by Satan, He made plain to men the character of God's law and the nature of His service. His life testifies that it is possible for us also to obey the law of God.

By His humanity, Christ touched humanity; by His divinity, He lays hold upon the throne of God. As the Son of man, He gave us an example of obedience; as the Son of

I Am the assurance of every promise. I Am; be not afraid. "God with us" is the surety of our deliverance from sin, the assurance of our power to obey the law of heaven.

God, He gives us power to obey. It was Christ who from the bush on Mount Horeb spoke to Moses saying, "I Am That I Am. ... Thus shalt thou say unto the children of Israel, I Am hath sent me unto you." Exodus 3:14. This was the pledge of Israel's deliverance. So when He came "in the likeness of men," He declared Himself the I Am. The Child of Bethlehem, the meek and lowly Saviour, is God "manifest in the flesh." 1 Timothy 3:16. And to us He says: "I Am the Good Shepherd." "I Am the living Bread." "I Am the Way, the Truth, and the Life." "All power is given unto Me in heaven and in earth." John 10:11; 6:51; 14:6; Matthew 28:18. I Am the assurance of every promise. I Am; be not afraid. "God with us" is the surety of our deliverance from sin, the assurance of our power to obey the law of heaven.

In stooping to take upon Himself humanity, Christ revealed a character the opposite of the character of Satan. But He stepped still lower in the path of humiliation. "Being found in fashion as a man, He humbled Himself, and became obedient unto death, even the death of the cross." Philippians 2:8. As the high priest laid aside his gorgeous pontifical robes, and officiated in the white linen dress of the common priest, so Christ took the form of a servant, and offered sacrifice, Himself the priest, Himself the victim. "He was wounded for our transgressions, He was bruised for our iniquities: the chastisement of our peace was upon Him." Isaiah 53:5.

Christ was treated as we deserve, that we might be treated as He deserves. He was condemned for our sins, in which He had no share, that we might be justified by His righteousness, in which we had no share. He suffered the death which was ours, that we might receive the life which was His. "With His stripes we are healed."

By His life and His death, Christ has achieved even more than recovery from the ruin wrought through sin. It was Satan's purpose to bring about an eternal separation between God and man; but in Christ we become more closely united to God than if we had never fallen. In taking our nature, the Saviour has bound Himself to humanity by a tie that is never to be broken. Through the eternal ages He is linked with us. "God so loved the world, that He gave His only-begotten Son." John 3:16. He gave Him not only to bear our sins, and to die as our sacrifice; He gave Him to the fallen race. To assure us of His immutable counsel of peace, God gave His only-begotten Son to become one of the human family, forever to retain His human nature. This is the pledge that God will fulfill His word. "Unto us a child is born, unto us a son is given: and the government shall be upon His shoulder." God has adopted human nature in the person of His Son, and has carried the same into the highest heaven. It is the "Son of man" who shares the throne of the universe. It is the "Son of man" whose name shall be called, "Wonderful, Counselor, The mighty God, The everlasting Father, The Prince of Peace." Isaiah 9:6. The I Am is the Daysman between God and humanity, laying His hand upon both. He who is "holy, harmless, undefiled, separate from sinners," is not ashamed to call us brethren. Hebrews 7:26; 2:11. In Christ the family of earth and the family of heaven are

bound together. Christ glorified is our brother. Heaven is enshrined in humanity, and humanity is enfolded in the bosom of Infinite Love.

Of His people God says, "They shall be as the stones of a crown, lifted up as an ensign upon His land. For how great is His goodness, and how great is His beauty!" Zechariah 9:16, 17. The exaltation of the redeemed will be an eternal testimony to God's mercy. "In the ages to come," He will "show the exceeding riches of His grace in His kindness toward us through Christ Jesus." "To the intent that ... unto the principalities and the powers in the heavenly places might be made known ... the manifold wisdom of God, according to the eternal purpose which He purposed in Christ Jesus our Lord." Ephesians 2:7; 3:10, 11, RV.

Through Christ's redeeming work the government of God stands justified. The Omnipotent One is made known as the God of love. Satan's charges are refuted, and his character unveiled. Rebellion can never again arise. Sin can never again enter the universe. Through eternal ages all are secure from apostasy. By love's self-sacrifice, the inhabitants of earth and heaven are bound to their Creator in bonds of indissoluble union.

The work of redemption will be complete. In the place where sin abounded, God's grace much more abounds. The earth itself, the very field that Satan claims as his, is to be not only ransomed but exalted. Our little world, under the curse of sin the one dark blot in His glorious creation, will be honored above all other worlds in the universe of God. Here, where the Son of God tabernacled in humanity; where the King of glory lived and suffered and died,—here, when He shall make all things new, the tabernacle of God shall be with men, "and He will dwell with them, and they shall be His people, and God Himself shall be with them, and be their God." And through endless ages as the redeemed walk in the light of the Lord, they will praise Him for His unspeakable Gift,—Immanuel, "God with us."

The Old Testament contains over 400 prophecies about the coming Messiah. These predictions were very specific, including the place and time of the Messiah's birth, His family line, when and how He would die, and more. Jesus Christ perfectly fulfilled every one of these predictions, even though they were made hundreds of years before His birth. What are the odds of this happening?

ONE-IN-A-LOT

A math professor named Peter Stoner worked with 600 students to determine the probability of one person fulfilling just eight of the more than 400 prophecies. For each prophecy, students estimated the odds of a person fulfilling that prophecy on accident. Then Professor Stoner took the most conservative averages of these 600 students. What do you think the chances were? One in a million? One in a trillion?

THE PERFECT MATCH

Let's take a look at their math:

1. **The Messiah would be born in Bethlehem (Micah 5:2).**

   Fulfilled in Mathew 2:1-6

By dividing the average population of Bethlehem by the average population of the earth since prophet Micah's time, Professor Stoner suggested that 1 man in 280,000 was born in Bethlehem.

2. **The Messiah would have a special messenger from God to prepare His way (Malachi 3:1, Isaiah 40:3).**

   Fulfilled in Matthew 3:3, Matthew 11:10, Mark 1:2, Luke 7:27

Students conservatively estimated that only 1 in 1000 people could say there was a special messenger who prepared the way for their work. John the Baptist claimed that he was God's messenger to prepare the way for the Messiah. When Jesus began His work, John was content for his own work to fade in popularity, telling his own jealous disciples that Jesus must "increase" while he must "decrease" (John 3:28–30).

3. **The Messiah would enter Jerusalem as a king riding on a donkey (Zechariah 9:9).**

   Fulfilled in Matthew 21:5–11, Mark 11:1–11, Luke 19:28–40, John 12:12–19

Of those rulers who have entered Jerusalem, how many did so riding on a donkey? Professor Stoner estimated 1 in 100. After all, most modern rulers would use a more comfortable mode of transportation! In fact, the prophet Zechariah made it clear that this donkey ride would be a profound expression of the Messiah's humility.

4. **Christ would be betrayed by a friend and wounded in His hands (Zechariah 13:6).**

   Fulfilled in Matthew 26:14–16

The professor's classes settled on 1 in 1000 for this prophecy. Students felt that a betrayal resulting in wounded hands would be quite rare! Judas, one of Jesus' own disciples, betrayed Him in an attempt to force Him into a kingly role. But rather than assert His power and become king on earth, Jesus submitted to crucifixion.

5. **The price paid for the Messiah would be 30 pieces of silver (Zechariah 11:12).**

   Fulfilled in Matthew 26:14–16

Judas was paid exactly 30 pieces of silver. Professor Stoner chose 1 in 1000 as an estimated probability for being betrayed for exactly that amount.

6. **The betrayal price would be thrown down in the Lord's house, then given to a potter (Zechariah 11:13).**

   Fulfilled in Matthew 27:3–9

The students judged such a specific requirement as extremely rare—just in 1 in 100,000! Matthew records the sad ending to Judas's story: when he realized Jesus would allow himself to be killed, Judas threw the money on the temple floor and hung himself. Unwilling to put the blood money back into the temple treasury, the leaders bought a field to use as a burial place for strangers—and that field belonged to a potter!

7. **The Messiah, though oppressed and afflicted, would remain silent (Isaiah 53:7).**

   Fulfilled in Matthew 26:63, Matthew 27:11–14, Mark 14:61, John 19:9

How many men, innocently on trial for their lives, would choose not to defend themselves and remain silent? Professor Stoner conservatively chose 1 in 1000.

8. **The Messiah would have his hands and feet pierced (Psalm 22:16).**

   Fulfilled in Matthew 27:35, Mark 15:24, Luke 23:33, Luke 24:40

Professor Stoner's students considered the various methods of execution used throughout history before placing the probability of death by crucifixion at 1 in 10,000.

PRACTICALLY IMPOSSIBLE

So what are the chances of one person accidentally fulfilling all 8 of these prophecies? One in a million? One in a trillion? Not even close! If we multiply these individual probabilities together and then divide by the number of people who have lived since the time the prophecies were given, the final result is actually one in a hundred quadrillion, also known as 1 in 10^{17}!

How much exactly is 10 to the 17th power? That many silver dollars could cover the face of Texas two feet deep! Now imagine one of those silver dollars has been painted blue. What is the probability of a blindfolded man randomly selecting the blue silver dollar on his first try? It's the very same as the chances of Jesus fulfilling just these 8 prophecies.

Jesus was truly one-of-a-kind!

Stoner, Peter W. "Chapter 3, The Christ of Prophecy." *Science Speaks: Online Edition*, Moody Press, 2002, sciencespeaks.dstoner.net/Christ_of_Prophecy.html#c9.

8

As A Child

This chapter is based on Luke 2:39, 40.

. . . .

The childhood and youth of Jesus were spent in a little mountain village. There was no place on earth that would not have been honored by His presence. The palaces of kings would have been privileged in receiving Him as a guest. But He passed by the homes of wealth, the courts of royalty, and the renowned seats of learning, to make His home in obscure and despised Nazareth.

Wonderful in its significance is the brief record of His early life: "The child grew, and waxed strong in spirit, filled with wisdom: and the grace of God was upon Him." In the sunlight of His Father's countenance, Jesus "increased in wisdom and stature, and in favor with God and man." Luke 2:52. His mind was active and penetrating, with a thoughtfulness and wisdom beyond His years. Yet His character was beautiful in its symmetry. The powers of mind and body developed gradually, in keeping with the laws of childhood.

As a child, Jesus manifested a peculiar loveliness of disposition. His willing hands were ever ready to serve others. He manifested a patience that nothing could disturb, and a truthfulness that would never sacrifice integrity. In principle firm as a rock, His life revealed the grace of unselfish courtesy.

With deep earnestness the mother of Jesus watched the unfolding of His powers, and beheld the impress of perfection upon His character. With delight she sought to encourage that bright, receptive mind. Through the Holy Spirit she received wisdom to co-operate with the heavenly agencies in the development of this child, who could claim only God as His Father.

From the earliest times the faithful in Israel had given much care to the education of the youth. The Lord had directed that even from babyhood the children should be taught of His goodness and His greatness, especially as revealed in His law, and shown in the history of Israel. Song and prayer and lessons from the Scriptures were to be adapted to the opening mind. Fathers and mothers were to instruct their children that the law of God is an expression of His character, and that as they received the principles of the law into the heart, the image of God was traced on mind and soul. Much of the teaching was oral; but the youth also learned to read the Hebrew writings; and the parchment rolls of the Old Testament Scriptures were open to their study.

In the days of Christ the town or city that did not provide for the religious instruction of the young was regarded as under the curse of God. Yet the teaching had become formal. Tradition had in a great degree supplanted the Scriptures. True education would lead the youth to "seek the Lord, if haply they might feel after Him, and find Him." Acts 17:27. But the Jewish teachers gave their attention to matters of ceremony. The mind was crowded with material that was worthless to the learner, and that would not be recognized in the higher school of the courts above. The experience which is obtained through a personal acceptance of God's word had no place in the educational system. Absorbed in the round of externals, the students found no quiet hours to spend with God. They did not hear His voice speaking to the heart. In their search after knowledge, they turned away from the Source of wisdom. The great essentials of the service of God were neglected. The principles of the law were obscured. That which was regarded as superior education was the greatest hindrance to real development. Under the training of the rabbis the powers of the youth were repressed. Their minds became cramped and narrow.

The child Jesus did not receive instruction in the synagogue schools. His mother was His first human teacher. From her lips and from the scrolls of the prophets, He learned of heavenly things. The very words which He Himself had spoken to Moses for Israel He was now taught at His mother's knee. As He advanced from childhood to youth, He did not seek the schools of the rabbis. He needed not the education to be obtained from such sources; for God was His instructor.

The question asked during the Saviour's ministry, "How knoweth this man letters, having never learned?" does not indicate that Jesus was unable to read, but merely that He had not received a rabbinical education (John 7:15). Since He gained knowledge as we may do, His intimate acquaintance with the Scriptures shows how diligently His early years were given to the study of God's word. And spread out before Him was the great library of God's created works. He who had made all things studied the lessons which His own hand had written in earth and sea and sky. Apart from the unholy ways of the world, He gathered stores of scientific knowledge from nature. He studied the life of plants and animals, and the life of man. From His earliest years He was possessed of one purpose; He lived to bless others. For this He found resources in nature; new ideas of ways and means flashed into His mind as He studied plant life and animal life. Continually He was seeking to draw from things seen illustrations by which to present the living oracles of God. The parables by which, during His ministry, He loved to teach His lessons of truth show how open His spirit was to the influences of nature, and how He had gathered the spiritual teaching from the surroundings of His daily life.

Thus to Jesus the significance of the word and the works of God was unfolded, as He was trying to understand the reason of things. Heavenly beings were His attendants, and the culture of holy thoughts and communings was His. From the first dawning of intelligence He was constantly growing in spiritual grace and knowledge of truth.

Every child may gain knowledge as Jesus did. As we try to become acquainted with our heavenly Father through His word, angels will draw near, our minds will be strengthened, our characters will be elevated and refined. We shall become more like our Saviour. And as we behold the beautiful and grand in nature, our affections go out after God. While the spirit is awed, the soul is invigorated by coming in contact with the Infinite through His works. Communion with God through prayer develops the mental and moral faculties, and the spiritual powers strengthen as we cultivate thoughts upon spiritual things.

The life of Jesus was a life in harmony with God. While He was a child, He thought and spoke as a child; but no trace of sin marred the image of God within Him. Yet He was not exempt from temptation. The inhabitants of Nazareth were proverbial for their wickedness. The low estimate in which they were generally held is shown by Nathanael's question, "Can there any good thing come out of Nazareth?" John 1:46. Jesus was placed where His character would be tested. It was necessary for Him to be constantly on guard in order to preserve His purity. He was subject to all the conflicts which we have to meet, that He might be an example to us in childhood, youth, and manhood.

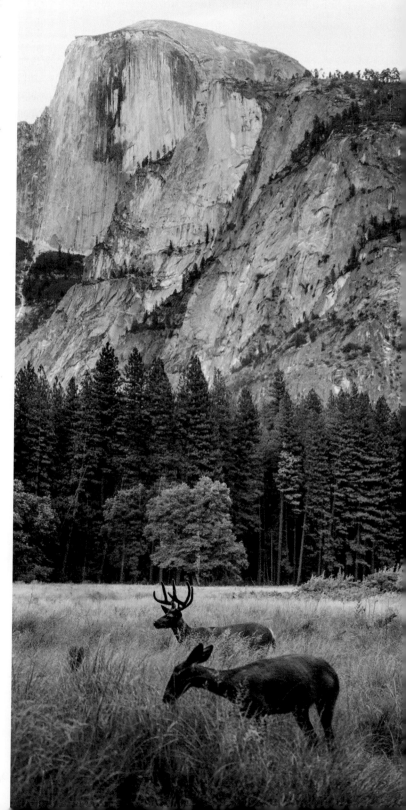

He who had made all things studied the lessons which His own hand had written in earth and sea and sky.

Satan was unwearied in his efforts to overcome the Child of Nazareth. From His earliest years Jesus was guarded by heavenly angels, yet His life was one long struggle against the powers of darkness. That there should be upon the earth one life free from the defilement of evil was an offense and a perplexity to the prince of darkness. He left no means untried to ensnare Jesus. No child of humanity will ever be called to live a holy life amid so fierce a conflict with temptation as was our Saviour.

Christ was the only sinless one who ever dwelt on earth; yet for nearly thirty years He lived among the wicked inhabitants of Nazareth. This fact is a rebuke to those who think themselves dependent upon place, fortune, or prosperity, in order to live a blameless life. Temptation, poverty, adversity, is the very discipline needed to develop purity and firmness.

Jesus lived in a peasant's home, and faithfully and cheerfully acted His part in bearing the burdens of the household. He had been the Commander of heaven, and

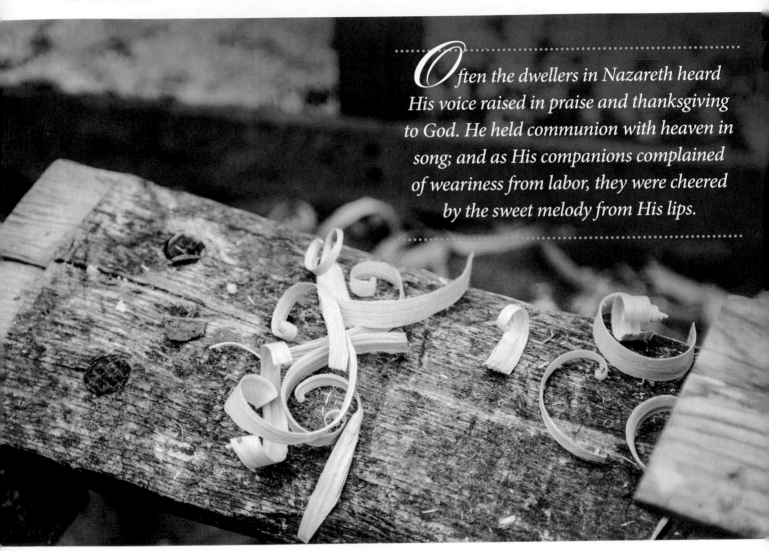

Often the dwellers in Nazareth heard His voice raised in praise and thanksgiving to God. He held communion with heaven in song; and as His companions complained of weariness from labor, they were cheered by the sweet melody from His lips.

The parents of Jesus were poor, and dependent upon their daily toil. He was familiar with poverty, self-denial, and privation. This experience was a safeguard to Him. In His industrious life there were no idle moments to invite temptation. No aimless hours opened the way for corrupting associations. So far as possible, He closed the door to the tempter. Neither gain nor pleasure, applause nor censure, could induce Him to consent to a wrong act. He was wise to discern evil, and strong to resist it.

angels had delighted to fulfill His word; now He was a willing servant, a loving, obedient son. He learned a trade, and with His own hands worked in the carpenter's shop with Joseph. In the simple garb of a common laborer He walked the streets of the little town, going to and returning from His humble work. He did not employ His divine power to lessen His burdens or to lighten His toil.

As Jesus worked in childhood and youth, mind and body were developed. He did not use His physical powers recklessly, but in such a way as to keep them in health, that He might do the best work in every line. He was not willing to be defective, even in the handling of tools. He was perfect as a workman, as He was perfect in character. By His own example He taught that it is our duty to be industrious, that our work should be performed with exactness and thoroughness, and that such labor is honorable. The exercise that teaches the hands to be useful and trains the young to bear their share of life's burdens gives physical strength, and develops every faculty. All should find something to do that will be beneficial to themselves and helpful to others. God appointed work as a blessing, and only the diligent worker finds the true glory and joy of life. The approval of God rests with loving assurance upon children and youth who cheerfully take their part in the duties of the household, sharing the burdens of father and mother. Such children will go out from the home to be useful members of society.

Throughout His life on earth, Jesus was an earnest and constant worker. He expected much; therefore He attempted much. After He had entered on His ministry, He said, "I must work the works of Him that sent Me, while it is day: the night cometh, when no man can work." John 9:4. Jesus did not shirk care and responsibility, as do many who profess to be His followers. It is because they seek to evade this discipline that so many are weak and inefficient. They may possess precious and amiable traits, but they are nerveless and almost useless when difficulties are to be met or obstacles surmounted. The positiveness and energy, the solidity and strength of character, manifested in Christ are to be developed in us, through the same discipline that He endured. And the grace that He received is for us.

So long as He lived among men, our Saviour shared the lot of the poor. He knew by experience their cares and hardships, and He could comfort and encourage all humble workers. Those who have a true conception of the teaching of His life will never feel that a distinction must be made between classes, that the rich are to be honored above the worthy poor.

Jesus carried into His labor cheerfulness and tact. It requires much patience and spirituality to bring Bible religion into the home life and into the workshop, to bear the strain of worldly business, and yet keep the eye single to the glory of God. This is where Christ was a helper. He was never so full of worldly care as to have no time or thought for heavenly things. Often He expressed the gladness of His heart by singing psalms and heavenly songs. Often the dwellers in Nazareth heard His voice raised in praise and thanksgiving to God. He held communion with heaven in song; and as His companions complained of weariness from labor, they were cheered by the sweet melody from His lips. His praise seemed to banish the evil angels, and, like incense, fill the place with fragrance. The minds of His hearers were carried away from their earthly exile, to the heavenly home.

Jesus was the fountain of healing mercy for the world; and through all those secluded years at Nazareth, His life flowed out in currents of sympathy and tenderness. The aged, the sorrowing, and the sin-burdened, the children at play in their innocent joy, the little creatures of the groves, the patient beasts of burden—all were happier for His presence. He whose word of power upheld the worlds would stoop to relieve a wounded bird. There was nothing beneath His notice, nothing to which He disdained to minister.

Thus as He grew in wisdom and stature, Jesus increased in favor with God and man. He drew the sympathy of all hearts by showing Himself capable of sympathizing with all. The atmosphere of hope and courage that surrounded Him made Him a blessing in every home. And often in the synagogue on the Sabbath day He was called upon to read the lesson from the prophets, and the hearts of the hearers thrilled as a new light shone out from the familiar words of the sacred text.

Yet Jesus shunned display. During all the years of His stay in Nazareth, He made no exhibition of His miraculous power. He sought no high position and assumed no titles. His quiet and simple life, and even the silence of the Scriptures concerning His early years, teach an important lesson. The more quiet and simple the life of the child—the more free from artificial excitement, and the more in harmony with nature—the more favorable is it to physical and mental vigor and to spiritual strength.

Jesus is our example. There are many who dwell with interest upon the period of His public ministry, while they pass unnoticed the teaching of His early years. But it is in His home life that He is the pattern for all children and youth. The Saviour condescended to poverty, that He might teach how closely we in a humble lot may walk with God. He lived to please, honor, and glorify His Father in the common things of life. His work began in consecrating the lowly trade of the craftsmen who toil for their daily bread. He was doing God's service just as much when laboring at the carpenter's bench as when working miracles for the multitude. And every youth who follows Christ's example of faithfulness and obedience in His lowly home may claim those words spoken of Him by the Father through the Holy Spirit, "Behold My Servant, whom I uphold; Mine Elect, in whom My soul delighteth." Isaiah 42:1.

Jesus did not receive baptism as a confession of guilt on His own account. He identified Himself with sinners, taking the steps that we are to take, and doing the work that we must do.

9

The Baptism

This chapter is based on Matthew 3:13–17; Mark 1:9–11; Luke 3:21, 22.

. . . .

Tidings of the wilderness prophet and his wonderful announcement, spread throughout Galilee. The message reached the peasants in the remotest hill towns, and the fisher folk by the sea, and in these simple, earnest hearts found its truest response. In Nazareth it was told in the carpenter shop that had been Joseph's, and One recognized the call. His time had come. Turning from His daily toil, He bade farewell to His mother, and followed in the steps of His countrymen who were flocking to the Jordan.

Jesus and John the Baptist were cousins, and closely related by the circumstances of their birth; yet they had had no direct acquaintance with each other. The life of Jesus had been spent at Nazareth in Galilee; that of John, in the wilderness of Judea. Amid widely different surroundings they had lived in seclusion, and had had no communication with each other. Providence had ordered this. No occasion was to be given for the charge that they had conspired together to support each other's claims.

John was acquainted with the events that had marked the birth of Jesus. He had heard of the visit to Jerusalem in His boyhood, and of what had passed in the school of the rabbis. He knew of His sinless life, and believed Him to be the Messiah; but of this he had no positive assurance. The fact that Jesus had for so many years remained in obscurity, giving no special evidence of His mission, gave occasion for doubt as to whether He could be the Promised One. The Baptist, however, waited in faith, believing that in God's own time all would be made plain. It had been revealed to him that the Messiah would seek baptism at his hands, and that a sign of His divine character should then be given. Thus he would be enabled to present Him to the people.

When Jesus came to be baptized, John recognized in Him a purity of character that he had never before perceived in any man. The very atmosphere of His presence was holy and awe-inspiring. Among the multitudes that had gathered about him at the Jordan, John had heard dark tales of crime, and had met souls bowed down with the burden of myriad sins; but never had he come in contact with a human being from whom there breathed an influence so divine. All this was in harmony with what had been revealed to John regarding the Messiah. Yet he shrank from granting the request of Jesus. How could he, a sinner, baptize the Sinless One? And why should He who needed no repentance submit to a rite that was a confession of guilt to be washed away?

As Jesus asked for baptism, John drew back, exclaiming, "I have need to be baptized of Thee, and comest Thou to me?" With firm yet gentle authority, Jesus answered, "Suffer it to be so now: for thus it becometh us to fulfill all righteousness." And John, yielding, led the Saviour down into the Jordan, and buried Him beneath the water. "And straightway coming up out of the water," Jesus "saw the heavens opened, and the Spirit like a dove descending upon Him."

Jesus did not receive baptism as a confession of guilt on His own account. He identified Himself with sinners, taking the steps that we are to take, and doing the work that we must do. His life of suffering and patient endurance after His baptism was also an example to us.

Upon coming up out of the water, Jesus bowed in prayer on the river bank. A new and important era was opening before Him. He was now, upon a wider stage, entering on the conflict of His life. Though He was the Prince of Peace, His coming must be as the unsheathing of a sword. The kingdom He had come to establish was the opposite of that which the Jews desired. He who was the foundation of the ritual and economy of Israel would be looked upon as its enemy and destroyer. He who had proclaimed the law upon Sinai would be condemned as a transgressor. He who had come to break the power of Satan would be denounced as Beelzebub. No one upon earth had understood Him, and during His ministry He must still walk alone. Throughout His life His mother and His brothers did not comprehend His mission. Even His disciples did not understand Him. He had dwelt in eternal light, as one with God, but His life on earth must be spent in solitude.

As one with us, He must bear the burden of our guilt and woe. The Sinless One must feel the shame of sin. The Peace Lover must dwell with strife, the truth must abide with falsehood, purity with vileness. Every sin, every discord, every defiling lust that transgression had brought, was torture to His spirit.

Alone He must tread the path; alone He must bear the burden. Upon Him who had laid off His glory and accepted the weakness of humanity the redemption of the world must rest. He saw and felt it all, but His purpose remained steadfast. Upon His arm depended the salvation of the fallen race, and He reached out His hand to grasp the hand of Omnipotent Love.

The Saviour's glance seems to penetrate heaven as He pours out His soul in prayer. Well He knows how sin has hardened the hearts of men, and how difficult it will be for them to discern His mission, and accept the gift of salvation. He pleads with the Father for power to overcome their unbelief, to break the fetters with which Satan has enthralled them, and in their behalf to conquer the destroyer. He asks for the witness that God accepts humanity in the person of His Son.

Never before have the angels listened to such a prayer. They are eager to bear to their loved Commander a message of assurance and comfort. But no; the Father Himself will answer the petition of His Son. Direct from the throne issue the beams of His glory. The heavens are opened, and upon the Saviour's head descends a dovelike form of purest light—fit emblem of Him, the meek and lowly One.

Of the vast throng at the Jordan, few except John discerned the heavenly vision. Yet the solemnity of the divine Presence rested upon the assembly. The people stood silently gazing upon Christ. His form was bathed in the light that ever surrounds the throne of God. His upturned face was glorified as they had never before seen the face of man. From the open heavens a voice was heard saying, "This is My beloved Son, in whom I am well pleased."

These words of confirmation were given to inspire faith in those who witnessed the scene, and to strengthen the Saviour for His mission. Notwithstanding that the sins of a guilty world were laid upon Christ, notwithstanding the humiliation of taking upon Himself our fallen nature, the voice from heaven declared Him to be the Son of the Eternal.

John had been deeply moved as he saw Jesus bowed as a suppliant, pleading with tears for the approval of the Father. As the glory of God encircled Him, and the voice from heaven was heard, John recognized the token which God had promised. He knew that it was the world's Redeemer whom he had baptized. The Holy Spirit rested upon him, and with outstretched hand pointing to Jesus, he cried, "Behold the Lamb of God, which taketh away the sin of the world."

None among the hearers, and not even the speaker himself, discerned the import of these words, "the Lamb of God." Upon Mount Moriah, Abraham had heard the question of his son, "My father, … where is the lamb for a burnt offering?" The father answered, "My son, God will provide Himself a lamb for a burnt offering." Genesis 22:7, 8. And in the ram divinely provided in the place of Isaac, Abraham saw a symbol of Him who was to die for the sins of men. The Holy Spirit through Isaiah, taking up the illustration, prophesied of the Saviour, "He is brought as a lamb to the slaughter," "and the Lord hath laid on Him the iniquity of us all" (Isaiah 53:7, 6); but the people of Israel had not understood the lesson. Many of them regarded the sacrificial offerings much as the heathen looked upon their sacrifices,—as gifts by which they themselves might propitiate the Deity. God desired to teach them that from His own love comes the gift which reconciles them to Himself.

And the word that was spoken to Jesus at the Jordan, "This is My beloved Son, in whom I am well pleased," embraces humanity. God spoke to Jesus as our representative. With all our sins and weaknesses, we are not cast aside as worthless. "He hath made us accepted in the Beloved." Ephesians 1:6. The glory that rested upon Christ is a pledge of the love of God for us. It tells us of the power of prayer—how the human voice may reach the ear of God, and our petitions find acceptance in the courts of heaven. By sin, earth was cut off from heaven, and alienated from its communion; but Jesus has connected it again with the sphere of glory. His love has encircled man, and reached the highest heaven. The light which fell from the open portals upon the head of our Saviour will fall upon us as we pray for help to resist temptation. The voice which spoke to Jesus says to every believing soul, This is My beloved child, in whom I am well pleased.

"Beloved, now are we the sons of God, and it doth not yet appear what we shall be: but we know that, when He shall appear, we shall be like Him; for we shall see Him as He is." 1 John 3:2. Our Redeemer has opened the way so that the most sinful, the most needy, the most oppressed and despised, may find access to the Father. All may have a home in the mansions which Jesus has gone to prepare. "These things saith He that is holy, He that is true, He that hath the key of David, He that openeth, and no man shutteth; and shutteth, and no man openeth; … behold, I have set before thee an open door, and no man can shut it." Revelation 3:7, 8.

10

The Temptation

This chapter is based on Matthew 4:1–11; Mark 1:12, 13; Luke 4:1–13.

············

"And Jesus being full of the Holy Ghost returned from Jordan, and was led by the Spirit into the wilderness." The words of Mark are still more significant. He says, "Immediately the Spirit driveth Him into the wilderness. And He was there in the wilderness forty days, tempted of Satan; and was with the wild beasts." "And in those days He did eat nothing."

When Jesus was led into the wilderness to be tempted, He was led by the Spirit of God. He did not invite temptation. He went to the wilderness to be alone, to contemplate His mission and work. By fasting and prayer He was to brace Himself for the bloodstained path He must travel. But Satan knew that the Saviour had gone into the wilderness, and he thought this the best time to approach Him.

Mighty issues for the world were at stake in the conflict between the Prince of light and the leader of the kingdom of darkness. After tempting man to sin, Satan claimed the earth as his, and styled himself the prince of this world. Having conformed to his own nature the father and mother of our race, he thought to establish here his empire. He declared that men had chosen him as their sovereign. Through his control of men, he held dominion over the world. Christ had come to disprove Satan's claim. As the Son of man, Christ would stand loyal to God. Thus it would be shown that Satan had not gained complete control of the human race, and that his claim to the world was false. All who desired deliverance from his power would be set free. The dominion that Adam had lost through sin would be recovered.

Since the announcement to the serpent in Eden, "I will put enmity between thee and the woman, and between thy seed and her seed" (Genesis 3:15), Satan had known that he did not hold absolute sway over the world. There was seen in men the working of a power that withstood his dominion. With intense interest he watched the sacrifices offered by Adam and his sons. In these ceremonies he discerned a symbol of communion between earth and heaven. He set himself to intercept this communion. He misrepresented God, and misinterpreted the rites that pointed to the Saviour. Men were led to fear God as one who delighted in their destruction. The sacrifices that should have revealed His love were offered only to appease His wrath. Satan excited the evil passions of men, in order to fasten his rule upon them. When God's written word was given, Satan studied the prophecies of the Saviour's advent. From generation to generation he worked to blind the people to these prophecies, that they might reject Christ at His coming.

At the birth of Jesus, Satan knew that One had come with a divine commission to dispute his dominion. He trembled at the angel's message attesting the authority of the newborn King. Satan well knew the position that Christ had held in heaven as the Beloved of the Father. That the Son of God should come to this earth as a man filled him with amazement and with apprehension. He could not fathom the mystery of this great sacrifice. His selfish soul could not understand such love for the deceived race. The glory and peace of heaven, and the joy of communion with God, were but dimly comprehended by men; but they were well known to Lucifer, the covering cherub. Since he had lost heaven, he was determined to find revenge by causing others to share his fall. This he would do by causing them to undervalue heavenly things, and to set the heart upon things of earth.

Not without hindrance was the Commander of heaven to win the souls of men to His kingdom. From the time when He was a babe in Bethlehem, He was continually assailed by the evil one. The image of God was manifest in Christ, and in the councils of Satan it was determined that He should be overcome. No human being had come into the world and escaped the power of the deceiver. The forces of the confederacy of evil were set upon His track to engage in warfare against Him, and if possible to prevail over Him.

At the Saviour's baptism, Satan was among the witnesses. He saw the Father's glory overshadowing His Son. He heard the voice of Jehovah testifying to the divinity of Jesus. Ever since Adam's sin, the human race had been cut off from direct communion with God; the intercourse between heaven and earth had been through Christ; but now that Jesus had come "in the likeness of sinful flesh" (Romans 8:3), the Father Himself spoke. He had before communicated with humanity through Christ; now He communicated with humanity in Christ. Satan had hoped that God's abhorrence of evil would bring an eternal separation between heaven and earth. But now it was manifest that the connection between God and man had been restored.

Satan saw that he must either conquer or be conquered. The issues of the conflict involved too much to be entrusted to his confederate angels. He must personally conduct the warfare. All the energies of apostasy were rallied against the Son of God. Christ was made the mark of every weapon of hell.

was to redeem Adam's failure. But when Adam was assailed by the tempter, none of the effects of sin were upon him. He stood in the strength of perfect manhood, possessing the full vigor of mind and body. He was surrounded with the glories of Eden, and was in daily communion with heavenly beings. It was not thus with Jesus when He entered the wilderness to cope with Satan. For four thousand years the race had been decreasing in physical strength, in mental power, and in moral worth; and Christ took upon Him the infirmities of degenerate humanity. Only thus could He rescue man from the lowest depths of his degradation.

Many claim that it was impossible for Christ to be overcome by temptation. Then He could not have been placed in Adam's position; He could not have gained the victory that

Satan saw that he must either conquer or be conquered. The issues of the conflict involved too much to be entrusted to his confederate angels. He must personally conduct the warfare. All the energies of apostasy were rallied against the Son of God. Christ was made the mark of every weapon of hell.

Many look on this conflict between Christ and Satan as having no special bearing on their own life; and for them it has little interest. But within the domain of every human heart this controversy is repeated. Never does one leave the ranks of evil for the service of God without encountering the assaults of Satan. The enticements which Christ resisted were those that we find it so difficult to withstand. They were urged upon Him in as much greater degree as His character is superior to ours. With the terrible weight of the sins of the world upon Him, Christ withstood the test upon appetite, upon the love of the world, and upon that love of display which leads to presumption. These were the temptations that overcame Adam and Eve, and that so readily overcome us.

Satan had pointed to Adam's sin as proof that God's law was unjust, and could not be obeyed. In our humanity, Christ

Adam failed to gain. If we have in any sense a more trying conflict than had Christ, then He would not be able to succor us. But our Saviour took humanity, with all its liabilities. He took the nature of man, with the possibility of yielding to temptation. We have nothing to bear which He has not endured.

With Christ, as with the holy pair in Eden, appetite was the ground of the first great temptation. Just where the ruin began, the work of our redemption must begin. As by the indulgence of appetite Adam fell, so by the denial of appetite Christ must overcome. "And when He had fasted forty days and forty nights, He was afterward an hungred. And when the tempter came to Him, he said, If Thou be the Son of God, command that these stones be made bread. But He answered and said, It is written, Man shall not live by bread alone, but by every word that proceedeth out of the mouth of God."

From the time of Adam to that of Christ, self-indulgence had increased the power of the appetites and passions, until they had almost unlimited control. Thus men had become debased and diseased, and of themselves it was impossible for them to overcome. In man's behalf, Christ conquered by enduring the severest test. For our sake He exercised a self-control stronger than hunger or death. And in this first victory were involved other issues that enter into all our conflicts with the powers of darkness.

When Jesus entered the wilderness, He was shut in by the Father's glory. Absorbed in communion with God, He was lifted above human weakness. But the glory departed, and He was left to battle with temptation. It was pressing upon Him every moment. His human nature shrank from the conflict that awaited Him. For forty days He fasted and prayed. Weak and emaciated from hunger, worn and haggard with mental agony, "His visage was so marred more than any man, and His form more than the sons of men." Isaiah 52:14. Now was Satan's opportunity. Now he supposed that he could overcome Christ.

There came to the Saviour, as if in answer to His prayers, one in the guise of an angel from heaven. He claimed to have a commission from God to declare that Christ's fast was at an end. As God had sent an angel to stay the hand of Abraham from offering Isaac, so, satisfied with Christ's willingness to enter the bloodstained path, the Father had sent an angel to deliver Him; this was the message brought to Jesus. The Saviour was faint from hunger, He was craving for food, when Satan came suddenly upon Him. Pointing to the stones which strewed the desert, and which had the appearance of loaves, the tempter said, "If Thou be the Son of God, command that these stones be made bread."

Though he appears as an angel of light, these first words betray his character. "If Thou be the Son of God." Here is the insinuation of distrust. Should Jesus do what Satan suggests, it would be an acceptance of the doubt. The tempter plans to overthrow Christ by the same means that were so successful with the human race in the beginning. How artfully had Satan approached Eve in Eden! "Yea, hath God said, Ye shall not eat of every tree of the garden?" Genesis 3:1. Thus far the tempter's words were truth; but in his manner of speaking them there was a disguised contempt for the words of God. There was a covert negative, a doubt of the divine truthfulness. Satan sought to instill into the mind of Eve the thought that God would not do as He had said; that the withholding of such beautiful fruit was a contradiction of His love and compassion for man. So now the tempter seeks to inspire Christ with his own sentiments. "If Thou be the Son of God."

The words rankle with bitterness in his mind. In the tones of his voice is an expression of utter incredulity. Would God treat His own Son thus? Would He leave Him in the desert with wild beasts, without food, without companions, without comfort? He insinuates that God never meant His Son to be in such a state as this. "If Thou be the Son of God," show Thy power by relieving Thyself of this pressing hunger. Command that this stone be made bread.

The words from heaven, "This is My beloved Son, in whom I am well pleased" (Matthew 3:17), were still sounding in the ears of Satan. But he was determined to make Christ disbelieve this testimony. The word of God was Christ's assurance of His divine mission. He had come to live as a man among men, and it was the word that declared His connection with heaven. It was Satan's purpose to cause Him to doubt that word. If Christ's confidence in God could be shaken, Satan knew that the victory in the whole controversy would be his. He could overcome Jesus. He hoped that under the force of despondency and extreme hunger, Christ would lose faith in His Father, and work a miracle in His own behalf. Had He done this, the plan of salvation would have been broken.

When Satan and the Son of God first met in conflict, Christ was the commander of the heavenly hosts; and Satan, the leader of revolt in heaven, was cast out. Now their condition is apparently reversed, and Satan makes the most of his supposed advantage. One of the most powerful of the angels, he says, has been banished from heaven. The appearance of Jesus indicates that He is that fallen angel, forsaken by God, and deserted by man. A divine being would be able to sustain his claim by working a miracle; "if Thou be the Son of God, command this stone that it be made bread." Such an act of creative power, urges the tempter, would be conclusive evidence of divinity. It would bring the controversy to an end.

Not without a struggle could Jesus listen in silence to the arch-deceiver. But the Son of God was not to prove His divinity to Satan, or to explain the reason of His humiliation. By conceding to the demands of the rebel, nothing for the good of man or the glory of God would be gained. Had Christ complied with the suggestion of the enemy, Satan would still have said, Show me a sign that I may believe you to be the Son of God. Evidence would have been worthless to break the power of rebellion in his heart. And Christ was not to exercise divine power for His own benefit. He had come to bear trial as we must do, leaving us an example of faith and submission. Neither here nor at any subsequent time in His earthly life did He work a miracle in His own behalf. His wonderful works were all for the good of others. Though Jesus recognized Satan from the beginning, He was not provoked to enter into controversy with him. Strengthened with the memory of the voice from heaven, He rested in His Father's love. He would not parley with temptation.

Jesus met Satan with the words of Scripture. "It is written," He said. In every temptation the weapon of His warfare was the word of God. Satan demanded of Christ a miracle as a sign of His divinity. But that which is greater than all miracles, a firm reliance upon a "Thus saith the Lord," was a sign that could not be controverted. So long as Christ held to this position, the tempter could gain no advantage.

It was in the time of greatest weakness that Christ was assailed by the fiercest temptations. Thus Satan thought to prevail. By this policy he had gained the victory over men. When strength failed, and the will power weakened, and faith ceased to repose in God, then those who had stood long and valiantly for the right were overcome. Moses was wearied with the forty years' wandering of Israel, when for the moment his faith let go its hold upon infinite power. He failed just upon the borders of the Promised Land. So with Elijah, who had stood undaunted before King Ahab, who had faced the whole nation of Israel, with the four hundred and fifty prophets of Baal at their head. After that terrible day upon Carmel, when the false prophets had been slain, and the people had declared their allegiance to God, Elijah fled for his life before the threats of the idolatrous Jezebel. Thus Satan has taken advantage of the weakness of humanity. And he will still work in the same way. Whenever one is encompassed with clouds, perplexed by circumstances, or afflicted by poverty or distress, Satan is at hand to tempt and annoy. He attacks our weak points of character. He seeks to shake our confidence in God, who suffers such a condition of things to exist. We are tempted to distrust God, to question His love. Often the tempter comes to us as he came to Christ, arraying before us our weakness and infirmities. He hopes to discourage the soul, and to break our hold on God. Then he is sure of his prey. If we would meet him as Jesus did, we should escape many a defeat. By parleying with the enemy, we give him an advantage.

When Christ said to the tempter, "Man shall not live by bread alone, but by every word that proceedeth out of the mouth of God," He repeated the words that, more than fourteen hundred years before, He had spoken to Israel: "The Lord thy God led thee these forty years in the wilderness. … And He humbled thee, and suffered thee to hunger, and fed thee with manna, which thou knewest not, neither did thy fathers know; that He might make thee know that man doth not live by bread only, but by every word that proceedeth out of the mouth of the Lord doth man live." Deuteronomy 8:2, 3. In the wilderness, when all means of sustenance failed, God sent His people manna from heaven; and a sufficient and constant supply was given. This provision was to teach them that while they trusted in God and walked in His ways He would not forsake them. The Saviour now practiced the lesson He had taught to Israel. By the word of God succor had been given to the Hebrew host, and by the same word it would be given to Jesus. He awaited God's time to bring relief. He was in the wilderness in obedience to God, and He would not obtain food by following the suggestions of Satan. In the presence of the witnessing universe, He testified that it is a less calamity to suffer whatever may befall than to depart in any manner from the will of God.

"Man shall not live by bread alone, but by every word of God." Often the follower of Christ is brought where he cannot serve God and carry forward his worldly enterprises. Perhaps it appears that obedience to some plain requirement of God will cut off his means of support. Satan would make him believe that he must sacrifice his conscientious convictions. But the only thing in our world upon which we can rely is the word of God. "Seek ye first the kingdom of God, and His righteousness; and all these things shall be added unto you." Matthew 6:33. Even in this life it is not for our good to depart from the will of our Father in heaven. When we learn the power of His word, we shall not follow the suggestions of Satan in order to obtain food or to save our lives. Our only questions will be, What is God's command? and what His promise? Knowing these, we shall obey the one, and trust the other.

In the last great conflict of the controversy with Satan those who are loyal to God will see every earthly support cut off. Because they refuse to break His law in obedience to earthly powers, they will be forbidden to buy or sell. It will finally be decreed that they shall be put to death. See Revelation 13:11–17. But to the obedient is given the promise, "He shall dwell on high: his place of defense shall be the munitions of rocks: bread shall be given him; his waters shall be sure." Isaiah 33:16. By this promise the children of God will live. When the earth shall be wasted with famine, they shall be fed. "They shall not be ashamed in the evil time: and in the days of famine they shall be satisfied." Psalm 37:19. To that time of distress the prophet Habakkuk looked forward, and his words express the faith of the church: "Although the fig tree shall not blossom, neither shall fruit be in the vines; the labor of the olive shall fail, and the fields shall yield no meat; the flock shall be cut off from the fold, and there shall be no herd in the stalls: yet I will rejoice in the Lord, I will joy in the God of my salvation." Habakkuk 3:17,18.

Of all the lessons to be learned from our Lord's first great temptation none is more important than that bearing upon the control of the appetites and passions. In all ages, temptations appealing to the physical nature have been most effectual in corrupting and degrading mankind. Through intemperance, Satan works to destroy the mental and moral powers that God gave to man as a priceless endowment. Thus it becomes impossible for men to appreciate things of eternal worth. Through sensual indulgence, Satan seeks to blot from the soul every trace of likeness to God.

The uncontrolled indulgence and consequent disease and degradation that existed at Christ's first advent will again exist, with intensity of evil, before His second coming. Christ declares that the condition of the world will be as in the days before the Flood, and as in Sodom and Gomorrah. Every imagination of the thoughts of the heart will be evil continually. Upon the very verge of that fearful time we are now living, and to us should come home the lesson of the Saviour's fast. Only by the inexpressible anguish which Christ endured can we estimate the evil of unrestrained indulgence. His example declares that our only hope of eternal life is through bringing the appetites and passions into subjection to the will of God.

In our own strength it is impossible for us to deny the clamors of our fallen nature. Through this channel Satan will bring temptation upon us. Christ knew that the enemy would come to every human being, to take advantage of hereditary weakness, and by his false insinuations to ensnare all whose trust is not in God. And by passing over the ground which man must travel, our Lord has prepared the way for us to overcome. It is not His will that we should be placed at a disadvantage in the conflict with Satan. He would not have us intimidated and discouraged by the assaults of the serpent. "Be of good cheer," He says; "I have overcome the world." John 16:33.

Let him who is struggling against the power of appetite look to the Saviour in the wilderness of temptation. See Him in His agony upon the cross, as He exclaimed, "I thirst." He has endured all that it is possible for us to bear. His victory is ours.

Jesus rested upon the wisdom and strength of His heavenly Father. He declares, "The Lord God will help Me; therefore shall I not be confounded: … and I know that I shall not be ashamed…. Behold, the Lord God will help Me." Pointing to His own example, He says to us, "Who is among you that feareth the Lord, … that walketh in darkness, and hath no light? let him trust in the name of the Lord, and stay upon his God." Isaiah 50:7–10.

"The prince of this world cometh," said Jesus, "and hath nothing in Me." John 14:30. There was in Him nothing that responded to Satan's sophistry. He did not consent to sin. Not even by a thought did He yield to temptation. So it may be with us. Christ's humanity was united with divinity; He was fitted for the conflict by the indwelling of the Holy Spirit. And He came to make us partakers of the divine nature. So long as we are united to Him by faith, sin has no more dominion over us. God reaches for the hand of faith in us to direct it to lay fast hold upon the divinity of Christ, that we may attain to perfection of character.

And how this is accomplished, Christ has shown us. By what means did He overcome in the conflict with Satan? By the word of God. Only by the word could He resist temptation. "It is written," He said. And unto us are given "exceeding great and precious promises: that by these ye might be partakers of the divine nature, having escaped the corruption that is in the world through lust." 2 Peter 1:4. Every promise in God's word is ours. "By every word that proceedeth out of the mouth of God" are we to live. When assailed by temptation, look not to circumstances or to the weakness of self, but to the power of the word. All its strength is yours. "Thy word," says the psalmist, "have I hid in mine heart, that I might not sin against Thee." "By the word of Thy lips I have kept me from the paths of the destroyer." Psalm 119:11; 17:4.

> *By what means did He overcome in the conflict with Satan? By the word of God. Only by the word could He resist temptation.*

The Victory

This chapter is based on Matthew 4:5-11; Mark 1:12, 13; Luke 4:5-13.

....

Then the devil taketh Him up into the holy city, and setteth Him on a pinnacle of the temple, and saith unto Him, If Thou be the Son of God, cast Thyself down: for it is written—

"He shall give His angels charge concerning Thee:
And in their hands they shall bear Thee up,
Lest at any time Thou dash Thy foot against a stone."

Satan now supposes that he has met Jesus on His own ground. The wily foe himself presents words that proceeded from the mouth of God. He still appears as an angel of light, and he makes it evident that he is acquainted with the Scriptures, and understands the import of what is written. As Jesus before used the word of God to sustain His faith, the tempter now uses it to countenance his deception. He claims that he has been only testing the fidelity of Jesus, and he now commends His steadfastness. As the Saviour has manifested trust in God, Satan urges Him to give still another evidence of His faith.

But again the temptation is prefaced with the insinuation of distrust, "If Thou be the Son of God." Christ was tempted to answer the "if;" but He refrained from the slightest acceptance of the doubt. He would not imperil His life in order to give evidence to Satan.

The tempter thought to take advantage of Christ's humanity, and urge Him to presumption. But while Satan can solicit, he cannot compel to sin. He said to Jesus, "Cast Thyself down," knowing that he could not cast Him down; for God would interpose to deliver Him. Nor could Satan force Jesus to cast Himself down. Unless Christ should consent to temptation, He could not be overcome. Not all the power of earth or hell could force Him in the slightest degree to depart from the will of His Father.

The tempter can never compel us to do evil. He cannot control minds unless they are yielded to his control. The will must consent, faith must let go its hold upon Christ, before Satan can exercise his power upon us. But every sinful desire we cherish affords him a foothold. Every point in which we fail of meeting the divine standard is an open door by which he can enter to tempt and destroy us. And every failure or defeat on our part gives occasion for him to reproach Christ.

When Satan quoted the promise, "He shall give His angels charge over Thee," he omitted the words, "to keep Thee in all Thy ways;" that is, in all the ways of God's choosing. Jesus refused to go outside the path of obedience. While manifesting perfect trust in His Father, He would not place Himself, unbidden, in a position that would necessitate the interposition of His Father to save Him from death. He would not force Providence to come to His rescue, and thus fail of giving man an example of trust and submission.

Jesus declared to Satan, "It is written again, Thou shalt not tempt the Lord thy God." These words were spoken by Moses to the children of Israel when they thirsted in the desert, and demanded that Moses should give them water, exclaiming, "Is the Lord among us, or not?" Exodus 17:7. God had wrought marvelously for them; yet in trouble they doubted Him, and demanded evidence that He was with them. In their unbelief they sought to put Him to the test. And Satan was urging Christ to do the same thing. God had already testified that Jesus was His Son; and now to ask for proof that He was the Son of God would be putting God's word to the test—tempting Him. And the same would be true of asking for that which God had not promised. It would manifest distrust, and be really proving, or tempting, Him. We should not present our petitions to God to prove whether He will fulfill His word, but because He will fulfill it; not to prove that He loves us, but because He loves us. "Without faith it is impossible to please Him: for he that cometh to God must believe that He is, and that He is a rewarder of them that diligently seek Him." Hebrews 11:6.

But faith is in no sense allied to presumption. Only he who has true faith is secure against presumption. For presumption is Satan's counterfeit of faith. Faith claims God's promises, and brings forth fruit in obedience. Presumption also claims the promises, but uses them as Satan did, to excuse transgression. Faith would have led our first parents to trust the love of God, and to obey His commands. Presumption led them to transgress His law, believing that His great love would save them from the consequence of their sin. It is not faith that claims the favor of Heaven without complying with the conditions on which mercy is to be granted. Genuine faith has its foundation in the promises and provisions of the Scriptures.

Often when Satan has failed of exciting distrust, he succeeds in leading us to presumption. If he can cause us to place ourselves unnecessarily in the way of temptation, he knows that the victory is his. God will preserve all who walk in the path of obedience; but to depart from it is to venture on Satan's ground. There we are sure to fall. The Saviour has bidden us, "Watch ye and pray, lest ye enter into temptation." Mark 14:38. Meditation and prayer would keep us from rushing unbidden into the way of danger, and thus we should be saved from many a defeat.

Yet we should not lose courage when assailed by temptation. Often when placed in a trying situation we doubt that the Spirit of God has been leading us. But it was the Spirit's leading that brought Jesus into the wilderness to be tempted by Satan. When God brings us into trial, He has a purpose to accomplish for our good. Jesus did not presume on God's promises by going unbidden into temptation, neither did He give up to despondency when temptation came upon Him. Nor should we. "God is faithful, who will not suffer you to be tempted above that ye are able; but will with the temptation also make a way to escape, that ye may be able to bear it." He says, "Offer unto God thanksgiving; and pay thy vows unto the Most High: and call upon Me in the day of trouble: I will deliver thee, and thou shalt glorify Me." 1 Corinthians 10:13; Psalm 50:14, 15.

Jesus was victor in the second temptation, and now Satan manifests himself in his true character. But he does not appear as a hideous monster, with cloven feet and bat's wings. He is a mighty angel, though fallen. He avows himself the leader of rebellion and the god of this world.

Placing Jesus upon a high mountain, Satan caused the kingdoms of the world, in all their glory, to pass in panoramic view before Him. The sunlight lay on templed cities, marble palaces, fertile fields, and fruit-laden vineyards. The traces of evil were hidden. The eyes of Jesus, so lately greeted by gloom and desolation, now gazed upon a scene of unsurpassed loveliness and prosperity. Then the tempter's voice was heard: "All this power will I give Thee, and the glory of them: for that is delivered unto me; and to whomsoever I will I give it. If Thou therefore wilt worship me, all shall be Thine."

Christ's mission could be fulfilled only through suffering. Before Him was a life of sorrow, hardship, and conflict, and an ignominious death. He must bear the sins of the whole world. He must endure separation from His Father's love. Now the tempter offered to yield up the power he had usurped. Christ might deliver Himself from the dreadful future by acknowledging the supremacy of Satan. But to do this was to yield the victory in the great controversy. It was in seeking to exalt himself above the Son of God that Satan had sinned in heaven. Should he prevail now, it would be the triumph of rebellion.

When Satan declared to Christ, The kingdom and glory of the world are delivered unto me, and to whomsoever I will I give it, he stated what was true only in part, and he declared it to serve his own purpose of deception. Satan's dominion was that wrested from Adam, but Adam was the vicegerent of the Creator. His was not an independent rule. The earth is God's, and He has committed all things to His Son. Adam was to reign subject to Christ. When Adam betrayed his sovereignty into Satan's hands, Christ still remained the rightful King. Thus the Lord had said to King Nebuchadnezzar, "The Most High ruleth in the kingdom of men, and giveth it to whomsoever He will." Daniel 4:17. Satan can exercise his usurped authority only as God permits.

When the tempter offered to Christ the kingdom and glory of the world, he was proposing that Christ should yield up the real kingship of the world, and hold dominion subject to Satan. This was the same dominion upon which the hopes of the Jews were set. They desired the kingdom of this world. If Christ had consented to offer them such a kingdom, they would gladly have received Him. But the curse of sin, with all its woe, rested upon it. Christ declared to the tempter, "Get thee behind Me, Satan: for it is written, Thou shalt worship the Lord thy God, and Him only shalt thou serve."

> *The tempter can never compel us to do evil. He cannot control minds unless they are yielded to his control. The will must consent, faith must let go its hold upon Christ, before Satan can exercise his power upon us.*

By the one who had revolted in heaven the kingdoms of this world were offered Christ, to buy His homage to the principles of evil; but He would not be bought; He had come to establish a kingdom of righteousness, and He would not abandon His purpose. With the same temptation Satan approaches men, and here he has better success than with Christ. To men he offers the kingdom of this world on condition that they will acknowledge his supremacy. He requires that they sacrifice integrity, disregard conscience, indulge selfishness. Christ bids them seek first the kingdom of God, and His righteousness; but Satan walks by their side and says: Whatever may be true in regard to life eternal, in order to make a success in this world you must serve me. I hold your welfare in my hands. I can give you riches, pleasures, honor, and happiness. Hearken to my counsel. Do not allow yourselves to be carried away with whimsical notions of honesty or self-sacrifice. I will prepare the way before you. Thus multitudes are deceived. They consent to live for the service of self, and Satan is satisfied. While he allures them with the hope of worldly dominion, he gains dominion over the soul. But he offers that which is not his to bestow, and which is soon to be wrested from him. In return he beguiles them of their title to the inheritance of the sons of God.

Satan had questioned whether Jesus was the Son of God. In his summary dismissal he had proof that he could not gainsay. Divinity flashed through suffering humanity. Satan had no power to resist the command. Writhing with humiliation and rage, he was forced to withdraw from the presence of the world's Redeemer. Christ's victory was as complete as had been the failure of Adam.

So we may resist temptation, and force Satan to depart from us. Jesus gained the victory through submission and faith in God, and

Never can the cost of our redemption be realized until the redeemed shall stand with the Redeemer before the throne of God.

by the apostle He says to us, "Submit yourselves therefore to God. Resist the devil, and he will flee from you. Draw nigh to God, and He will draw nigh to you." James 4:7, 8. We cannot save ourselves from the tempter's power; he has conquered humanity, and when we try to stand in our own strength, we shall become a prey to his devices; but "the name of the Lord is a strong tower: the righteous runneth into it, and is safe." Proverbs 18:10. Satan trembles and flees before the weakest soul who finds refuge in that mighty name.

After the foe had departed, Jesus fell exhausted to the earth, with the pallor of death upon His face. The angels of heaven had watched the conflict, beholding their loved Commander as He passed through inexpressible suffering to make a way of escape for us. He had endured the test, greater than we shall ever be called to endure. The angels now ministered to the Son of God as He lay like one dying. He was strengthened with food, comforted with the message of His Father's love and the assurance that all heaven triumphed in His victory. Warming to life again, His great heart goes out in sympathy for man, and He goes forth to complete the work He has begun; to rest not until the foe is vanquished, and our fallen race redeemed.

Never can the cost of our redemption be realized until the redeemed shall stand with the Redeemer before the throne of God. Then as the glories of the eternal home burst upon our enraptured senses we shall remember that Jesus left all this for us, that He not only became an exile from the heavenly courts, but for us took the risk of failure and eternal loss. Then we shall cast our crowns at His feet, and raise the song, "Worthy is the Lamb that was slain to receive power, and riches, and wisdom, and strength, and honor, and glory, and blessing." Revelation 5:12.

At the Marriage Feast

This chapter is based on John 2:1–11.

. . . .

Jesus did not begin His ministry by some great work before the Sanhedrin at Jerusalem. At a household gathering in a little Galilean village His power was put forth to add to the joy of a wedding feast. Thus He showed His sympathy with men, and His desire to minister to their happiness. In the wilderness of temptation He Himself had drunk the cup of woe. He came forth to give to men the cup of blessing, by His benediction to hallow the relations of human life.

From the Jordan, Jesus had returned to Galilee. There was to be a marriage at Cana, a little town not far from Nazareth; the parties were relatives of Joseph and Mary; and Jesus, knowing of this family gathering, went to Cana, and with His disciples was invited to the feast.

Again He met His mother, from whom He had for some time been separated. Mary had heard of the manifestation at the Jordan, at His baptism. The tidings had been carried to Nazareth, and had brought to her mind afresh the scenes that for so many years had been hidden in her heart. In common with all Israel, Mary was deeply stirred by the mission of John the Baptist. Well she remembered the prophecy given at his birth. Now his connection with Jesus kindled her hopes anew. But tidings had reached her also of the mysterious departure of Jesus to the wilderness, and she was oppressed with troubled forebodings.

From the day when she heard the angel's announcement in the home at Nazareth Mary had treasured every evidence that Jesus was the Messiah. His sweet, unselfish life assured her that He could be no other than the Sent of God. Yet there came to her also doubts and disappointments, and she had longed for the time when His glory should be revealed. Death had separated her from Joseph, who had shared her knowledge of the mystery of the birth of Jesus. Now there was no one to whom she could confide her hopes and fears. The past two months had been very sorrowful. She had been parted from Jesus, in whose sympathy she found comfort; she pondered upon the words of Simeon, "A sword shall pierce through thy own soul also" (Luke 2:35); she recalled the three days of agony when she thought Jesus lost to her forever; and with an anxious heart she awaited His return.

At the marriage feast she meets Him, the same tender, dutiful son. Yet He is not the same. His countenance is changed. It bears the traces of His conflict in the wilderness, and a new expression of dignity and power gives evidence of His heavenly mission. With Him is a group of young men, whose eyes follow Him with reverence, and who call Him Master. These companions recount to Mary what they have seen and heard at the baptism and elsewhere. They conclude by declaring, "We have found Him, of whom Moses in the law, and the prophets, did write." John 1:45.

As the guests assemble, many seem to be preoccupied with some topic of absorbing interest. A suppressed excitement pervades the company. Little groups converse together in eager but quiet tones, and wondering glances are turned upon the Son of Mary. As Mary had heard the disciples' testimony in regard to Jesus, she had been gladdened with the assurance that her long-cherished hopes were not in vain. Yet she would have been more than human if there had not mingled with this holy joy a trace of the fond mother's natural pride. As she saw the many glances bent upon Jesus, she longed to have Him prove to the company that He was really the Honored of God. She hoped there might be opportunity for Him to work a miracle before them.

It was the custom of the times for marriage festivities to continue several days. On this occasion, before the feast ended it was found that the supply of wine had failed. This discovery caused much perplexity and regret. It was unusual to dispense with wine on festive occasions, and its absence would seem to indicate a want of hospitality. As a relative of the parties, Mary had assisted in the arrangements for the

danger that Mary would regard her relationship to Jesus as giving her a special claim upon Him, and the right, in some degree, to direct Him in His mission. For thirty years He had been to her a loving and obedient son, and His love was unchanged; but He must now go about His Father's work. As Son of the Most High, and Saviour of the world, no earthly ties must hold Him from His mission, or influence His conduct. He must stand free to do the will of God. This lesson is also for us. The claims of God are paramount even to the ties of human relationship. No earthly attraction should turn our feet from the path in which He bids us walk.

The only hope of redemption for our fallen race is in Christ; Mary could find salvation only through the Lamb of God. In herself she possessed no merit. Her connection

> *As Son of the Most High, and Saviour of the world, no earthly ties must hold Him from His mission, or influence His conduct. He must stand free to do the will of God. This lesson is also for us. The claims of God are paramount even to the ties of human relationship. No earthly attraction should turn our feet from the path in which He bids us walk.*

feast, and she now spoke to Jesus, saying, "They have no wine." These words were a suggestion that He might supply their need. But Jesus answered, "Woman, what have I to do with thee? Mine hour is not yet come."

This answer, abrupt as it seems to us, expressed no coldness or discourtesy. The Saviour's form of address to His mother was in accordance with Oriental custom. It was used toward persons to whom it was desired to show respect. Every act of Christ's earthly life was in harmony with the precept He Himself had given, "Honor thy father and thy mother." Exodus 20:12. On the cross, in His last act of tenderness toward His mother, Jesus again addressed her in the same way, as He committed her to the care of His best-loved disciple. Both at the marriage feast and upon the cross, the love expressed in tone and look and manner interpreted His words.

At His visit to the temple in His boyhood, as the mystery of His lifework opened before Him, Christ had said to Mary, "Wist ye not that I must be about My Father's business?" Luke 2:49. These words struck the keynote of His whole life and ministry. Everything was held in abeyance to His work, the great work of redemption which He had come into the world to accomplish. Now He repeated the lesson. There was

with Jesus placed her in no different spiritual relation to Him from that of any other human soul. This is indicated in the Saviour's words. He makes clear the distinction between His relation to her as the Son of man and as the Son of God. The tie of kinship between them in no way placed her on an equality with Him.

The words, "Mine hour is not yet come," point to the fact that every act of Christ's life on earth was in fulfillment of the plan that had existed from the days of eternity. Before He came to earth, the plan lay out before Him, perfect in all its details. But as He walked among men, He was guided, step by step, by the Father's will. He did not hesitate to act at the appointed time. With the same submission He waited until the time had come.

In saying to Mary that His hour had not yet come, Jesus was replying to her unspoken thought—to the expectation she cherished in common with her people. She hoped that He would reveal Himself as the Messiah, and take the throne of Israel. But the time had not come. Not as a King, but as "a Man of Sorrows, and acquainted with grief," had Jesus accepted the lot of humanity.

But though Mary had not a right conception of Christ's mission, she trusted Him implicitly. To this faith Jesus responded. It was to honor Mary's trust, and to strengthen the faith of His disciples, that the first miracle was performed. The disciples were to encounter many and great temptations to unbelief. To them the prophecies had made it clear beyond all controversy that Jesus was the Messiah. They looked for the religious leaders to receive Him with confidence even greater than their own. They declared among the people the wonderful works of Christ and their own confidence in His mission, but they were amazed and bitterly disappointed by the unbelief, the deep-seated prejudice, and the enmity to Jesus, displayed by the priests and rabbis. The Saviour's early miracles strengthened the disciples to stand against this opposition.

In nowise disconcerted by the words of Jesus, Mary said to those serving at table, "Whatsoever He saith unto you, do it." Thus she did what she could to prepare the way for the work of Christ.

Beside the doorway stood six large stone water jars, and Jesus bade the servants fill these with water. It was done. Then as the wine was wanted for immediate use, He said, "Draw out now, and bear unto the governor of the feast." Instead of the water with which the vessels had been filled, there flowed forth wine. Neither the ruler of the feast nor the guests generally were aware that the supply of wine had failed. Upon tasting that which the servants brought, the ruler found it superior to any he had ever before drunk, and very different from that served at the beginning of the feast. Turning to the bridegroom, he said, "Every man at the beginning doth set forth good wine; and when men have well drunk, then that which is worse: but thou hast kept the good wine until now."

As men set forth the best wine first, then afterward that which is worse, so does the world with its gifts. That which it offers may please the eye and fascinate the senses, but it proves to be unsatisfying. The wine turns to bitterness, the gaiety to gloom. That which was begun with songs and mirth ends in weariness and disgust. But the gifts of Jesus are ever fresh and new. The feast that He provides for the soul never fails to give satisfaction and joy. Each new gift increases the capacity of the receiver to appreciate and enjoy the blessings of the Lord. He gives grace for grace. There can be no failure of supply. If you abide in Him, the fact that you receive a rich gift today insures the reception of a richer gift tomorrow. The words of Jesus to Nathanael express the law of God's dealing with the children of faith. With every fresh revelation of His love, He declares to the receptive heart, "Believest thou? thou shalt see greater things than these." John 1:50.

The gift of Christ to the marriage feast was a symbol. The water represented baptism into His death; the wine, the shedding of His blood for the sins of the world. The water to fill the jars was brought by human hands, but the word of Christ alone could impart to it life-giving virtue. So with the rites which point to the Saviour's death. It is only by the power of Christ, working through faith, that they have efficacy to nourish the soul.

The word of Christ supplied ample provision for the feast. So abundant is the provision of His grace to blot out the iniquities of men, and to renew and sustain the soul.

At the first feast He attended with His disciples, Jesus gave them the cup that symbolized His work for their salvation. At the last supper He gave it again, in the institution of that sacred rite by which His death was to be shown forth "till He come." 1 Corinthians 11:26. And the sorrow of the disciples at parting from their Lord was comforted with the promise of reunion, as He said, "I will not drink henceforth of this fruit of the vine, until that day when I drink it new with you in My Father's kingdom." Matthew 26:29.

The wine which Christ provided for the feast, and that which He gave to the disciples as a symbol of His own blood, was the pure juice of the grape. To this the prophet Isaiah refers when he speaks of the new wine "in the cluster," and says, "Destroy it not; for a blessing is in it." Isaiah 65:8.

It was Christ who in the Old Testament gave the warning to Israel, "Wine is a mocker, strong drink is raging: and whosoever is deceived thereby is not wise." Proverbs 20:1. And He Himself provided no such beverage. Satan tempts men to indulgence that will becloud reason and benumb the spiritual perceptions, but Christ teaches us to bring the lower nature into subjection. His whole life was an example of self-denial. In order to break the power of appetite, He suffered in our behalf the severest test that humanity could endure. It was Christ who directed that John the Baptist should drink neither wine nor strong drink. It was He who enjoined similar abstinence upon the wife of Manoah. And He pronounced a curse upon the man who should put the bottle to his neighbor's lips. Christ did not contradict His own teaching. The unfermented wine which He provided for the wedding guests was a wholesome and refreshing drink. Its effect was to bring the taste into harmony with a healthful appetite.

As the guests at the feast remarked upon the quality of the wine, inquiries were made that drew from the servants an account of the miracle. The company were for a time too much amazed to think of Him who had performed the wonderful work. When at length they looked for Him, it was found that He had withdrawn so quietly as to be unnoticed even by His disciples.

The attention of the company was now turned to the disciples. For the first time they had the opportunity of acknowledging their faith in Jesus. They told what they had seen and heard at the Jordan, and there was kindled in many hearts the hope that God had raised up a deliverer for His people. The news of the miracle spread through all that region, and was carried to Jerusalem. With new interest the priests and elders searched the prophecies pointing to Christ's coming. There was eager desire to learn the mission of this new teacher, who appeared among the people in so unassuming a manner.

The ministry of Christ was in marked contrast to that of the Jewish elders. Their regard for tradition and formalism had destroyed all real freedom of thought or action. They lived in continual dread of defilement. To avoid contact with the "unclean," they kept aloof, not only from the Gentiles, but from the majority of their own people, seeking neither to benefit them nor to win their friendship. By dwelling constantly on these matters, they had dwarfed their minds and narrowed the orbit of their lives. Their example encouraged egotism and intolerance among all classes of the people.

Jesus began the work of reformation by coming into close sympathy with humanity. While He showed the greatest reverence for the law of God, He rebuked the pretentious piety of the Pharisees, and tried to free the people from the senseless rules that bound them. He was seeking to break down the barriers which separated the different classes of society, that He might bring men together as children of one family. His attendance at the marriage feast was designed to be a step toward effecting this.

God had directed John the Baptist to dwell in the wilderness, that he might be shielded from the influence of the priests and rabbis, and be prepared for a special mission. But the austerity and isolation of his life were not an example for the people. John himself had not directed his hearers to forsake their former duties. He bade them give evidence of their repentance by faithfulness to God in the place where He had called them.

Jesus reproved self-indulgence in all its forms, yet He was social in His nature. He accepted the hospitality of all classes, visiting the homes of the rich and the poor, the learned and the ignorant, and seeking to elevate their thoughts from questions of commonplace life to those things that are spiritual and eternal. He gave no license to dissipation, and no shadow of worldly levity marred His conduct; yet He found pleasure in scenes of innocent happiness, and by His presence sanctioned the social gathering. A Jewish marriage was an impressive occasion, and its joy was not displeasing to the Son of man. By attending this feast, Jesus honored marriage as a divine institution.

In both the Old and the New Testament, the marriage relation is employed to represent the tender and sacred union that exists between Christ and His people. To the mind of Jesus the gladness of the wedding festivities pointed forward to the rejoicing of that day when He shall bring home His bride to the Father's house, and the redeemed with the Redeemer shall sit down to the marriage supper of the Lamb. He says, "As the bridegroom rejoiceth over the bride, so shall thy God rejoice over thee." "Thou shalt no more be termed Forsaken; … but thou shalt be called My Delight; … for the Lord delighteth in thee." "He will rejoice over thee with joy; He will rest in His love, He will joy over thee with singing." Isaiah 62:5, 4, margin; Zephaniah 3:17. When the vision of heavenly things was granted to John the apostle, he wrote: "I heard as it were the voice of a great multitude, and as the voice of many waters, and as the voice of mighty thunderings, saying, Alleluia: for the Lord God omnipotent reigneth. Let us be glad and rejoice, and give honor to Him: for the marriage of the Lamb is come, and His wife hath made herself ready." "Blessed are they which are called unto the marriage supper of the Lamb." Revelation 19:6, 7, 9.

Jesus saw in every soul one to whom must be given the call to His kingdom. He reached the hearts of the people by going among them as one who desired their good. He sought them in the public streets, in private houses, on the boats, in the synagogue, by the shores of the lake, and at the marriage feast. He met them at their daily vocations, and manifested an interest in their secular affairs. He carried His instruction into the household, bringing families in their own homes under the influence of His divine presence. His strong personal sympathy helped to win hearts. He often repaired to the mountains for solitary prayer, but this was a preparation for His labor among men in active life. From these seasons He came forth to relieve the sick, to instruct the ignorant, and to break the chains from the captives of Satan.

It was by personal contact and association that Jesus trained His disciples. Sometimes He taught them, sitting among them on the mountainside; sometimes beside the sea, or walking with them by the way, He revealed the mysteries of the kingdom of God. He did not sermonize as men do today. Wherever hearts were open to receive the divine message, He unfolded the truths of the way of salvation. He did not command His disciples to do this or that, but said, "Follow Me." On His journeys through country and cities He took them with Him, that they might see how He taught the

In both the Old and the New Testament, the marriage relation is employed to represent the tender and sacred union that exists between Christ and His people.

people. He linked their interest with His, and they united with Him in the work.

The example of Christ in linking Himself with the interests of humanity should be followed by all who preach His word, and by all who have received the gospel of His grace. We are not to renounce social communion. We should not seclude ourselves from others. In order to reach all classes, we must meet them where they are. They will seldom seek us of their own accord. Not alone from the pulpit are the hearts of men touched by divine truth. There is another field of labor, humbler, it may be, but fully as promising. It is found in the home of the lowly, and in the mansion of the great; at the hospitable board, and in gatherings for innocent social enjoyment.

As disciples of Christ we shall not mingle with the world from a mere love of pleasure, to unite with them in folly. Such associations can result only in harm. We should never give sanction to sin by our words or our deeds, our silence or our presence. Wherever we go, we are to carry Jesus with us, and to reveal to others the preciousness of our Saviour. But those who try to preserve their religion by hiding it within stone walls lose precious opportunities of doing good. Through the social relations, Christianity comes in contact with the world. Everyone who has

received the divine illumination is to brighten the pathway of those who know not the Light of life.

We should all become witnesses for Jesus. Social power, sanctified by the grace of Christ, must be improved in winning souls to the Saviour. Let the world see that we are not selfishly absorbed in our own interests, but that we desire others to share our blessings and privileges. Let them see that our religion does not make us unsympathetic or exacting. Let all who profess to have found Christ, minister as He did for the benefit of men.

We should never give to the world the false impression that Christians are a gloomy, unhappy people. If our eyes are fixed on Jesus, we shall see a compassionate Redeemer, and shall catch light from His countenance. Wherever His Spirit reigns, there peace abides. And there will be joy also, for there is a calm, holy trust in God.

Christ is pleased with His followers when they show that, though human, they are partakers of the divine nature. They are not statues, but living men and women. Their hearts, refreshed by the dews of divine grace, open and expand to the Sun of Righteousness. The light that shines upon them they reflect upon others in works that are luminous with the love of Christ.

The Sermon On the Mount

This chapter is based on Matthew 5; 6; 7.

. . . .

Christ seldom gathered His disciples alone to receive His words. He did not choose for His audience those only who knew the way of life. It was His work to reach the multitudes who were in ignorance and error. He gave His lessons of truth where they could reach the darkened understanding. He Himself was the Truth, standing with girded loins and hands ever outstretched to bless, and in words of warning, entreaty, and encouragement, seeking to uplift all who would come unto Him.

The Sermon on the Mount, though given especially to the disciples, was spoken in the hearing of the multitude. After the ordination of the apostles, Jesus went with them to the seaside. Here in the early morning the people had begun to assemble. Besides the usual crowds from the Galilean towns, there were people from Judea, and even from Jerusalem itself; from Perea, from Decapolis, from Idumea, away to the south of Judea; and from Tyre and Sidon, the Phoenician cities on the shore of the Mediterranean. "When they had heard what great things He did," they "came to hear Him, and to be healed of their diseases: … there went virtue out of Him, and healed them all." Mark 3:8; Luke 6:17–19.

The narrow beach did not afford even standing room within reach of His voice for all who desired to hear Him, and Jesus led the way back to the mountainside. Reaching a level space that offered a pleasant gathering place for the vast assembly, He seated Himself on the grass, and the disciples and the multitude followed His example.

The disciples' place was always next to Jesus. The people constantly pressed upon Him, yet the disciples understood that they were not to be crowded away from His presence. They sat close beside Him, that they might not lose a word of His instruction. They were attentive listeners, eager to understand the truths they were to make known to all lands and all ages.

With a feeling that something more than usual might be expected, they now pressed about their Master. They believed that the kingdom was soon to be established, and from the events of the morning they gathered assurance that some announcement concerning it was about to be made. A feeling of expectancy pervaded the multitude also, and eager faces gave evidence of the deep interest. As the people sat upon the green hillside, awaiting the words of the divine Teacher, their hearts were filled with thoughts of future glory. There were scribes and Pharisees who looked forward to the day when they should have dominion over the hated Romans, and possess the riches and splendor of the world's great empire. The poor peasants and fishermen hoped to hear the assurance that their wretched hovels, the scanty food, the life of toil, and fear of want were to be exchanged for mansions of plenty and days of ease. In place of the one coarse garment which was their covering by day, and their blanket at night, they hoped that Christ would give them the rich and costly robes of their conquerors. All hearts thrilled with the proud hope that Israel was soon to be honored before the nations as the chosen of the Lord, and Jerusalem exalted as the head of a universal kingdom.

Christ disappointed the hope of worldly greatness. In the Sermon on the Mount He sought to undo the work that had been wrought by false education, and to give His hearers a right conception of His kingdom and of His own character. Yet He did not make a direct attack on the errors of the people. He saw the misery of the world on account of sin, yet He did not present before them a vivid delineation of their wretchedness. He taught them of something infinitely better than they had known. Without combating their ideas of the kingdom of God, He told them the conditions of entrance therein, leaving them to draw their own conclusions as to its nature. The truths He taught are no less important to us than to the multitude that followed Him. We no less than they need to learn the foundation principles of the kingdom of God.

Christ's first words to the people on the mount were words of blessing. Happy are they, He said, who recognize their spiritual poverty, and feel their need of redemption.

The proud heart strives to earn salvation; but both our title to heaven and our fitness for it are found in the righteousness of Christ. The Lord can do nothing toward the recovery of man until, convinced of his own weakness, and stripped of all self-sufficiency, he yields himself to the control of God.

The gospel is to be preached to the poor. Not to the spiritually proud, those who claim to be rich and in need of nothing, is it revealed, but to those who are humble and contrite. One fountain only has been opened for sin, a fountain for the poor in spirit.

The proud heart strives to earn salvation; but both our title to heaven and our fitness for it are found in the righteousness of Christ. The Lord can do nothing toward the recovery of man until, convinced of his own weakness, and stripped of all self-sufficiency, he yields himself to the control of God. Then he can receive the gift that God is waiting to bestow. From the soul that feels his need, nothing is withheld. He has unrestricted access to Him in whom all fullness dwells. "For thus saith the high and lofty One that inhabiteth eternity, whose name is Holy; I dwell in the high and holy place, with him also that is of a contrite and humble spirit, to revive the spirit of the humble, and to revive the heart of the contrite ones." Isaiah 57:15.

"Blessed are they that mourn: for they shall be comforted." By these words Christ does not teach that mourning in itself has power to remove the guilt of sin. He gives no sanction to pretense or to voluntary humility. The mourning of which He speaks does not consist in melancholy and lamentation. While we sorrow on account of sin, we are to rejoice in the precious privilege of being children of God.

We often sorrow because our evil deeds bring unpleasant consequences to ourselves; but this is not repentance. Real sorrow for sin is the result of the working of the Holy Spirit. The Spirit reveals the ingratitude of the heart that has slighted and grieved the Saviour, and brings us in contrition to the foot of the cross. By every sin Jesus is wounded afresh; and as we look upon Him whom we have pierced, we mourn for the sins that have brought anguish upon Him. Such mourning will lead to the renunciation of sin.

The worldling may pronounce this sorrow a weakness; but it is the strength which binds the penitent to the Infinite One with links that cannot be broken. It shows that the angels of God are bringing back to the soul the graces that were lost through hardness of heart and transgression. The tears of the penitent are only the raindrops that precede the sunshine of holiness. This sorrow heralds a joy which will be a living fountain in the soul. "Only acknowledge thine iniquity, that thou hast transgressed against the Lord thy God;" "and I will not cause Mine anger to fall upon you: for I am merciful, saith the Lord." Jeremiah 3:13, 12. "Unto them that mourn in Zion," He has appointed to give "beauty for ashes, the oil of joy for mourning, the garment of praise for the spirit of heaviness." Isaiah 61:3.

And for those also who mourn in trial and sorrow there is comfort. The bitterness of grief and humiliation is better than the indulgences of sin. Through affliction God reveals to us the plague spots in our characters, that by His grace we may overcome our faults. Unknown chapters in regard to ourselves are opened to us, and the test comes, whether we will accept the reproof and the counsel of God. When brought into trial, we are not to fret and complain. We should not rebel, or worry ourselves out of the hand of Christ. We are to humble the soul before God. The ways of the Lord are obscure to him who desires to see things in a light pleasing to himself. They appear dark and joyless to our human nature. But God's ways are ways of mercy and the end is salvation. Elijah knew not what he was doing when in the desert he said that he had had enough of life, and prayed that he might die. The Lord in His mercy did not take him at his word. There was yet a great work for Elijah to do; and when his work was done, he was not to perish in discouragement and solitude in the wilderness. Not for him the descent into the dust of death, but the ascent in glory, with the convoy of celestial chariots, to the throne on high.

God's word for the sorrowing is, "I have seen his ways, and will heal him: I will lead him also, and restore comforts unto him and to his mourners." "I will turn their mourning into joy, and will comfort them, and make them rejoice from their sorrow." Isaiah 57:18; Jeremiah 31:13.

"Blessed are the meek." The difficulties we have to encounter may be very much lessened by that meekness which hides itself in Christ. If we possess the humility of our Master, we shall rise above the slights, the rebuffs, the annoyances, to which we are daily exposed, and they will cease to cast a gloom over the spirit. The highest evidence of nobility in a Christian is self-control. He who under abuse or cruelty fails to maintain a calm and trustful spirit robs God of His right to reveal in him His own perfection of character. Lowliness of heart is the strength that gives victory to the followers of Christ; it is the token of their connection with the courts above.

"Though the Lord be high, yet hath He respect unto the lowly." Psalm 138:6. Those who reveal the meek and lowly spirit of Christ are tenderly regarded by God. They may be looked upon with scorn by the world, but they are of great value in His sight. Not only the wise, the great, the beneficent, will gain a passport to the heavenly courts; not only the busy worker, full of zeal and restless activity. No; the poor in spirit, who crave the presence of an abiding Christ, the humble in heart, whose highest ambition is to do God's will,—these will gain an abundant entrance. They will be among that number who have washed their robes and made them white in the blood of the Lamb. "Therefore are they before the throne of God, and serve Him day and night in His temple: and He that sitteth on the throne shall dwell among them." Revelation 7:15.

"Blessed are they which do hunger and thirst after righteousness." The sense of unworthiness will lead the heart to hunger and thirst for righteousness, and this desire will not be disappointed. Those who make room in their hearts for Jesus will realize His love. All who long to bear the likeness of the character of God shall be satisfied. The Holy Spirit never leaves unassisted the soul who is looking unto Jesus. He takes of the things of Christ and shows them unto him. If the eye is kept fixed on Christ, the work of the Spirit ceases not until the soul is conformed to His image. The pure element of love will expand the soul, giving it a capacity for higher attainments, for increased knowledge of heavenly things, so that it will not rest short of the fullness. "Blessed are they which do hunger and thirst after righteousness; for they shall be filled."

The merciful shall find mercy, and the pure in heart shall see God. Every impure thought defiles the soul, impairs the moral sense, and tends to obliterate the impressions of the Holy Spirit. It dims the spiritual vision, so that men cannot behold God. The Lord may and does forgive the repenting sinner; but though forgiven, the soul is marred. All impurity of speech or of thought must be shunned by him who would have clear discernment of spiritual truth.

But the words of Christ cover more than freedom from sensual impurity, more than freedom from that ceremonial defilement which the Jews so rigorously shunned. Selfishness prevents us from beholding God. The self-seeking spirit judges of God as altogether such a one as itself. Until we have renounced this, we cannot understand Him who is love. Only the unselfish heart, the humble and trustful spirit, shall see God as "merciful and gracious, long-suffering, and abundant in goodness and truth." Exodus 34:6.

"Blessed are the peacemakers." The peace of Christ is born of truth. It is harmony with God. The world is at enmity with the law of God; sinners are at enmity with their Maker; and as a result they are at enmity with one another. But the psalmist declares, "Great peace have they which love Thy law: and nothing shall offend them." Psalm 119:165. Men cannot manufacture peace. Human plans for the purification and uplifting of individuals or of society will fail of producing peace, because they do not reach the heart. The only power that can create or perpetuate true peace is the grace of Christ. When this is implanted in the heart, it will cast out the evil passions that cause strife and dissension. "Instead of the thorn shall come up the fir tree, and instead of the brier shall come up the myrtle tree;" and life's desert "shall rejoice, and blossom as the rose." Isaiah 55:13; 35:1.

The multitudes were amazed at this teaching, which was so at variance with the precepts and example of the Pharisees.

The people had come to think that happiness consisted in the possession of the things of this world, and that fame and the honor of men were much to be coveted. It was very pleasing to be called "Rabbi," and to be extolled as wise and religious, having their virtues paraded before the public. This was regarded as the crown of happiness. But in the presence of that vast throng, Jesus declared that earthly gain and honor were all the reward such persons would ever receive. He spoke with certainty, and a convincing power attended His words. The people were silenced, and a feeling of fear crept over them. They looked at one another doubtfully. Who of them would be saved if this Man's teachings were true? Many were convicted that this remarkable Teacher was actuated by the Spirit of God, and that the sentiments He uttered were divine.

After explaining what constitutes true happiness, and how it may be obtained, Jesus more definitely pointed out the duty of His disciples, as teachers chosen of God to lead others into the path of righteousness and eternal life. He knew that they would often suffer from disappointment and discouragement, that they would meet with decided opposition, that they would be insulted, and their testimony rejected. Well He knew that in the fulfillment of their mission, the humble men who listened so attentively to His words were to bear calumny, torture, imprisonment, and death, and He continued:

"Blessed are they which are persecuted for righteousness' sake: for theirs is the kingdom of heaven. Blessed are ye, when men shall revile you, and persecute you, and shall say all manner of evil against you falsely, for My sake. Rejoice, and be exceeding glad: for great is your reward in heaven: for so persecuted they the prophets which were before you."

The world loves sin, and hates righteousness, and this was the cause of its hostility to Jesus. All who refuse His infinite love will find Christianity a disturbing element. The light of Christ sweeps away the darkness that covers their sins, and the need of reform is made manifest. While those who yield to the influence of the Holy Spirit begin war with themselves, those who cling to sin war against the truth and its representatives.

Thus strife is created, and Christ's followers are accused as troublers of the people. But it is fellowship with God that brings them the world's enmity. They are bearing the reproach of Christ. They are treading the path that has been trodden by the noblest of the earth. Not with sorrow, but with rejoicing, should they meet persecution. Each fiery trial is God's

agent for their refining. Each is fitting them for their work as colaborers with Him. Each conflict has its place in the great battle for righteousness, and each will add to the joy of their final triumph. Having this in view, the test of their faith and patience will be cheerfully accepted rather than dreaded and avoided. Anxious to fulfill their obligation to the world, fixing their desire upon the approval of God, His servants are to fulfill every duty, irrespective of the fear or the favor of men.

"Ye are the salt of the earth," Jesus said. Do not withdraw yourselves from the world in order to escape persecution. You are to abide among men, that the savor of the divine love may be as salt to preserve the world from corruption.

Hearts that respond to the influence of the Holy Spirit are the channels through which God's blessing flows. Were those who serve God removed from the earth, and His Spirit withdrawn from among men, this world would be left to desolation and destruction, the fruit of Satan's dominion. Though the wicked know it not, they owe even the blessings of this life to the presence, in the world, of God's people whom they despise and oppress. But if Christians are such in name only, they are like the salt that has lost its savor. They have no influence for good in the world. Through their misrepresentation of God they are worse than unbelievers.

"Ye are the light of the world." The Jews thought to confine the benefits of salvation to their own nation; but Christ showed them that salvation is like the sunshine. It belongs to the whole world. The religion of the Bible is not to be confined between the covers of a book, nor within the walls of a church. It is not to be brought out occasionally for our own benefit, and then to be carefully laid aside again. It is to sanctify the daily life, to manifest itself in every business transaction and in all our social relations.

True character is not shaped from without, and put on; it radiates from within. If we wish to direct others in the path of righteousness, the principles of righteousness must be enshrined in our own hearts. Our profession of faith may proclaim the theory of religion, but it is our practical piety that holds forth the word of truth. The consistent life, the holy conversation, the unswerving integrity, the active, benevolent spirit, the godly example,—these are the mediums through which light is conveyed to the world.

Jesus had not dwelt on the specifications of the law, but He did not leave His hearers to conclude that He had come to set aside its requirements. He knew that spies stood ready

> *Hearts that respond to the influence of the Holy Spirit are the channels through which God's blessing flows.*

to seize upon every word that might be wrested to serve their purpose. He knew the prejudice that existed in the minds of many of His hearers, and He said nothing to unsettle their faith in the religion and institutions that had been committed to them through Moses. Christ Himself had given both the moral and the ceremonial law. He did not come to destroy confidence in His own instruction. It was because of His great reverence for the law and the prophets that He sought to break through the wall of traditional requirements which hemmed in the Jews. While He set aside their false interpretations of the law, He carefully guarded His disciples against yielding up the vital truths committed to the Hebrews.

The Pharisees prided themselves on their obedience to the law; yet they knew so little of its principles through everyday practice that to them the Saviour's words sounded like heresy. As He swept away the rubbish under which the truth had been buried, they thought He was sweeping away the truth itself. They whispered to one another that He was making light of the law. He read their thoughts, and answered them, saying—

"Think not that I am come to destroy the law, or the prophets: I am not come to destroy, but to fulfill." Here Jesus refutes the charge of the Pharisees. His mission to the world is to vindicate the sacred claims of that law which they charge Him with breaking. If the law of God could have been changed or abrogated, then Christ need not have suffered the consequences of our transgression. He came to explain the relation of the law to man, and to illustrate its precepts by His own life of obedience.

God has given us His holy precepts, because He loves mankind. To shield us from the results of transgression, He reveals the principles of righteousness. The law is an expression of the thought of God; when received in Christ, it becomes our thought. It lifts us above the power of natural desires and tendencies, above temptations that lead to sin. God desires us to be happy, and He gave us the precepts of the law that in obeying them we might have joy. When at Jesus' birth the angels sang—

"Glory to God in the highest,
 And on earth peace, good will
  toward men" (Luke 2:14),

they were declaring the principles of the law which He had come to magnify and make honorable.

When the law was proclaimed from Sinai, God made known to men the holiness of His character, that by contrast they might see the sinfulness of their own. The law was given to convict them of sin, and reveal their need of a Saviour. It would do this as its principles were applied to the heart by the Holy Spirit. This work it is still to do. In the life of Christ the principles of the law are made plain; and as the Holy Spirit of God touches the heart, as the light of Christ reveals to men their need of His cleansing blood and His justifying righteousness, the law is still an agent in bringing us to Christ,

The righteousness which Christ taught is conformity of heart and life to the revealed will of God.

that we may be justified by faith. "The law of the Lord is perfect, converting the soul." Psalm 19:7.

"Till heaven and earth pass," said Jesus, "one jot or one tittle shall in nowise pass from the law, till all be fulfilled." The sun shining in the heavens, the solid earth upon which you dwell, are God's witnesses that His law is changeless and eternal. Though they may pass away, the divine precepts shall endure. "It is easier for heaven and earth to pass, than one tittle of the law to fail." Luke 16:17. The system of types that pointed to Jesus as the Lamb of God was to be abolished at His death; but the precepts of the Decalogue are as immutable as the throne of God.

Since "the law of the Lord is perfect," every variation from it must be evil. Those who disobey the commandments of God, and teach others to do so, are condemned by Christ. The Saviour's life of obedience maintained the claims of the law; it proved that the law could be kept in humanity, and showed the excellence of character that obedience would develop. All who obey as He did are likewise declaring that the law is "holy, and just, and good." Romans 7:12. On the other hand, all who break God's commandments are sustaining Satan's claim that the law is unjust, and cannot be obeyed. Thus they second the deceptions of the great adversary, and cast dishonor upon God. They are the children of the wicked one, who was the first rebel against God's law. To admit them into heaven would again bring in the elements of discord and rebellion, and imperil the well-being of the universe. No man who willfully disregards one principle of the law shall enter the kingdom of heaven.

The rabbis counted their righteousness a passport to heaven; but Jesus declared it to be insufficient and unworthy. External ceremonies and a theoretical knowledge of truth constituted Pharisaical righteousness. The rabbis claimed to be holy through their own efforts in keeping the law; but their works had divorced righteousness from religion. While they were punctilious in ritual observances, their lives were immoral and debased. Their so-called righteousness could never enter the kingdom of heaven.

The greatest deception of the human mind in Christ's day was that a mere assent to the truth constitutes righteousness. In all human experience a theoretical knowledge of the truth has been proved to be insufficient for the saving of the soul. It does not bring forth the fruits of righteousness. A jealous regard for what is termed theological truth often accompanies a hatred of genuine truth as made manifest in life. The darkest chapters of history are burdened with the record of crimes committed by bigoted religionists. The Pharisees claimed to be children of Abraham, and boasted of their possession of the oracles of God; yet these advantages did not preserve them from selfishness, malignity, greed for gain, and the basest hypocrisy. They thought themselves the greatest religionists of the world, but their so-called orthodoxy led them to crucify the Lord of glory.

The same danger still exists. Many take it for granted that they are Christians, simply because they subscribe to certain theological tenets. But they have not brought the truth into practical life. They have not believed and loved it, therefore they have not received the power and grace that come through sanctification of the truth. Men may profess faith in the truth; but if it does not make them sincere, kind, patient, forbearing, heavenly-minded, it is a curse to its possessors, and through their influence it is a curse to the world.

The righteousness which Christ taught is conformity of heart and life to the revealed will of God. Sinful men can become righteous only as they have faith in God and maintain a vital connection with Him. Then true godliness will elevate the thoughts and ennoble the life. Then the external forms of religion accord with the Christian's internal purity. Then the ceremonies required in the service of God are not meaningless rites, like those of the hypocritical Pharisees.

Jesus takes up the commandments separately, and explains the depth and breadth of their requirement. Instead of removing one jot of their force, He shows how far-reaching their principles are, and exposes the fatal mistake of the Jews in their outward show of obedience. He declares that by the evil thought or the lustful look the law of God is transgressed. One who becomes a party to the least injustice is breaking the law and degrading his own moral nature. Murder first exists in the mind. He who gives hatred a place in his heart is setting his feet in the path of the murderer, and his offerings are abhorrent to God.

The Jews cultivated a spirit of retaliation. In their hatred of the Romans they gave utterance to hard denunciations, and pleased the wicked one by manifesting his attributes. Thus they were training themselves to do the terrible deeds to which he led them on. In the religious life of the Pharisees there was nothing to recommend piety to the Gentiles. Jesus bade them not to deceive themselves with the thought that they could in heart rise up against their oppressors, and cherish the longing to avenge their wrongs.

It is true there is an indignation that is justifiable, even in the followers of Christ. When they see that God is dishonored, and His service brought into disrepute, when they see the innocent oppressed, a righteous indignation stirs the soul. Such anger, born of sensitive morals, is not a sin. But those who at any supposed provocation feel at liberty to indulge anger or resentment are opening the heart to Satan. Bitterness and animosity must be banished from the soul if we would be in harmony with heaven.

The Saviour goes farther than this. He says, "If thou bring thy gift to the altar, and there rememberest that thy brother hath aught against thee; leave there thy gift before the altar, and go thy way; first be reconciled to thy brother, and then come and offer thy gift." Many are zealous in religious services, while between them and their brethren are unhappy differences which they might reconcile. God requires them to do all in their power to restore harmony. Until they do this, He cannot accept their services. The Christian's duty in this matter is clearly pointed out.

God pours His blessings upon all. "He maketh His sun to rise on the evil and on the good, and sendeth rain on the just and on the unjust." He is "kind unto the unthankful and to the evil." Luke 6:35. He bids us to be like Him. "Bless them that curse you," said Jesus; "do good to them that hate you, … that ye may be the children of your Father which is in heaven." These are the principles of the law, and they are the wellsprings of life.

God's ideal for His children is higher than the highest human thought can reach. "Be ye therefore perfect, even as your Father which is in heaven is perfect." This command is a promise. The plan of redemption contemplates our complete recovery from the power of Satan. Christ always separates the contrite soul from sin. He came to destroy the works of the devil, and He has made provision that the Holy Spirit shall be imparted to every repentant soul, to keep him from sinning.

The tempter's agency is not to be accounted an excuse for one wrong act. Satan is jubilant when he hears the professed followers of Christ making excuses for their deformity of character. It is these excuses that lead to sin. There is no excuse for sinning. A holy temper, a Christlike life, is accessible to every repenting, believing child of God.

The ideal of Christian character is Christlikeness. As the Son of man was perfect in His life, so His followers are to be perfect in their life. Jesus was in all things made like unto His brethren. He became flesh, even as we are. He was hungry and thirsty and weary. He was sustained by food and refreshed by sleep. He shared the lot of man; yet He was the blameless Son of God. He was God in the flesh. His character is to be ours. The Lord says of those who believe in Him, "I will dwell in them, and walk in them; and I will be their God, and they shall be My people." 2 Corinthians 6:16.

Christ is the ladder that Jacob saw, the base resting on the earth, and the topmost round reaching to the gate of heaven, to the very threshold of glory. If that ladder had failed by a single step of reaching the earth, we should have been lost. But Christ reaches us where we are. He took our nature and overcame, that we through taking His nature might overcome. Made "in the likeness of sinful flesh" (Romans 8:3), He lived a sinless life. Now by His divinity He lays hold upon the throne of heaven, while by His humanity He reaches us. He bids us by faith in Him attain to the glory of the character of God. Therefore are we to be perfect, even as our "Father which is in heaven is perfect."

Jesus had shown in what righteousness consists, and had pointed to God as its source. Now He turned to practical duties. In almsgiving, in prayer, in fasting, He said, let nothing be done to attract attention or win praise to self. Give in sincerity, for the benefit of the suffering poor. In prayer, let the soul commune with God. In fasting, go not with the head bowed down, and heart filled with thoughts of self. The heart of the Pharisee is a barren and profitless soil, in which no seeds of divine life can flourish. It is he who yields himself most unreservedly to God that will render Him the most acceptable service. For through fellowship with God men become workers together with Him in presenting His character in humanity.

The service rendered in sincerity of heart has great recompense. "Thy Father which seeth in secret Himself shall reward thee openly." By the life we live through the grace of Christ the character is formed. The original loveliness begins to be restored to the soul. The attributes of the character of Christ are imparted, and the image of the Divine begins to shine forth. The faces of men and women who walk and work with God express the peace of heaven. They are surrounded with the atmosphere of heaven. For these souls the kingdom of God has begun. They have Christ's joy, the joy of being a blessing to humanity. They have the honor of being accepted for the Master's use; they are trusted to do His work in His name.

"No man can serve two masters." We cannot serve God with a divided heart. Bible religion is not one influence among many others; its influence is to be supreme, pervading and controlling every other. It is not to be like a dash of color brushed here and there upon the canvas, but it is to pervade the whole life, as if the canvas were dipped into the color, until every thread of the fabric were dyed a deep, unfading hue.

"If therefore thine eye be single, thy whole body shall be full of light. But if thine eye be evil, thy whole body shall be full of darkness." Purity and steadfastness of purpose are the conditions of receiving light from God. He who desires to know the truth must be willing to accept all that it reveals.

He can make no compromise with error. To be wavering and halfhearted in allegiance to truth is to choose the darkness of error and satanic delusion.

Worldly policy and the undeviating principles of righteousness do not blend into each other imperceptibly, like the colors of the rainbow. Between the two a broad, clear line is drawn by the eternal God. The likeness of Christ stands out as distinct from that of Satan as midday in contrast with midnight. And only those who live the life of Christ are His co-workers. If one sin is cherished in the soul, or one wrong practice retained in the life, the whole being is contaminated.

directions for their life journey at once, lest they should become confused. He tells them just as much as they can remember and perform. The strength and wisdom imparted are for the present emergency. "If any of you lack wisdom"—for today—"let him ask of God, that giveth to all men liberally, and upbraideth not; and it shall be given him." James 1:5.

"Judge not, that ye be not judged." Do not think yourself better than other men, and set yourself up as their judge. Since you cannot discern motive, you are incapable of judging another. In criticizing him, you are passing sentence upon yourself; for you show that you are a participant with

We are to follow Christ day by day. God does not bestow help for tomorrow. He does not give His children all the directions for their life journey at once, lest they should become confused. He tells them just as much as they can remember and perform. The strength and wisdom imparted are for the present emergency.

The man becomes an instrument of unrighteousness.

All who have chosen God's service are to rest in His care. Christ pointed to the birds flying in the heavens, to the flowers of the field, and bade His hearers consider these objects of God's creation. "Are not ye of much more value than they?" He said. Matthew 6:26, RV. The measure of divine attention bestowed on any object is proportionate to its rank in the scale of being. The little brown sparrow is watched over by Providence. The flowers of the field, the grass that carpets the earth, share the notice and care of our heavenly Father. The great Master Artist has taken thought for the lilies, making them so beautiful that they outshine the glory of Solomon. How much more does He care for man, who is the image and glory of God. He longs to see His children reveal a character after His similitude. As the sunbeam imparts to the flowers their varied and delicate tints, so does God impart to the soul the beauty of His own character.

All who choose Christ's kingdom of love and righteousness and peace, making its interest paramount to all other, are linked to the world above, and every blessing needed for this life is theirs. In the book of God's providence, the volume of life, we are each given a page. That page contains every particular of our history; even the hairs of the head are numbered. God's children are never absent from His mind.

"Be not therefore anxious for the morrow." Matthew 6:34, RV. We are to follow Christ day by day. God does not bestow help for tomorrow. He does not give His children all the

Satan, the accuser of the brethren. The Lord says, "Examine yourselves, whether ye be in the faith; prove your own selves." This is our work. "If we would judge ourselves, we should not be judged." 2 Corinthians 13:5; 1 Corinthians 11:31.

The good tree will produce good fruit. If the fruit is unpalatable and worthless, the tree is evil. So the fruit borne in the life testifies as to the condition of the heart and the excellence of the character. Good works can never purchase salvation, but they are an evidence of the faith that acts by love and purifies the soul. And though the eternal reward is not bestowed because of our merit, yet it will be in proportion to the work that has been done through the grace of Christ.

Thus Christ set forth the principles of His kingdom, and showed them to be the great rule of life. To impress the lesson He adds an illustration. It is not enough, He says, for you to hear My words. By obedience you must make them the foundation of your character. Self is but shifting sand. If you build upon human theories and inventions, your house will fall. By the winds of temptation, the tempests of trial, it will be swept away. But these principles that I have given will endure. Receive Me; build on My words.

"Everyone therefore which heareth these words of Mine, and doeth them, shall be likened unto a wise man, which built his house upon the rock: and the rain descended, and the floods came, and the winds blew, and beat upon that house; and it fell not: for it was founded upon the rock." Matthew 7:24, 25, RV.

The Sabbath

....

The Sabbath was hallowed at the creation. As ordained for man, it had its origin when "the morning stars sang together, and all the sons of God shouted for joy." Job 38:7. Peace brooded over the world; for earth was in harmony with heaven. "God saw everything that He had made, and, behold, it was very good;" and He rested in the joy of His completed work (Genesis 1:31).

Because He had rested upon the Sabbath, "God blessed the seventh day, and sanctified it"—set it apart to a holy use. He gave it to Adam as a day of rest. It was a memorial of the work of creation, and thus a sign of God's power and His love. The Scripture says, "He hath made His wonderful works to be remembered." "The things that are made," declare "the invisible things of Him since the creation of the world," "even His everlasting power and divinity." Genesis 2:3; Psalm 111:4; Romans 1:20, RV.

All things were created by the Son of God. "In the beginning was the Word, and the Word was with God. … All things were made by Him; and without Him was not anything made that was made." John 1:1–3. And since the Sabbath is a memorial of the work of creation, it is a token of the love and power of Christ.

The Sabbath calls our thoughts to nature, and brings us into communion with the Creator. In the song of the bird, the sighing of the trees, and the music of the sea, we still may hear His voice who talked with Adam in Eden in the cool of the day. And as we behold His power in nature we find comfort, for the word that created all things is that which speaks life to the soul. He "who commanded the light to shine out of darkness, hath shined in our hearts, to give the light of the knowledge of the glory of God in the face of Jesus Christ." 2 Corinthians 4:6.

It was this thought that awoke the song,—

"Thou, Lord, hast made me glad through Thy work;
I will triumph in the works of Thy hands.

O Lord, how great are Thy works!
And Thy thoughts are very deep." Psalm 92:4, 5.

And the Holy Spirit through the prophet Isaiah declares: "To whom then will ye liken God? or what likeness will ye compare unto Him? … Have ye not known? have ye not heard? hath it not been told you from the beginning? have ye not understood from the foundations of the earth? It is He that sitteth upon the circle of the earth, and the inhabitants thereof are as grasshoppers; that stretcheth out the heavens as a curtain, and spreadeth them out as a tent to dwell in. … To whom then will ye liken Me, or shall I be equal? saith the Holy One. Lift up your eyes on high, and behold who hath created these things, that bringeth out their host by number: He calleth them all by names by the greatness of His might, for that He is strong in power; not one faileth. Why sayest thou, O Jacob, and speakest, O Israel, My way is hid from the Lord, and my judgment is passed over from my God? Hast thou not known? hast thou not heard, that the everlasting God, the Lord, the Creator of the ends of the earth, fainteth not, neither is weary? … He giveth power to the faint; and to them that have no might He increaseth strength." "Fear thou not; for I am with thee: be not dismayed; for I am thy God: I will strengthen thee; yea, I will help thee; yea, I will uphold thee with the right hand of My righteousness." "Look unto Me, and be ye saved, all the ends of the earth: for I am God, and there is none else." This is the message written in nature, which the Sabbath is appointed to keep in memory. When the Lord bade Israel hallow His Sabbaths, He said, "They shall be a sign between Me and you, that ye may know that I am Jehovah your God." Isaiah 40:18–29; 41:10; 45:22; Ezekiel 20:20, RV.

The Sabbath was embodied in the law given from Sinai; but it was not then first made known as a day of rest. The people of Israel had a knowledge of it before they came to Sinai. On the way thither the Sabbath was kept. When some profaned it, the Lord reproved them, saying, "How long refuse ye to keep My commandments and My laws?" Exodus 16:28.

The Sabbath was not for Israel merely, but for the world. It had been made known to man in Eden, and, like the other precepts of the Decalogue, it is of imperishable obligation. Of that law of which the fourth commandment forms a part, Christ declares, "Till heaven and earth pass, one jot or one tittle shall in nowise pass from the law." So long as the heavens and the earth endure, the Sabbath will continue as a sign of the Creator's power. And when Eden shall bloom on earth again, God's holy rest day will be honored by all beneath the sun. "From one Sabbath to another" the inhabitants of the glorified new earth shall go up "to worship before Me, saith the Lord." Matthew 5:18; Isaiah 66:23.

No other institution which was committed to the Jews tended so fully to distinguish them from surrounding nations as did the Sabbath. God designed that its observance should designate them as His worshipers. It was to be a token of their separation from idolatry, and their connection with the true God. But in order to keep the Sabbath holy, men must themselves be holy. Through faith they must become partakers of the righteousness of Christ. When the command was given to Israel, "Remember the Sabbath day, to keep it holy," the Lord said also to them, "Ye shall be holy men unto Me." Exodus 20:8; 22:31. Only thus could the Sabbath distinguish Israel as the worshipers of God.

As the Jews departed from God, and failed to make the righteousness of Christ their own by faith, the Sabbath lost its significance to them. Satan was seeking to exalt himself and to draw men away from Christ, and he worked to pervert the Sabbath, because it is the sign of the power of Christ. The Jewish leaders accomplished the will of Satan by surrounding God's rest day with burdensome requirements. In the days of Christ the Sabbath had become so perverted that its observance reflected the character of selfish and arbitrary men rather than the character of the loving heavenly Father. The rabbis virtually represented God as giving laws which it was impossible for men to obey. They led the people to look upon God as a tyrant, and to think that the observance of the Sabbath, as He required it, made men hard-hearted and cruel. It was the work of Christ to clear away these misconceptions. Although the rabbis followed Him with merciless hostility, He did not even appear to conform to their requirements, but went straight forward, keeping the Sabbath according to the law of God.

The Sabbath calls our thoughts to nature, and brings us into communion with the Creator. In the song of the bird, the sighing of the trees, and the music of the sea, we still may hear His voice who talked with Adam in Eden in the cool of the day.

Upon one Sabbath day, as the Saviour and His disciples returned from the place of worship, they passed through a field of ripening grain. Jesus had continued His work to a late hour, and while passing through the fields, the disciples began to gather the heads of grain, and to eat the kernels after rubbing them in their hands. On any other day this act would have excited no comment, for one passing through a field of grain, an orchard, or a vineyard, was at liberty to gather what he desired to eat. See Deuteronomy 23:24, 25. But to do this on the Sabbath was held to be an act of desecration. Not only was the gathering of the grain a kind of reaping, but the rubbing of it in the hands was a kind of threshing. Thus, in the opinion of the rabbis, there was a double offense.

The spies at once complained to Jesus, saying, "Behold, Thy disciples do that which is not lawful to do upon the Sabbath day."

When accused of Sabbathbreaking at Bethesda, Jesus defended Himself by affirming His Sonship to God, and declaring that He worked in harmony with the Father. Now that the disciples are attacked, He cites His accusers to examples from the Old Testament, acts performed on the Sabbath by those who were in the service of God.

The Jewish teachers prided themselves on their knowledge of the Scriptures, and in the Saviour's answer there was an implied rebuke for their ignorance of the Sacred Writings. "Have ye not read so much as this," He said, "what David did, when himself was an hungered, and they which were with him; how he went into the house of God, and did take and eat the shewbread, … which it is not lawful to eat but for the priests alone?" "And He said unto

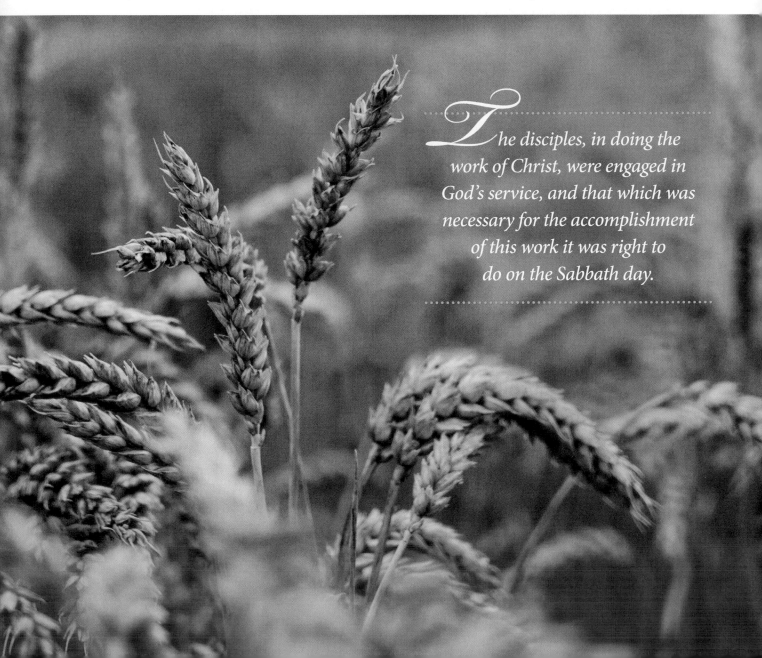

The disciples, in doing the work of Christ, were engaged in God's service, and that which was necessary for the accomplishment of this work it was right to do on the Sabbath day.

them, The Sabbath was made for man, and not man for the Sabbath." "Have ye not read in the law, how that on the Sabbath days the priests in the temple profane the Sabbath, and are blameless? But I say unto you, That in this place is one greater than the temple." "The Son of man is Lord also of the Sabbath." Luke 6:3, 4; Mark 2:27, 28; Matthew 12:5, 6.

If it was right for David to satisfy his hunger by eating of the bread that had been set apart to a holy use, then it was right for the disciples to supply their need by plucking the grain upon the sacred hours of the Sabbath. Again, the priests in the temple performed greater labor on the Sabbath than upon other days. The same labor in secular business would be sinful; but the work of the priests was in the service of God. They were performing those rites that pointed to the redeeming power of Christ, and their labor was in harmony with the object of the Sabbath. But now Christ Himself had come. The disciples, in doing the work of Christ, were engaged in God's service, and that which was necessary for the accomplishment of this work it was right to do on the Sabbath day.

Christ would teach His disciples and His enemies that the service of God is first of all. The object of God's work in this world is the redemption of man; therefore that which is necessary to be done on the Sabbath in the accomplishment of this work is in accord with the Sabbath law. Jesus then crowned His argument by declaring Himself the "Lord of the Sabbath"—One above all question and above all law. This infinite Judge acquits the disciples of blame, appealing to the very statutes they are accused of violating.

Jesus did not let the matter pass with administering a rebuke to His enemies. He declared that in their blindness they had mistaken the object of the Sabbath. He said, "If ye had known what this meaneth, I will have mercy, and not sacrifice, ye would not have condemned the guiltless." Matthew 12:7. Their many heartless rites could not supply the lack of that truthful integrity and tender love which will ever characterize the true worshiper of God.

Again Christ reiterated the truth that the sacrifices were in themselves of no value. They were a means, and not an end. Their object was to direct men to the Saviour, and thus to bring them into harmony with God. It is the service of love that God values. When this is lacking, the mere round of ceremony is an offense to Him. So with the Sabbath. It was designed to bring men into communion with God; but when the mind was absorbed with wearisome rites, the object of the Sabbath was thwarted. Its mere outward observance was a mockery.

Upon another Sabbath, as Jesus entered a synagogue, He saw there a man who had a withered hand. The Pharisees watched Him, eager to see what He would do. The Saviour well knew that in healing on the Sabbath He would be regarded as a transgressor, but He did not hesitate to break down the wall of traditional requirements that barricaded the Sabbath. Jesus bade the afflicted man stand forth, and then asked, "It is lawful to do good on the Sabbath days, or to do evil? to save life, or to kill?" It was a maxim among the Jews that a failure to do good, when one had opportunity, was to do evil; to neglect to save life was to kill. Thus Jesus met the rabbis on their own ground. "But they held their peace. And when He had looked round about on them with anger, being grieved for the hardness of their hearts, He saith unto the man, Stretch forth thine hand. And he stretched it out: and his hand was restored whole as the other." Mark 3:4, 5.

When questioned, "Is it lawful to heal on the Sabbath days?" Jesus answered, "What man shall there be among you, that shall have one sheep, and if it fall into a pit on the Sabbath day, will he not lay hold on it, and lift it out? How much then is a man better than a sheep? Wherefore it is lawful to do well on the Sabbath days." Matthew 12:10–12.

The spies dared not answer Christ in the presence of the multitude, for fear of involving themselves in difficulty. They knew that He had spoken the truth. Rather than violate their traditions, they would leave a man to suffer, while they would relieve a brute because of the loss to the owner if it were neglected. Thus greater care was shown for a dumb animal than for man, who is made in the image of God. This illustrates the working of all false religions. They originate in man's desire to exalt himself above God, but they result in degrading man below the brute. Every religion that wars against the sovereignty of God defrauds man of the glory which was his at the creation, and which is to be restored to him in Christ. Every false religion teaches its adherents to be careless of human needs, sufferings, and rights. The gospel places a high value upon humanity as the purchase of the blood of Christ, and it teaches a tender regard for the wants and woes of man. The Lord says, "I will make a man more precious than fine gold; even a man than the golden wedge of Ophir." Isaiah 13:12.

When Jesus turned upon the Pharisees with the question whether it was lawful on the Sabbath day to do good or to do evil, to save life or to kill, He confronted them with their own wicked purposes. They were hunting His life with bitter hatred, while He was saving life and bringing happiness to multitudes. Was it better to slay upon the Sabbath, as they were planning to do, than to heal the afflicted, as He had done? Was it more righteous to have murder in the heart upon God's holy day than love to all men, which finds expression in deeds of mercy?

In the healing of the withered hand, Jesus condemned the custom of the Jews, and left the fourth commandment standing as God had given it. "It is lawful to do well on the Sabbath days," He declared. By sweeping away the senseless restrictions of the Jews, Christ honored the Sabbath, while those who complained of Him were dishonoring God's holy day.

Those who hold that Christ abolished the law teach that He broke the Sabbath and justified His disciples in doing the same. Thus they are really taking the same ground as did the caviling Jews. In this they contradict the testimony of Christ Himself, who declared, "I have kept My Father's commandments, and abide in His love." John 15:10. Neither the Saviour nor His followers broke the law of the Sabbath. Christ was a living representative of the law. No violation of its holy precepts was found in His life. Looking upon a nation of witnesses who were seeking occasion to condemn Him, He could say unchallenged, "Which of you convicteth Me of sin?" John 8:46, RV.

The Saviour had not come to set aside what patriarchs and prophets had spoken; for He Himself had spoken through these representative men. All the truths of God's word came from Him. But these priceless gems had been placed in false settings. Their precious light had been made to minister to error. God desired them to be removed from their settings of error and replaced in the framework of truth. This work only a divine hand could accomplish. By its connection with error, the truth had been serving the cause of the enemy of God and man. Christ had come to place it where it would glorify God, and work the salvation of humanity.

"The Sabbath was made for man, and not man for the Sabbath," Jesus said. The institutions that God has established are for the benefit of mankind. "All things are for your sakes." "Whether Paul, or Apollos, or Cephas, or the world, or life, or death, or things present, or things to come; all are yours; and ye are Christ's; and Christ is God's." 2 Corinthians 4:15; 1 Corinthians 3:22, 23. The law of Ten Commandments, of which the Sabbath forms a part, God gave to His people as a blessing. "The Lord commanded

The institutions that God has established are for the benefit of mankind.

us," said Moses, "to do all these statutes, to fear the Lord our God, for our good always, that He might preserve us alive." Deuteronomy 6:24. And through the psalmist the message was given to Israel, "Serve the Lord with gladness: come before His presence with singing. Know ye that the Lord He is God: it is He that hath made us, and not we ourselves; we are His people, and the sheep of His pasture. Enter into His gates with thanksgiving, and into His courts with praise." Psalm 100:2–4. And of all who keep "the Sabbath from polluting it," the Lord declares, "Even them will I bring to My holy mountain, and make them joyful in My house of prayer." Isaiah 56:6, 7.

"Wherefore the Son of man is Lord also of the Sabbath." These words are full of instruction and comfort. Because the Sabbath was made for man, it is the Lord's day. It belongs to Christ. For "all things were made by Him; and without Him was not anything made that was made." John 1:3. Since He made all things, He made the Sabbath. By Him it was set apart as a memorial of the work of creation. It points to Him as both the Creator and the Sanctifier. It declares that He who created all things in heaven and in earth, and by whom all things hold together, is the head of the church, and that by His power we are reconciled to God. For, speaking of Israel, He said, "I gave them My Sabbaths, to be a sign between Me and them, that they might know that I am the Lord that sanctify them"—make them holy. Ezekiel 20:12. Then the Sabbath is a sign of Christ's power to make us holy. And it is given to all whom Christ makes holy. As a sign of His sanctifying power, the Sabbath is given to all who through Christ become a part of the Israel of God.

And the Lord says, "If thou turn away thy foot from the Sabbath, from doing thy pleasure on My holy day; and call the Sabbath a delight, the holy of the Lord, honorable; … then shalt thou delight thyself in the Lord." Isaiah 58:13, 14. To all who receive the Sabbath as a sign of Christ's creative and redeeming power, it will be a delight. Seeing Christ in it, they delight themselves in Him. The Sabbath points them to the works of creation as an evidence of His mighty power in redemption. While it calls to mind the lost peace of Eden, it tells of peace restored through the Saviour. And every object in nature repeats His invitation, "Come unto Me, all ye that labor and are heavy-laden, and I will give you rest." Matthew 11:28.

The Feast At Simon's House

This chapter is based on Matthew 26:6–13; Mark 14:3–11; Luke 7:36–50; John 11:55–57; 12:1–11.

. . . .

Simon of Bethany was accounted a disciple of Jesus. He was one of the few Pharisees who had openly joined Christ's followers. He acknowledged Jesus as a teacher, and hoped that He might be the Messiah, but he had not accepted Him as a Saviour. His character was not transformed; his principles were unchanged.

Simon had been healed of the leprosy, and it was this that had drawn him to Jesus. He desired to show his gratitude, and at Christ's last visit to Bethany he made a feast for the Saviour and His disciples. This feast brought together many of the Jews. There was at this time much excitement at Jerusalem. Christ and His mission were attracting greater attention than ever before. Those who had come to the feast closely watched His movements, and some of them with unfriendly eyes.

The Saviour had reached Bethany only six days before the Passover, and according to His custom had sought rest at the home of Lazarus. The crowds of travelers who passed on to the city spread the tidings that He was on His way to Jerusalem, and that He would rest over the Sabbath at Bethany. Among the people there was great enthusiasm. Many flocked to Bethany, some out of sympathy with Jesus, and others from curiosity to see one who had been raised from the dead.

Many expected to hear from Lazarus a wonderful account of scenes witnessed after death. They were surprised that he told them nothing.

He had nothing of this kind to tell. Inspiration declares, "The dead know not anything. … Their love, and their hatred, and their envy, is now perished." Ecclesiastes 9:5, 6. But Lazarus did have a wonderful testimony to bear in regard to the work of Christ. He had been raised from the dead for this purpose. With assurance and power he declared that Jesus was the Son of God.

The reports carried back to Jerusalem by the visitors to Bethany increased the excitement. The people were eager to see and hear Jesus. There was a general inquiry as to whether Lazarus would accompany Him to Jerusalem, and if the prophet would be crowned king at the Passover. The priests and rulers saw that their hold upon the people was still weakening, and their rage against Jesus grew more bitter. They could hardly wait for the opportunity of removing Him forever from their way. As time passed, they began to fear that after all He might not come to Jerusalem. They remembered how often He had baffled their murderous designs, and they were fearful that He had now read their purposes against Him, and would remain away. They could ill conceal their anxiety, and questioned among themselves, "What think ye, that He will not come to the feast?"

A council of the priests and Pharisees was called. Since the raising of Lazarus the sympathies of the people were so fully with Christ that it would be dangerous to seize upon Him openly. So the authorities determined to take Him secretly, and carry on the trial as quietly as possible. They hoped that when His condemnation became known, the fickle tide of public opinion would set in their favor.

Thus they proposed to destroy Jesus. But so long as Lazarus lived, the priests and rabbis knew that they were not secure. The very existence of a man who had been four days in the grave, and who had been restored by a word from Jesus, would sooner or later cause a reaction. The people would be avenged on their leaders for taking the life of One who could perform such a miracle. The Sanhedrin therefore decided that Lazarus also must die. To such lengths do envy and prejudice lead their slaves. The hatred and unbelief of the Jewish leaders had increased until they would even take the life of one whom infinite power had rescued from the grave.

While this plotting was going on at Jerusalem, Jesus and His friends were invited to Simon's feast. At the table the Saviour sat with Simon, whom He had cured of a loathsome disease, on one side, and Lazarus, whom He had raised from the dead, on the other. Martha served at the table, but Mary was earnestly listening to every word from the lips of Jesus. In His mercy, Jesus had pardoned her sins, He had called forth her beloved brother from the grave, and Mary's heart was filled with gratitude. She had heard Jesus speak of His approaching death, and in her deep love and sorrow she had longed to show Him honor. At great personal sacrifice she had purchased an alabaster box of "ointment of spikenard, very costly," with which to anoint His body. But now many were declaring that He was about to be crowned king. Her grief was turned to joy, and she was eager to be first in honoring her Lord. Breaking her box of ointment, she poured its contents upon the head and feet of Jesus; then, as she knelt weeping, moistening them with her tears, she wiped His feet with her long, flowing hair.

She had sought to avoid observation, and her movements might have passed unnoticed, but the ointment filled the room with its fragrance, and published her act to all present. Judas looked upon this act with great displeasure. Instead of waiting to hear what Christ would say of the matter, he began to whisper his complaints

The fragrant gift which Mary had thought to lavish upon the dead body of the Saviour she poured upon His living form. At the burial its sweetness could only have pervaded the tomb; now it gladdened His heart with the assurance of her faith and love.

to those near him, throwing reproach upon Christ for suffering such waste. Craftily he made suggestions that would be likely to cause disaffection.

Judas was treasurer for the disciples, and from their little store he had secretly drawn for his own use, thus narrowing down their resources to a meager pittance. He was eager to put into the bag all that he could obtain. The treasure in the bag was often drawn upon to relieve the poor; and when something that Judas did not think essential was bought, he would say, Why is this waste? why was not the cost of this put into the bag that I carry for the poor? Now the act of Mary was in such marked contrast to his selfishness that he was put to shame; and according to his custom, he sought to assign a worthy motive for his objection to her gift. Turning to the disciples, he asked, "Why was not this ointment sold for three hundred pence, and given to the poor? This he said, not that he cared for the poor; but because he was a thief, and had the bag, and bare what was put therein." Judas had no heart for the poor. Had Mary's ointment been sold, and the proceeds fallen into his possession, the poor would have received no benefit.

Judas had a high opinion of his own executive ability. As a financier he thought himself greatly superior to his fellow disciples, and he had led them to regard him in the same light. He had gained their confidence, and had a strong influence over them. His professed sympathy for the poor deceived them, and his artful insinuation caused them to look distrustfully upon Mary's devotion. The murmur passed round the table, "To what purpose is this waste? For this ointment might have been sold for much, and given to the poor."

Mary heard the words of criticism. Her heart trembled within her. She feared that her sister would reproach her for extravagance. The Master, too, might think her improvident. Without apology or excuse she was about to shrink away, when the voice of her Lord was heard, "Let her alone; why trouble ye her?" He saw that she was embarrassed and distressed. He knew that in this act of service she had expressed her gratitude for the forgiveness of her sins, and He brought relief to her mind. Lifting His voice above the murmur of criticism, He said, "She hath wrought a good work on Me. For ye have the poor with you always, and whensoever ye will ye may do them good: but Me ye have not always. She hath done what she could: she is come aforehand to anoint My body to the burying."

The fragrant gift which Mary had thought to lavish upon the dead body of the Saviour she poured upon His living form. At the burial its sweetness could only have pervaded the tomb; now it gladdened His heart with the assurance of her faith and love. Joseph of Arimathaea and Nicodemus offered not their gift of love to Jesus in His life. With bitter tears they brought their costly spices for His cold, unconscious form. The women who bore spices to the tomb found their errand in vain, for He had risen. But Mary, pouring out her love upon the Saviour while He was conscious of her devotion, was anointing Him for the burial. And as He went down into the darkness of His great trial, He carried with Him the memory of that deed, an earnest of the love that would be His from His redeemed ones forever.

Many there are who bring their precious gifts for the dead. As they stand about the cold, silent form, words of love are freely spoken. Tenderness, appreciation, devotion, all are lavished upon one who sees not nor hears. Had these words been spoken when the weary spirit needed them so much, when the ear could hear and the heart could feel, how precious would have been their fragrance!

Mary knew not the full significance of her deed of love. She could not answer her accusers. She could not explain why she had chosen that occasion for anointing Jesus. The Holy Spirit had planned for her, and she had obeyed His promptings. Inspiration stoops to give no reason. An unseen presence, it speaks to mind and soul, and moves the heart to action. It is its own justification.

Christ told Mary the meaning of her act, and in this He gave her more than He had received. "In that she hath poured this ointment on My body," He said, "she did it for My burial." As the alabaster box was broken, and filled the whole house with its fragrance, so Christ was to die, His body was to be broken; but He was to rise from the tomb, and the fragrance of His life was to fill the earth. Christ "hath loved us, and hath given Himself for us an offering and a sacrifice to God for a sweet-smelling savor." Ephesians 5:2.

"Verily I say unto you," Christ declared, "Wheresoever this gospel shall be preached throughout the whole world, this also that she hath done shall be spoken of for a memorial of her." Looking into the future, the Saviour spoke with certainty concerning His gospel. It was to be preached throughout the world. And as far as the gospel extended, Mary's gift would shed its fragrance, and hearts would be blessed through her unstudied act. Kingdoms would rise and fall; the names of monarchs and conquerors would be forgotten; but this woman's deed would be immortalized upon the pages of sacred history. Until time should be no more, that broken alabaster box would tell the story of the abundant love of God for a fallen race.

Mary's act was in marked contrast with that which Judas was about to do. What a sharp lesson Christ might have given him who had dropped the seed of criticism and evil thinking into the minds of the disciples! How justly the accuser might have been accused! He who reads the motives of every heart, and understands every action, might have opened before those at the feast dark chapters in the experience of Judas. The hollow pretense on which the traitor based his words might have been laid bare; for, instead of sympathizing with the poor, he was robbing them of the money intended for their relief. Indignation might have been excited against him for his oppression of the widow, the orphan, and the hireling. But had Christ unmasked Judas, this would have been urged as a reason for the betrayal. And though charged with being a thief, Judas would have gained sympathy, even among the disciples. The Saviour reproached him not, and thus avoided giving him an excuse for his treachery.

But the look which Jesus cast upon Judas convinced him that the Saviour penetrated his hypocrisy, and read his base, contemptible character. And in commending Mary's action, which had been so severely condemned, Christ had rebuked Judas. Prior to this, the Saviour had never given him a direct rebuke. Now the reproof rankled in his heart. He determined to be revenged. From the supper he went directly to the palace of the high priest, where he found the council assembled, and he offered to betray Jesus into their hands.

The priests were greatly rejoiced. These leaders of Israel had been given the privilege of receiving Christ as their Saviour, without money and without price. But they refused the precious gift offered them in the most tender spirit of constraining love. They refused to accept that salvation which is of more value than gold, and bought their Lord for thirty pieces of silver.

Judas had indulged avarice until it overpowered every good trait of his character. He grudged the offering made to Jesus. His heart burned with envy that the Saviour should be the recipient of a gift suitable for the monarchs of the earth. For a sum far less than the box of ointment cost, he betrayed his Lord.

The disciples were not like Judas. They loved the Saviour. But they did not rightly appreciate His exalted character. Had they realized what He had done for them, they would have felt that nothing bestowed upon Him was wasted. The wise men from the East, who knew so little of Jesus, had shown a truer appreciation of the honor due Him. They brought precious gifts to the Saviour, and bowed in homage before Him when He was but a babe, and cradled in a manger.

Christ values acts of heartfelt courtesy. When anyone did Him a favor, with heavenly politeness He blessed the actor. He did not refuse the simplest flower plucked by the hand of a child, and offered to Him in love. He accepted the offerings of children, and blessed the givers, inscribing their names in the book of life. In the Scriptures, Mary's anointing of Jesus is mentioned as distinguishing her from the other Marys. Acts of love and reverence for Jesus are an evidence of faith in Him as the Son of God. And the Holy Spirit mentions, as evidences of woman's loyalty to Christ: "If she have washed the saints' feet, if she have relieved the afflicted, if she have diligently followed every good work." 1 Timothy 5:10.

Christ delighted in the earnest desire of Mary to do the will of her Lord. He accepted the wealth of pure affection which His disciples did not, would not, understand. The desire that Mary had to do this service for her Lord was of more value to Christ than all the precious ointment in the world, because it expressed her appreciation of the world's Redeemer. It was the love of Christ that constrained her. The matchless excellence of the character of Christ filled her soul. That ointment was a symbol of the heart of the giver. It was the outward demonstration of a love fed by heavenly streams until it overflowed.

The work of Mary was just the lesson the disciples needed to show them that the expression of their love for Him would be pleasing to Christ. He had been everything to them, and they did not realize that soon they would be deprived of His presence, that soon they could offer Him no token of their gratitude for His great love. The loneliness of Christ, separated from the heavenly courts, living the life of humanity, was never understood or appreciated by the disciples as it should have been. He was often grieved because His disciples did not give Him that which He should have received from them. He knew that if they were under the influence of the heavenly angels that accompanied Him, they too would think no offering of sufficient value to declare the heart's spiritual affection.

Their afterknowledge gave them a true sense of the many things they might have done for Jesus expressive of the love and gratitude of their hearts, while they were near Him. When Jesus was no longer with them, and they felt indeed as sheep without a shepherd, they began to see how they might have shown Him attentions that would have brought gladness to His heart. They no longer cast blame upon Mary, but upon themselves. Oh, if they could have taken back their censuring, their presenting the poor as more worthy of the gift than was Christ! They felt the reproof keenly as they took from the cross the bruised body of their Lord.

The same want is evident in our world today. But few appreciate all that Christ is to them. If they did, the great

> *Christ values acts of heartfelt courtesy. When anyone did Him a favor, with heavenly politeness He blessed the actor. He did not refuse the simplest flower plucked by the hand of a child, and offered to Him in love. He accepted the offerings of children, and blessed the givers, inscribing their names in the book of life.*

love of Mary would be expressed, the anointing would be freely bestowed. The expensive ointment would not be called a waste. Nothing would be thought too costly to give for Christ, no self-denial or self-sacrifice too great to be endured for His sake.

The words spoken in indignation, "To what purpose is this waste?" brought vividly before Christ the greatest sacrifice ever made—the gift of Himself as the propitiation for a lost world. The Lord would be so bountiful to His human family that it could not be said of Him that He could do more. In the gift of Jesus, God gave all heaven. From a human point of view, such a sacrifice was a wanton waste. To human reasoning the whole plan of salvation is a waste of mercies and resources. Self-denial and wholehearted sacrifice meet us everywhere. Well may the heavenly host look with amazement upon the human family who refuse to be uplifted and enriched with the boundless love expressed in Christ. Well may they exclaim, Why this great waste?

But the atonement for a lost world was to be full, abundant, and complete. Christ's offering was exceedingly abundant to reach every soul that God had created. It could not be restricted so as not to exceed the number who would accept the great Gift. All men are not saved; yet the plan of redemption is not a waste because it does not accomplish all that its liberality has provided for. There must be enough and to spare.

Simon the host had been influenced by the criticism of Judas upon Mary's gift, and he was surprised at the conduct of Jesus. His Pharisaic pride was offended. He knew that many of his guests were looking upon Christ with distrust and displeasure. Simon said in his heart, "This Man, if He were a prophet, would have known who and what manner of woman this is that toucheth Him: for she is a sinner."

By curing Simon of leprosy, Christ had saved him from a living death. But now Simon questioned whether the Saviour were a prophet. Because Christ allowed this woman to approach Him, because He did not indignantly spurn her as one whose sins were too great to be forgiven, because He did not show that He realized she had fallen, Simon was tempted to think that He was not a prophet. Jesus knows nothing of this woman who is so free in her demonstrations, he thought, or He would not allow her to touch Him.

But it was Simon's ignorance of God and of Christ that led him to think as he did. He did not realize that God's Son must act in God's way, with compassion, tenderness, and mercy. Simon's way was to take no notice of Mary's penitent service. Her act of kissing Christ's feet and anointing them with ointment was exasperating to his hardheartedness. He

thought that if Christ were a prophet, He would recognize sinners and rebuke them.

To this unspoken thought the Saviour answered: "Simon, I have somewhat to say unto thee. … There was a certain creditor which had two debtors: the one owed five hundred pence, and the other fifty. And when they had nothing to pay, he frankly forgave them both. Tell Me therefore, which of them will love him most? Simon answered and said, I suppose that he, to whom he forgave most. And He said unto him, Thou hast rightly judged."

As did Nathan with David, Christ concealed His home thrust under the veil of a parable. He threw upon His host the burden of pronouncing sentence upon himself. Simon had led into sin the woman he now despised. She had been deeply wronged by him. By the two debtors of the parable, Simon and the woman were represented. Jesus did not design to teach that different degrees of obligation should be felt by the two persons, for each owed a debt of gratitude that never could be repaid. But Simon felt himself more righteous than Mary, and Jesus desired him to see how great his guilt really was. He would show him that his sin was greater than hers, as much greater as a debt of five hundred pence exceeds a debt of fifty pence.

Simon now began to see himself in a new light. He saw how Mary was regarded by One who was more than a prophet. He saw that with keen prophetic eye Christ read her heart of love and devotion. Shame seized upon him, and he realized that he was in the presence of One superior to himself.

"I entered into thine house," Christ continued, "thou gavest Me no water for My feet;" but with tears of repentance, prompted by love, Mary hath washed My feet, and wiped them with the hair of her head. "Thou gavest Me no kiss: but this woman," whom you despise, "since the time I came in hath not ceased to kiss My feet." Christ recounted the opportunities Simon had had to show his love for his Lord, and his appreciation of what had been done for him. Plainly, yet with delicate politeness, the Saviour assured His disciples that His heart is grieved when His children neglect to show their gratitude to Him by words and deeds of love.

The Heart Searcher read the motive that led to Mary's action, and He saw also the spirit that prompted Simon's words. "Seest thou this woman?" He said to him. She is a sinner. "I say unto thee, Her sins, which are many, are forgiven; for she loved much: but to whom little is forgiven, the same loveth little."

Simon's coldness and neglect toward the Saviour showed how little he appreciated the mercy he had received. He had thought he honored Jesus by inviting Him to his house. But he now saw himself as he really was. While he thought himself reading his Guest, his Guest had been reading him. He saw how true Christ's judgment of him was. His religion had been a robe of Pharisaism. He had despised the compassion of Jesus. He had not recognized Him as the representative of God. While Mary was a sinner pardoned, he was a sinner unpardoned. The rigid rule of justice he had desired to enforce against her condemned him.

Simon was touched by the kindness of Jesus in not openly rebuking him before the guests. He had not been treated as he desired Mary to be treated. He saw that Jesus did not wish to expose his guilt to others, but sought by a true statement of the case to convince his mind, and by pitying kindness to

be realized. Through His grace she became a partaker of the divine nature. The one who had fallen, and whose mind had been a habitation of demons, was brought very near to the Saviour in fellowship and ministry. It was Mary who sat at His feet and learned of Him. It was Mary who poured upon His head the precious anointing oil, and bathed His feet with her tears. Mary stood beside the cross, and followed Him to the sepulcher. Mary was first at the tomb after His resurrection. It was Mary who first proclaimed a risen Saviour.

Jesus knows the circumstances of every soul. You may say, I am sinful, very sinful. You may be; but the worse you are, the more you need Jesus. He turns no weeping, contrite one away. He does not tell to any all that He might reveal, but He bids

> *He turns no weeping, contrite one away. He does not tell to any all that He might reveal, but He bids every trembling soul take courage. Freely will He pardon all who come to Him for forgiveness and restoration.*

subdue his heart. Stern denunciation would have hardened Simon against repentance, but patient admonition convinced him of his error. He saw the magnitude of the debt which he owed his Lord. His pride was humbled, he repented, and the proud Pharisee became a lowly, self-sacrificing disciple.

Mary had been looked upon as a great sinner, but Christ knew the circumstances that had shaped her life. He might have extinguished every spark of hope in her soul, but He did not. It was He who had lifted her from despair and ruin. Seven times she had heard His rebuke of the demons that controlled her heart and mind. She had heard His strong cries to the Father in her behalf. She knew how offensive is sin to His unsullied purity, and in His strength she had overcome.

When to human eyes her case appeared hopeless, Christ saw in Mary capabilities for good. He saw the better traits of her character. The plan of redemption has invested humanity with great possibilities, and in Mary these possibilities were to

every trembling soul take courage. Freely will He pardon all who come to Him for forgiveness and restoration.

Christ might commission the angels of heaven to pour out the vials of His wrath on our world, to destroy those who are filled with hatred of God. He might wipe this dark spot from His universe. But He does not do this. He is today standing at the altar of incense, presenting before God the prayers of those who desire His help.

The souls that turn to Him for refuge, Jesus lifts above the accusing and the strife of tongues. No man or evil angel can impeach these souls. Christ unites them to His own divine-human nature. They stand beside the great Sin Bearer, in the light proceeding from the throne of God. "Who shall lay anything to the charge of God's elect? It is God that justifieth. Who is he that condemneth? It is Christ that died, yea rather, that is risen again, who is even at the right hand of God, who also maketh intercession for us." Romans 8:33, 34.

Let Not Your Heart Be Troubled

This chapter is based on John 13:31–38; 14–17.

. . . .

Looking upon His disciples with divine love and with the tenderest sympathy, Christ said, "Now is the Son of man glorified, and God is glorified in Him." Judas had left the upper chamber, and Christ was alone with the eleven. He was about to speak of His approaching separation from them; but before doing this He pointed to the great object of His mission. It was this that He kept ever before Him. It was His joy that all His humiliation and suffering would glorify the Father's name. To this He first directs the thoughts of His disciples.

Then addressing them by the endearing term, "Little children," He said, "Yet a little while I am with you. Ye shall seek Me: and as I said unto the Jews, Whither I go, ye cannot come; so now I say to you."

The disciples could not rejoice when they heard this. Fear fell upon them. They pressed close about the Saviour. Their Master and Lord, their beloved Teacher and Friend, He was dearer to them than life. To Him they had looked for help in all their difficulties, for comfort in their sorrows and disappointments. Now He was to leave them, a lonely, dependent company. Dark were the forebodings that filled their hearts.

But the Saviour's words to them were full of hope. He knew that they were to be assailed by the enemy, and that Satan's craft is most successful against those who are depressed by difficulties. Therefore He pointed them away from "the things which are seen," to "the things which are not seen." 2 Corinthians 4:18. From earthly exile He turned their thoughts to the heavenly home.

"Let not your heart be troubled," He said; "ye believe in God, believe also in Me. In My Father's house are many mansions: if it were not so, I would have told you. I go to prepare a place for you. And if I go and prepare a place for you, I will come again, and receive you unto Myself; that were I am, there ye may be also. And whither I go ye know, and the way ye know." For your sake I came into the world. I am working in your behalf. When I go away, I shall still work earnestly for you. I came into the world to reveal Myself to you, that you

might believe. I go to the Father to co-operate with Him in your behalf. The object of Christ's departure was the opposite of what the disciples feared. It did not mean a final separation. He was going to prepare a place for them, that He might come again, and receive them unto Himself. While He was building mansions for them, they were to build characters after the divine similitude.

Still the disciples were perplexed. Thomas, always troubled by doubts, said, "Lord, we know not whither Thou goest; and how can we know the way? Jesus saith unto him, I am the way, the truth, and the life; no man cometh unto the Father, but by Me. If ye had known Me, ye should have known My Father also: and from henceforth ye know Him, and have seen Him."

There are not many ways to heaven. Each one may not choose his own way. Christ says, "I am the way: … no man cometh unto the Father, but by Me." Since the first gospel sermon was preached, when in Eden it was declared that the seed of the woman should bruise the serpent's head, Christ had been uplifted as the way, the truth, and the life. He was the way when Adam lived, when Abel presented to God the blood of the slain lamb, representing the blood of the Redeemer. Christ was the way by which patriarchs and prophets were saved. He is the way by which alone we can have access to God.

"If ye had known Me," Christ said, "ye should have known My Father also: and from henceforth ye know Him, and have seen Him." But not yet did the disciples understand. "Lord, show us the Father," exclaimed Philip, "and it sufficeth us."

Amazed at his dullness of comprehension, Christ asked with pained surprise, "Have I been so long time with you, and yet hast thou not known Me, Philip?" Is it possible that you do not see the Father in the works He does through Me? Do you not believe that I came to testify of the Father? "How sayest thou then, Show us the Father?" "He that hath seen Me hath seen the Father." Christ had not ceased to be God when He became man. Though He had humbled Himself to humanity, the Godhead was still His own. Christ alone could represent the Father to humanity, and this representation the disciples had been privileged to behold for over three years.

"Believe Me that I am in the Father, and the Father in Me: or else believe Me for the very works' sake." Their faith might safely rest on the evidence given in Christ's works, works that no man, of himself, ever had done, or ever could do. Christ's work testified to His divinity. Through Him the Father had been revealed.

If the disciples believed this vital connection between the Father and the Son, their faith would not forsake them when they saw Christ's suffering and death to save a perishing world. Christ was seeking to lead them from their low condition of faith to the experience they might receive if they truly realized what He was—God in human flesh. He desired them to see that their faith must lead up to God, and be anchored there. How earnestly and perseveringly our compassionate Saviour sought to prepare His disciples for the storm of temptation that was soon to beat upon them. He would have them hid with Him in God.

As Christ was speaking these words, the glory of God was shining from His countenance, and all present felt a sacred awe as they listened with rapt attention to His words. Their hearts were more decidedly drawn to Him; and as they were drawn to Christ in greater love, they were drawn to one another. They felt that heaven was very near, and that the words to which they listened were a message to them from their heavenly Father.

"Verily, verily, I say unto you," Christ continued, "He that believeth on Me, the works that I do shall he do also." The Saviour was deeply anxious for His disciples to understand for what purpose His divinity was united to humanity. He came to the world to display the glory of God, that man might be uplifted by its restoring power. God was manifested in Him that He might be manifested in them. Jesus revealed no qualities, and exercised no powers, that men may not have through faith in Him. His perfect humanity is that which all His followers may possess, if they will be in subjection to God as He was.

"And greater works than these shall he do; because I go unto My Father." By this Christ did not mean that the disciples' work would be of a more exalted character than His, but that it would have greater extent. He did not refer merely to miracle working, but to all that would take place under the working of the Holy Spirit.

After the Lord's ascension, the disciples realized the fulfillment of His promise. The scenes of the crucifixion, resurrection, and ascension of Christ were a living reality to them. They saw that the prophecies had been literally fulfilled. They searched the Scriptures, and accepted their teaching with a faith and assurance unknown before. They knew that the divine Teacher was all that He had claimed to be. As they told their experience, and exalted the love of God, men's hearts were melted and subdued, and multitudes believed on Jesus.

The Saviour's promise to His disciples is a promise to His church to the end of time. God did not design that His wonderful plan to redeem men should achieve only insignificant results. All who will go to work, trusting not in what they themselves can do, but in what God can do for and through them, will certainly realize the fulfillment of His promise. "Greater works than these shall ye do," He declares; "because I go unto My Father."

As yet the disciples were unacquainted with the Saviour's unlimited resources and power. He said to them, "Hitherto have ye asked nothing in My name." John 16:24. He explained that the secret of their success would be in asking for strength and grace in His name. He would be present before the Father to make request for them. The prayer of the humble suppliant He presents as His own desire in that soul's behalf. Every sincere prayer is heard in heaven. It may not be fluently expressed; but if the heart is in it, it will ascend to the sanctuary where Jesus ministers, and He will present it to the Father without one awkward, stammering word, beautiful and fragrant with the incense of His own perfection.

The path of sincerity and integrity is not a path free from obstruction, but in every difficulty we are to see a call to prayer. There is no one living who has any power that he has not received from God, and the source whence it comes is open to the weakest human being. "Whatsoever ye shall ask in My name," said Jesus, "that will I do, that the Father may be glorified in the Son. If ye shall ask anything in My name, I will do it."

"In My name," Christ bade His disciples pray. In Christ's name His followers are to stand before God. Through the value of the sacrifice made for them, they are of value in the Lord's sight. Because of the imputed righteousness of Christ they are accounted precious. For Christ's sake the Lord pardons those that fear Him. He does not see in them the vileness of the sinner. He recognizes in them the likeness of His Son, in whom they believe.

The Lord is disappointed when His people place a low estimate upon themselves. He desires His chosen heritage to value themselves according to the price He has placed upon them. God wanted them, else He would not have sent His Son on such an expensive errand to redeem them. He has a use for them, and He is well pleased when they make the very highest demands upon Him, that they may glorify His name. They may expect large things if they have faith in His promises.

But to pray in Christ's name means much. It means that we are to accept His character, manifest His spirit, and work His works. The Saviour's promise is given on condition. "If ye love Me," He says, "keep My commandments." He saves men, not in sin, but from sin; and those who love Him will show their love by obedience.

All true obedience comes from the heart. It was heart work with Christ. And if we consent, He will so identify Himself with our thoughts and aims, so blend our hearts and minds into conformity to His will, that when obeying Him we shall be but carrying out our own impulses. The will, refined and sanctified, will find its highest delight in doing His service. When we know God as it is our privilege to know Him, our life will be a life of continual obedience. Through an appreciation of the character of Christ, through communion with God, sin will become hateful to us.

As Christ lived the law in humanity, so we may do if we will take hold of the Strong for strength. But we are not to place the responsibility of our duty upon others, and wait for them to tell us what to do. We cannot depend for counsel upon humanity. The Lord will teach us our duty just as willingly as He will teach somebody else. If we come to Him in faith, He will speak His mysteries to us personally. Our hearts will often burn within us as One draws nigh to commune with us as He did with Enoch. Those who decide to do nothing in any line that will displease God, will know, after presenting their case before Him, just what course to pursue. And they will receive not only wisdom, but strength. Power for obedience, for service, will be imparted to them, as Christ has promised. Whatever was given to Christ—the "all things" to supply the need of fallen men—was given to Him as the head and representative of humanity. And "whatsoever we ask, we receive of Him, because we keep His commandments, and do those things that are pleasing in His sight." 1 John 3:22.

Before offering Himself as the sacrificial victim, Christ sought for the most essential and complete gift to bestow upon His followers, a gift that would bring within their reach the boundless resources of grace. "I will pray the Father," He said, "and He shall give you another Comforter, that He

> *The path of sincerity and integrity is not a path free from obstruction, but in every difficulty we are to see a call to prayer.*

may abide with you forever; even the Spirit of truth; whom the world cannot receive, because it seeth Him not, neither knoweth Him: but ye know Him; for He dwelleth with you, and shall be in you. I will not leave you orphans: I will come to you." John 14:16–18, margin.

Before this the Spirit had been in the world; from the very beginning of the work of redemption He had been moving upon men's hearts. But while Christ was on earth, the disciples had desired no other helper. Not until they were deprived of His presence would they feel their need of the Spirit, and then He would come.

The Holy Spirit is Christ's representative, but divested of the personality of humanity, and independent thereof. Cumbered with humanity, Christ could not be in every place personally. Therefore it was for their interest that He should go to the Father, and send the Spirit to be His successor on earth. No one could then have any advantage because of his location or his personal contact with Christ. By the Spirit the Saviour would be accessible to all. In this sense He would be nearer to them than if He had not ascended on high.

Cumbered with humanity, Christ could not be in every place personally. Therefore it was for their interest that He should go to the Father, and send the Spirit to be His successor on earth.

"He that loveth Me shall be loved of My Father, and I will love him, and will manifest Myself to him." Jesus read the future of His disciples. He saw one brought to the scaffold, one to the cross, one to exile among the lonely rocks of the sea, others to persecution and death. He encouraged them with the promise that in every trial He would be with them. That promise has lost none of its force. The Lord knows all about His faithful servants who for His sake are lying in prison or who are banished to lonely islands. He comforts them with His own presence. When for the truth's sake the believer stands at the bar of unrighteous tribunals, Christ stands by his side. All the reproaches that fall upon him, fall upon Christ. Christ is condemned over again in the person of His disciple. When one is incarcerated in prison walls, Christ ravishes the heart with His love. When one suffers death for His sake, Christ says, "I am He that liveth, and was dead; and, behold, I am alive forevermore, … and have the keys of hell and of death." Revelation 1:18. The life that is sacrificed for Me is preserved unto eternal glory.

At all times and in all places, in all sorrows and in all afflictions, when the outlook seems dark and the future perplexing, and we feel helpless and alone, the Comforter will be sent in answer to the prayer of faith. Circumstances may separate us from every earthly friend; but no circumstance, no distance, can separate us from the heavenly Comforter. Wherever we are, wherever we may go, He is always at our right hand to support, sustain, uphold, and cheer.

The disciples still failed to understand Christ's words in their spiritual sense, and again He explained His meaning. By the Spirit, He said, He would manifest Himself to them. "The Comforter, which is the Holy Ghost, whom the Father will send in My name, He shall teach you all things." No more will you say, I cannot comprehend. No longer will you see through a glass, darkly. You shall "be able to comprehend with all saints what is the breadth, and length, and depth, and height; and to know the love of Christ, which passeth knowledge." Ephesians 3:18, 19.

The disciples were to bear witness to the life and work of Christ. Through their word He was to speak to all the people on the face of the earth. But in the humiliation and death of Christ they were to suffer great trial and disappointment. That after this experience their word might be accurate, Jesus promised that the Comforter should "bring all things to your remembrance, whatsoever I have said unto you."

"I have yet many things to say unto you," He continued, "but ye cannot bear them now. Howbeit when He, the Spirit of truth, is come, He will guide you into all truth: for He shall not speak of Himself; but whatsoever He shall hear, that shall He speak: and He will show you things to come. He shall glorify Me: for He shall receive of Mine, and shall show it unto you." Jesus had opened before His disciples a vast tract of truth. But it was most difficult for them to keep His lessons distinct from the traditions and maxims of the scribes and Pharisees. They had been educated to accept the teaching of the rabbis as the voice of God, and it still held a power over their minds, and molded their sentiments. Earthly ideas, temporal things, still had a large place in their thoughts. They did not understand the spiritual nature of Christ's kingdom, though He had so often explained it to them. Their minds had become confused. They did not comprehend the value of the scriptures Christ presented. Many of His lessons seemed almost lost upon them. Jesus saw that they did not lay hold of the real meaning of His words. He compassionately promised that the Holy Spirit should recall these sayings to their minds. And He had left unsaid many things that could not be comprehended by the disciples. These also would be opened to them by the Spirit. The Spirit was to quicken their understanding, that they might have an appreciation of heavenly things. "When He, the Spirit of truth, is come," said Jesus, "He will guide you into all truth."

The Comforter is called "the Spirit of truth." His work is to define and maintain the truth. He first dwells in the heart as the Spirit of truth, and thus He becomes the Comforter. There is comfort and peace in the truth, but no real peace or comfort can be found in falsehood. It is through false theories and traditions that Satan gains his power over the mind. By directing men to false standards, he misshapes the character. Through the Scriptures the Holy Spirit speaks to the mind, and impresses truth upon the heart. Thus He exposes error, and expels it from the soul. It is by the Spirit of truth, working through the word of God, that Christ subdues His chosen people to Himself.

In describing to His disciples the office work of the Holy Spirit, Jesus sought to inspire them with the joy and hope that inspired His own heart. He rejoiced because of the abundant help He had provided for His church. The Holy Spirit was the highest of all gifts that He could solicit from His Father for the exaltation of His people. The Spirit was to be given as a regenerating agent, and without this the sacrifice of Christ would have been of no avail. The power of evil had been strengthening for centuries, and the submission of men to this satanic captivity was amazing. Sin could be resisted and overcome only through the mighty agency of the Third Person of the Godhead, who would come with no modified energy, but in the fullness of divine power. It is the Spirit that makes effectual what has been wrought out by the world's Redeemer. It is by the Spirit that the heart is made pure. Through the Spirit the believer becomes a partaker of the divine nature. Christ has given His Spirit as a divine power to overcome all hereditary and cultivated tendencies to evil, and to impress His own character upon His church.

Of the Spirit Jesus said, "He shall glorify Me." The Saviour came to glorify the Father by the demonstration of His love; so the Spirit was to glorify Christ by revealing His grace to the world. The very image of God is to be reproduced in humanity. The honor of God, the honor of Christ, is involved in the perfection of the character of His people.

"When He [the Spirit of truth] is come, He will reprove the world of sin, and of righteousness, and of judgment." The preaching of the word will be of no avail without the continual presence and aid of the Holy Spirit. This is the only effectual teacher of divine truth. Only when the truth is accompanied to the heart by the Spirit will it quicken the conscience or transform the life. One might be able to present the letter of the word of God, he might be familiar with all its commands and promises; but unless the Holy Spirit sets home the truth, no souls will fall on the Rock and be broken. No amount of education, no advantages, however great, can make one a channel of light without the co-operation of the Spirit of God. The sowing of the gospel seed will not be a success unless the seed is quickened into life by the dew of heaven. Before one book of the New Testament was written, before one gospel sermon had been preached after Christ's ascension, the Holy Spirit came upon the praying apostles. Then the testimony of their enemies was, "Ye have filled Jerusalem with your doctrine." Acts 5:28.

Christ has promised the gift of the Holy Spirit to His church, and the promise belongs to us as much as to the first disciples. But like every other promise, it is given on conditions. There are many who believe and profess to claim the Lord's promise; they talk about Christ and about the Holy Spirit, yet receive no benefit. They do not surrender the soul to be guided and controlled by the divine agencies. We cannot use the Holy Spirit. The Spirit is to use us. Through the Spirit God works in His people "to will and to do of His good pleasure." Philemon 2:13. But many will not submit to this. They want to manage themselves. This is why they do not receive the heavenly gift. Only to those who wait humbly upon God, who watch for His guidance and grace, is the Spirit given. The power of God awaits their demand and reception. This promised blessing, claimed by faith, brings all other blessings in its train. It is given according to the riches of the grace of Christ, and He is ready to supply every soul according to the capacity to receive.

In His discourse to the disciples, Jesus made no mournful allusion to His own sufferings and death. His last legacy to them was a legacy of peace. He said, "Peace I leave with you, My peace I give unto you: not as the world giveth, give I unto you. Let not your heart be troubled, neither let it be afraid."

Before leaving the upper chamber, the Saviour led His disciples in a song of praise. His voice was heard, not in the strains of some mournful lament, but in the joyful notes of the Passover hallel:

> "O praise the Lord, all ye nations:
> Praise Him, all ye people.
> For His merciful kindness is great toward us:
> And the truth of the Lord endureth forever.
> Praise ye the Lord." Psalm 117.

After the hymn, they went out. Through the crowded streets they made their way, passing out of the city gate toward the Mount of Olives. Slowly they proceeded, each busy with his own thoughts. As they began to descend toward the mount, Jesus said, in a tone of deepest sadness, "All ye shall be offended because of Me this night: for it is written, I will smite the shepherd, and the sheep of the flock shall be scattered abroad." Matthew 26:31. The disciples listened in sorrow and amazement. They remembered how in the synagogue at Capernaum, when Christ spoke of Himself as the bread of life, many had been offended, and had turned away from Him. But the twelve had not shown themselves unfaithful. Peter, speaking for his brethren, had then declared his loyalty to Christ. Then the Saviour had said, "Have not I chosen you twelve, and one of you is a devil?" John 6:70. In the upper chamber Jesus said that one of the twelve would betray Him, and that Peter would deny Him. But now His words include them all.

Now Peter's voice is heard vehemently protesting, "Although all shall be offended, yet will not I." In the upper chamber he had declared, "I will lay down my life for Thy sake." Jesus had warned him that he would that very night deny his Saviour. Now Christ repeats the warning: "Verily I say unto thee, That this day, even in this night, before the cock crow twice, thou shalt deny Me thrice." But Peter only "spake the more vehemently, If I should die with Thee, I will not deny Thee in anywise. Likewise also said they all." Mark 14:29, 30, 31. In their self-confidence they denied the repeated statement of Him who knew. They were unprepared for the test; when temptation should overtake them, they would understand their own weakness.

When Peter said he would follow his Lord to prison and to death, he meant it, every word of it; but he did not know himself. Hidden in his heart were elements of evil that circumstances would fan into life. Unless he was made conscious of his danger, these would prove his eternal ruin. The Saviour saw in him a self-love and assurance that would overbear even his love for Christ. Much of infirmity, of unmortified sin, carelessness of spirit, unsanctified temper, heedlessness in entering into temptation, had been revealed in his experience. Christ's solemn warning was a call to heart searching. Peter needed to distrust himself, and to have a deeper faith in Christ. Had he in humility received the warning, he would have appealed to the Shepherd of the flock to keep His sheep. When on the Sea of Galilee he was about to sink, he cried, "Lord, save me." Matthew 14:30. Then the hand of Christ was outstretched to grasp his hand. So now if he had cried to Jesus, Save me from myself, he would have been kept. But

Peter felt that he was distrusted, and he thought it cruel. He was already offended, and he became more persistent in his self-confidence.

Jesus looks with compassion on His disciples. He cannot save them from the trial, but He does not leave them comfortless. He assures them that He is to break the fetters of the tomb, and that His love for them will not fail. "After I am risen again," He says, "I will go before you into Galilee." Matthew 26:32. Before the denial, they have the assurance of forgiveness. After His death and resurrection, they knew that they were forgiven, and were dear to the heart of Christ.

Jesus and the disciples were on the way to Gethsemane, at the foot of Mount Olivet, a retired spot which He had often visited for meditation and prayer. The Saviour had been explaining to His disciples His mission to the world, and the spiritual relation to Him which they were to sustain. Now He illustrates the lesson. The moon is shining bright, and reveals to Him a flourishing grapevine. Drawing the attention of the disciples to it, He employs it as a symbol.

"I am the true Vine," He says. Instead of choosing the graceful palm, the lofty cedar, or the strong oak, Jesus takes the vine with its clinging tendrils to represent Himself. The palm tree, the cedar, and the oak stand alone. They require no support. But the vine entwines about the trellis, and thus climbs heavenward. So Christ in His humanity was dependent upon divine power. "I can of Mine own self do nothing," He declared (John 5:30).

"I am the true Vine." The Jews had always regarded the vine as the most noble of plants, and a type of all that was powerful, excellent, and fruitful. Israel had been represented as a vine which God had planted in the Promised Land. The Jews based their hope of salvation on the fact of their connection with Israel. But Jesus says, I am the real Vine. Think not that through a connection with Israel you may become partakers of the life of God, and inheritors of His promise. Through Me alone is spiritual life received.

"I am the true Vine, and My Father is the husbandman." On the hills of Palestine our heavenly Father had planted this goodly Vine, and He Himself was the husbandman. Many were attracted by the beauty of this Vine, and declared its heavenly origin. But to the leaders in Israel it appeared as a root out of a dry ground. They took the plant, and bruised it, and trampled it under their unholy feet. Their thought was to destroy it forever. But the heavenly Husbandman never lost sight of His plant. After men thought they had killed it, He took it, and replanted it on the other side of the wall. The vine stock was to be no longer visible. It was hidden from the rude assaults of men. But the branches of the Vine hung over the wall. They were to represent the Vine. Through them grafts might still be united to the Vine. From them fruit has been obtained. There has been a harvest which the passers-by have plucked.

"I am the Vine, ye are the branches," Christ said to His disciples. Though He was about to be removed from them, their spiritual union with Him was to be unchanged. The connection of the branch with the vine, He said, represents the relation you are to sustain to Me. The scion is engrafted into the living vine, and fiber by fiber, vein by vein, it grows into the vine stock. The life of the vine becomes the life of the branch. So the soul dead in trespasses and sins receives life through connection with Christ. By faith in Him as a personal Saviour the union is formed. The sinner unites his weakness to Christ's strength, his emptiness to Christ's fullness, his frailty to Christ's enduring might. Then he has the mind of Christ. The humanity of Christ has touched our humanity, and our humanity has touched divinity. Thus through the agency of the Holy Spirit man becomes a partaker of the divine nature. He is accepted in the Beloved.

This union with Christ, once formed, must be maintained. Christ said, "Abide in Me, and I in you. As the branch cannot bear fruit of itself, except it abide in the vine; no more can ye, except ye abide in Me." This is no casual touch, no off-and-on connection. The branch becomes a part of the living vine. The communication of life, strength, and fruitfulness from the root to the branches is unobstructed and constant. Separated from the vine, the branch cannot live. No more, said Jesus, can you live apart from Me. The life you have received from Me can be preserved only by continual communion. Without Me you cannot overcome one sin, or resist one temptation.

"Abide in Me, and I in you." Abiding in Christ means a constant receiving of His Spirit, a life of unreserved surrender to His service. The channel of communication must be open continually between man and his God. As the vine branch constantly draws the sap from the living vine, so are we to cling to Jesus, and receive from Him by faith the strength and perfection of His own character.

The root sends its nourishment through the branch to the outermost twig. So Christ communicates the current of spiritual strength to every believer. So long as the soul is united to Christ, there is no danger that it will wither or decay.

The life of the vine will be manifest in fragrant fruit on the branches. "He that abideth in Me," said Jesus, "and I in him, the same bringeth forth much fruit: for without Me ye can do nothing." When we live by faith on the Son of God, the fruits of the Spirit will be seen in our lives; not one will be missing.

"My Father is the husbandman. Every branch in Me that beareth not fruit He taketh away." While the graft is outwardly united with the vine, there may be no vital connection. Then there will be no growth or fruitfulness. So there may be an apparent connection with Christ without a real union with Him by faith. A profession of religion places men in the church, but the character and conduct show whether they are in connection with Christ. If they bear no fruit, they are false branches. Their separation from Christ involves a ruin as complete as that represented by the dead branch. "If a man abide not in Me," said Christ, "he is cast forth as a branch, and

> *Abiding in Christ means a constant receiving of His Spirit, a life of unreserved surrender to His service. The channel of communication must be open continually between man and his God.*

is withered; and men gather them, and cast them into the fire, and they are burned."

"And every branch that beareth fruit, He purgeth [pruneth] it, that it may bring forth more fruit." From the chosen twelve who had followed Jesus, one as a withered branch was about to be taken away; the rest were to pass under the pruning knife of bitter trial. Jesus with solemn tenderness explained the purpose of the husbandman. The pruning will cause pain, but it is the Father who applies the knife. He works with no wanton hand or indifferent heart. There are branches trailing upon the ground; these must be cut loose from the earthly supports to which their tendrils are fastening. They are to reach heavenward, and find their support in God. The excessive foliage that draws away the life current from the fruit must be pruned off. The overgrowth must be cut out, to give room for the healing beams of the Sun of Righteousness. The husbandman prunes away the harmful growth, that the fruit may be richer and more abundant.

"Herein is My Father glorified," said Jesus, "that ye bear much fruit." God desires to manifest through you the holiness, the benevolence, the compassion, of His own character. Yet the Saviour does not bid the disciples labor to bear fruit. He tells them to abide in Him. "If ye abide in Me," He says, "and My words abide in you, ye shall ask what ye will, and it shall be done unto you." It is through the word that Christ abides in His followers. This is the same vital union that is represented by eating His flesh and drinking His blood.

With prophetic eye Christ traced the scenes to take place in His last great conflict. He knew that when He should exclaim, "It is finished," all heaven would triumph.

The words of Christ are spirit and life. Receiving them, you receive the life of the Vine. You live "by every word that proceedeth out of the mouth of God." Matthew 4:4. The life of Christ in you produces the same fruits as in Him. Living in Christ, adhering to Christ, supported by Christ, drawing nourishment from Christ, you bear fruit after the similitude of Christ.

In this last meeting with His disciples, the great desire which Christ expressed for them was that they might love one another as He had loved them. Again and again He spoke of this. "These things I command you," He said repeatedly, "that ye love one another." His very first injunction when alone with them in the upper chamber was, "A new commandment I give unto you, That ye love one another; as I have loved you, that ye also love one another." To the disciples this commandment was new; for they had not loved one another as

Christ had loved them. He saw that new ideas and impulses must control them; that new principles must be practiced by them; through His life and death they were to receive a new conception of love. The command to love one another had a new meaning in the light of His self-sacrifice. The whole work of grace is one continual service of love, of self-denying, self-sacrificing effort. During every hour of Christ's sojourn upon the earth, the love of God was flowing from Him in irrepressible streams. All who are imbued with His Spirit will love as He loved. The very principle that actuated Christ will actuate them in all their dealing one with another.

This love is the evidence of their discipleship. "By this shall all men know that ye are My disciples," said Jesus, "if ye have love one to another." When men are bound together, not by force or self-interest, but by love, they show the working of an influence that is above every human influence. Where this oneness exists, it is evidence that the image of God is being restored in humanity, that a new principle of life has been implanted. It shows that there is power in the divine nature to withstand the supernatural agencies of evil, and that the grace of God subdues the selfishness inherent in the natural heart.

This love, manifested in the church, will surely stir the wrath of Satan. Christ did not mark out for His disciples an easy path. "If the world hate you," He said, "ye know that it hated Me before it hated you. If ye were of the world, the world would love his own: but because ye are not of the world, but I have chosen you out of the world, therefore the world hateth you. Remember the word that I said unto you, The servant is not greater than his lord. If they have persecuted Me, they will also persecute you; if they have kept My saying, they will keep yours also. But all these things will they do unto you for My name's sake, because they know not Him that sent Me." The gospel is to be carried forward by aggressive warfare, in the midst of opposition, peril, loss, and suffering. But those who do this work are only following in their Master's steps.

As the world's Redeemer, Christ was constantly confronted with apparent failure. He, the messenger of mercy to our world, seemed to do little of the work He longed to do in uplifting and saving. Satanic influences were constantly working to oppose His way. But He would not be discouraged. Through the prophecy of Isaiah He declares, "I have labored in vain, I have spent My strength for nought, and in vain: yet surely My judgment is with the Lord, and My work with My God. … Though Israel be not gathered, yet shall I be glorious in the eyes of the Lord, and My God shall be My strength." It is to Christ that the promise is given, "Thus saith the Lord, the Redeemer of Israel, and His Holy One, to Him whom man despiseth, to Him whom the nation abhorreth; … thus saith the Lord: … I will preserve Thee, and give Thee for a covenant of the people, to establish the earth, to cause to inherit the desolate heritages; that Thou mayest say to the prisoners, Go forth; to them that are in darkness, Show yourselves. … They shall not hunger nor thirst; neither shall the heat nor sun smite them: for He that hath mercy on them shall lead them, even by the springs of water shall He guide them." Isaiah 49:4, 5, 7–10.

Upon this word Jesus rested, and He gave Satan no advantage. When the last steps of Christ's humiliation were to be taken, when the deepest sorrow was closing about His soul, He said to His disciples, "The prince of this world cometh, and hath nothing in Me." "The prince of this world is judged." Now shall he be cast out. John 14:30; 16:11; 12:31. With prophetic eye Christ traced the scenes to take place in His last great conflict. He knew that when He should exclaim, "It is finished," all heaven would triumph. His ear caught the distant music and the shouts of victory in the heavenly courts. He knew that the knell of Satan's empire would then be sounded, and the name of Christ would be heralded from world to world throughout the universe.

Christ rejoiced that He could do more for His followers than they could ask or think. He spoke with assurance, knowing that an almighty decree had been given before the world was made. He knew that truth, armed with the omnipotence of the Holy Spirit, would conquer in the contest with evil; and that the bloodstained banner would wave triumphantly over His followers. He knew that the life of His trusting disciples would be like His, a series of uninterrupted victories, not seen to be such here, but recognized as such in the great hereafter.

"These things I have spoken unto you," He said, "that in Me ye might have peace. In the world ye shall have tribulation: but be of good cheer; I have overcome the world." Christ did not fail, neither was He discouraged, and His followers are to manifest a faith of the same enduring nature. They are to live as He lived, and work as He worked, because they depend on Him as the great Master Worker. Courage, energy, and perseverance they must possess. Though apparent impossibilities obstruct their way, by His grace they are to go forward. Instead of deploring difficulties, they are called upon to surmount them. They are to despair of nothing, and to hope for everything. With the golden chain of His matchless love Christ has bound them to the throne of God. It is His purpose that the highest influence in the universe, emanating from the source of all power, shall be theirs. They are to have power to resist evil, power that neither earth, nor death, nor hell can master, power that will enable them to overcome as Christ overcame.

Christ designs that heaven's order, heaven's plan of government, heaven's divine harmony, shall be represented in His church on earth. Thus in His people He is glorified. Through them the Sun of Righteousness will shine in undimmed luster to the world. Christ has given to His church ample facilities, that He may receive a large revenue of glory from His redeemed, purchased possession. He has bestowed upon His people capabilities and blessings that they may represent His own sufficiency. The church, endowed with the righteousness of Christ, is His depositary, in which the riches of His mercy, His grace, and His love, are to appear in full and final display. Christ looks upon His people in their purity and perfection, as the reward of His humiliation, and the supplement of His glory,—Christ, the great Center, from whom radiates all glory.

With strong, hopeful words the Saviour ended His instruction. Then He poured out the burden of His soul in prayer for His disciples. Lifting His eyes to heaven, He said, "Father, the hour is come; glorify Thy Son, that Thy Son also may glorify Thee: as Thou hast given Him power over all flesh, that He should give eternal life to as many as Thou hast given Him. And this is life eternal, that they might know Thee the only true God, and Jesus Christ, whom Thou hast sent."

Christ had finished the work that was given Him to do. He had glorified God on the earth. He had manifested the Father's name. He had gathered out those who were to continue His work among men. And He said, "I am glorified in them. And now I am no more in the world, but these are in the world, and I come to Thee. Holy Father, keep through Thine own name those whom Thou hast given Me, that they may be one, as We are." "Neither pray I for these alone, but for them also which shall believe on Me through their word; that they all may be one; … I in them, and Thou in Me, that they may be made perfect in one; and that the world may know that Thou hast sent Me, and hast loved them, as Thou hast loved Me."

Thus in the language of one who has divine authority, Christ gives His elect church into the Father's arms. As a consecrated high priest He intercedes for His people. As a faithful shepherd He gathers His flock under the shadow of the Almighty, in the strong and sure refuge. For Him there waits the last battle with Satan, and He goes forth to meet it.

Gethsemane

This chapter is based on Matthew 26:36–56; Mark 14:32–50; Luke 22:39–53; John 18:1–12.

. . . .

In company with His disciples, the Saviour slowly made His way to the garden of Gethsemane. The Passover moon, broad and full, shone from a cloudless sky. The city of pilgrims' tents was hushed into silence.

Jesus had been earnestly conversing with His disciples and instructing them; but as He neared Gethsemane, He became strangely silent. He had often visited this spot for meditation and prayer; but never with a heart so full of sorrow as upon this night of His last agony. Throughout His life on earth He had walked in the light of God's presence. When in conflict with men who were inspired by the very spirit of Satan, He could say, "He that sent Me is with Me: the Father hath not left Me alone; for I do always those things that please Him." John 8:29. But now He seemed to be shut out from the light of God's sustaining presence. Now He was numbered with the transgressors. The guilt of fallen humanity He must bear. Upon Him who knew no sin must be laid the iniquity of us all. So dreadful does sin appear to Him, so great is the weight of guilt which He must bear, that He is tempted to fear it will shut Him out forever from His Father's love. Feeling how terrible is the wrath of God against transgression, He exclaims, "My soul is exceeding sorrowful, even unto death."

As they approached the garden, the disciples had marked the change that came over their Master. Never before had they seen Him so utterly sad and silent. As He proceeded, this strange sadness deepened; yet they dared not question Him as to the cause. His form swayed as if He were about to fall. Upon reaching the garden, the disciples looked anxiously for His usual place of retirement, that their Master might rest. Every step that He now took was with labored effort. He groaned aloud, as if suffering under the pressure of a terrible burden. Twice His companions supported Him, or He would have fallen to the earth.

Near the entrance to the garden, Jesus left all but three of the disciples, bidding them pray for themselves and for Him. With Peter, James, and John, He entered its secluded recesses. These three disciples were Christ's closest companions. They had beheld His glory on the mount of transfiguration; they had seen Moses and Elijah talking with Him; they had heard the voice from heaven; now in His great struggle, Christ desired their presence near Him. Often they had passed the night with Him in this retreat. On these occasions, after a season of watching and prayer, they would sleep undisturbed at a little distance from their Master, until He awoke them in the morning to go forth anew to labor. But now He desired them to spend the night with Him in prayer. Yet He could not bear that even they should witness the agony He was to endure.

"Tarry ye here," He said, "and watch with Me."

He went a little distance from them—not so far but that they could both see and hear Him—and fell prostrate upon the ground. He felt that by sin He was being separated from His Father. The gulf was so broad, so black, so deep, that His spirit shuddered before it. This agony He must not exert His divine power to escape. As man He must suffer the consequences of man's sin. As man He must endure the wrath of God against transgression.

Christ was now standing in a different attitude from that in which He had ever stood before. His suffering can best be described in the words of the prophet, "Awake, O sword, against My shepherd, and against the man that is My fellow, saith the Lord of hosts." Zechariah 13:7. As the substitute and surety for sinful man, Christ was suffering under divine justice. He saw what justice meant. Hitherto He had been as an intercessor for others; now He longed to have an intercessor for Himself.

As Christ felt His unity with the Father broken up, He feared that in His human nature He would be unable to endure the coming conflict with the powers of darkness. In the wilderness of temptation the destiny of the human race had been at stake. Christ was then conqueror. Now the tempter had come for the last fearful struggle. For this he had been preparing during the three years of Christ's ministry. Everything was at stake with him. If he failed here, his hope of mastery was lost; the kingdoms of the world would finally become Christ's; he himself would be overthrown and cast out. But if Christ could be overcome, the earth would become Satan's kingdom, and the human race would be forever in his power. With the issues of the conflict before Him, Christ's soul was filled with dread of separation from God. Satan told Him that if He became the surety for a sinful world, the separation would be eternal. He would be identified with Satan's kingdom, and would nevermore be one with God.

And what was to be gained by this sacrifice? How hopeless appeared the guilt and ingratitude of men! In its hardest features Satan pressed the situation upon the Redeemer: The people who claim to be above all others in temporal and spiritual advantages have rejected You. They are seeking to destroy You, the foundation, the center and seal of the promises made to them as a peculiar people. One of Your own disciples, who has listened to Your instruction, and has been among the foremost in church activities, will betray You. One of Your most zealous followers will deny You. All will forsake You. Christ's whole being abhorred the thought. That those whom He had undertaken to save, those whom He loved so much, should unite in the plots of Satan, this pierced His soul. The conflict was terrible. Its measure was the guilt of His nation, of His accusers and betrayer, the guilt of a world lying in wickedness. The sins of men weighed heavily upon Christ, and the sense of God's wrath against sin was crushing out His life.

Behold Him contemplating the price to be paid for the human soul. In His agony He clings to the cold ground, as if to prevent Himself from being drawn farther from God. The chilling dew of night falls upon His prostrate form, but He heeds it not. From His pale lips comes the bitter cry, "O My Father, if it be possible, let this cup pass from Me." Yet even now He adds, "Nevertheless not as I will, but as Thou wilt."

The human heart longs for sympathy in suffering. This longing Christ felt to the very depths of His being. In the supreme agony of His soul He came to His disciples with a yearning desire to hear some words of comfort from those whom He had so often blessed and comforted, and shielded in sorrow and distress. The One who had always had words of sympathy for them was now suffering superhuman agony, and He longed to know that they were praying for Him and for themselves.

How dark seemed the malignity of sin! Terrible was the temptation to let the human race bear the consequences of its

own guilt, while He stood innocent before God. If He could only know that His disciples understood and appreciated this, He would be strengthened.

Rising with painful effort, He staggered to the place where He had left His companions. But He "findeth them asleep." Had He found them praying, He would have been relieved. Had they been seeking refuge in God, that satanic agencies might not prevail over them, He would have been comforted by their steadfast faith. But they had not heeded the repeated warning, "Watch and pray." At first they had been much troubled to see their Master, usually so calm and dignified, wrestling with a sorrow that was beyond comprehension. They had prayed as they heard the strong cries of the sufferer. They did not intend to forsake their Lord, but they seemed paralyzed by a stupor which they might have shaken off if they had continued pleading with God. They did not realize the necessity of watchfulness and earnest prayer in order to withstand temptation.

Just before He bent His footsteps to the garden, Jesus had said to the disciples, "All ye shall be offended because of Me this night." They had given Him the strongest assurance that they would go with Him to prison and to death. And poor, self-sufficient Peter had added, "Although all shall be offended, yet will not I." Mark 14:27, 29. But the disciples trusted to themselves. They did not look to the mighty Helper as Christ had counseled them to do. Thus when the Saviour was most in need of their sympathy and prayers, they were found asleep. Even Peter was sleeping.

And John, the loving disciple who had leaned upon the breast of Jesus, was asleep. Surely, the love of John for his Master should have kept him awake. His earnest prayers should have mingled with those of his loved Saviour in the time of His supreme sorrow. The Redeemer had spent entire nights praying for His disciples, that their faith might not fail. Should Jesus now put to James and John the question He had once asked them, "Are ye able to drink of the cup that I shall drink of, and to be baptized with the baptism that I am baptized with?" they would not have ventured to answer, "We are able." Matthew 20:22.

The disciples awakened at the voice of Jesus, but they hardly knew Him, His face was so changed by anguish. Addressing Peter, Jesus said, "Simon, sleepest thou? couldest not thou watch one hour? Watch ye and pray, lest ye enter into temptation. The spirit truly is ready, but the flesh is weak." The

> *The human heart longs for sympathy in suffering. This longing Christ felt to the very depths of His being.*

weakness of His disciples awakened the sympathy of Jesus. He feared that they would not be able to endure the test which would come upon them in His betrayal and death. He did not reprove them, but said, "Watch ye and pray, lest ye enter into temptation." Even in His great agony, He was seeking to excuse their weakness. "The spirit truly is ready," He said, "but the flesh is weak."

Again the Son of God was seized with superhuman agony, and fainting and exhausted, He staggered back to the place of His former struggle. His suffering was even greater than before. As the agony of soul came upon Him, "His sweat was as it were great drops of blood falling down to the ground." The cypress and palm trees were the silent witnesses of His anguish. From their leafy branches dropped heavy dew upon His stricken form, as if nature wept over its Author wrestling alone with the powers of darkness.

darkness. As one already glorified, He had claimed oneness with God. In unfaltering accents He had poured out His songs of praise. He had spoken to His disciples in words of courage and tenderness. Now had come the hour of the power of darkness. Now His voice was heard on the still evening air, not in tones of triumph, but full of human anguish. The words of the Saviour were borne to the ears of the drowsy disciples, "O My Father, if this cup may not pass away from Me, except I drink it, Thy will be done."

The first impulse of the disciples was to go to Him; but He had bidden them tarry there, watching unto prayer. When Jesus came to them, He found them still sleeping. Again He had felt a longing for companionship, for some words from His disciples which would bring relief, and break the spell of darkness that well-nigh overpowered Him. But their eyes were heavy; "neither wist they what to answer Him." His

The cypress and palm trees were the silent witnesses of His anguish. From their leafy branches dropped heavy dew upon His stricken form, as if nature wept over its Author wrestling alone with the powers of darkness.

A short time before, Jesus had stood like a mighty cedar, withstanding the storm of opposition that spent its fury upon Him. Stubborn wills, and hearts filled with malice and subtlety, had striven in vain to confuse and overpower Him. He stood forth in divine majesty as the Son of God. Now He was like a reed beaten and bent by the angry storm. He had approached the consummation of His work a conqueror, having at each step gained the victory over the powers of

presence aroused them. They saw His face marked with the bloody sweat of agony, and they were filled with fear. His anguish of mind they could not understand. "His visage was so marred more than any man, and His form more than the sons of men." Isaiah 52:14.

Turning away, Jesus sought again His retreat, and fell prostrate, overcome by the horror of a great darkness. The humanity of the Son of God trembled in that trying hour. He prayed not now for His disciples that their faith might not fail, but for His own tempted, agonized soul. The awful moment had come—that moment which was to decide the destiny of the world. The fate of humanity trembled in the balance. Christ might even now refuse to drink the cup apportioned to guilty man. It was not yet too late. He might wipe the bloody sweat from His brow, and leave man to perish in his iniquity. He might say, Let the transgressor receive the penalty of his sin, and I will go back to My Father. Will the Son of God drink the bitter cup of humiliation and agony? Will the innocent suffer the consequences of the curse of sin, to save the guilty? The words fall tremblingly from the pale lips of Jesus, "O My Father, if this cup may not pass away from Me, except I drink it, Thy will be done."

Three times has He uttered that prayer. Three times has humanity shrunk from the last, crowning sacrifice. But now the history of the human race comes up before the world's Redeemer. He sees that the transgressors of the law, if left to themselves, must perish. He sees the helplessness of man. He sees the power of sin. The woes and lamentations of a doomed world rise before Him. He beholds its impending fate, and His decision is made. He will save man at any cost to Himself. He accepts His baptism of blood, that through Him perishing millions may gain everlasting life. He has left the courts of heaven, where all is purity, happiness, and glory, to save the one lost sheep, the one world that has fallen by transgression. And He will not turn from His mission. He will become the propitiation of a race that has willed to sin. His prayer now breathes only submission: "If this cup may not pass away from Me, except I drink it, Thy will be done."

Having made the decision, He fell dying to the ground from which He had partially risen. Where now were His disciples, to place their hands tenderly beneath the head of their fainting Master, and bathe that brow, marred indeed more than the sons of men? The Saviour trod the wine press alone, and of the people there was none with Him.

But God suffered with His Son. Angels beheld the Saviour's agony. They saw their Lord enclosed by legions of satanic forces, His nature weighed down with a shuddering, mysterious dread. There was silence in heaven. No harp was touched. Could mortals have viewed the amazement of the angelic host as in silent grief they watched the Father separating His beams of light, love, and glory from His beloved Son, they would better understand how offensive in His sight is sin.

The worlds unfallen and the heavenly angels had watched with intense interest as the conflict drew to its close. Satan and his confederacy of evil, the legions of apostasy, watched intently this great crisis in the work of redemption.

The powers of good and evil waited to see what answer would come to Christ's thrice-repeated prayer. Angels had longed to bring relief to the divine sufferer, but this might not be. No way of escape was found for the Son of God. In this awful crisis, when everything was at stake, when the mysterious cup trembled in the hand of the sufferer, the heavens opened, a light shone forth amid the stormy darkness of the crisis hour, and the mighty angel who stands in God's presence, occupying the position from which Satan fell, came to the side of Christ. The angel came not to take the cup from Christ's hand, but to strengthen Him to drink it, with the assurance of the Father's love. He came to give power to the divine-human suppliant. He pointed Him to the open heavens, telling Him of the souls that would be saved as the result of His sufferings. He assured Him that His Father is greater and more powerful than Satan, that His death would result in the utter discomfiture of Satan, and that the kingdom of this world would be given to the saints of the Most High. He told Him that He would see of the travail of His soul, and be satisfied, for He would see a multitude of the human race saved, eternally saved.

Christ's agony did not cease, but His depression and discouragement left Him. The storm had in nowise abated, but He who was its object was strengthened to meet its fury. He came forth calm and serene. A heavenly peace rested upon His bloodstained face. He had borne that which no human being could ever bear; for He had tasted the sufferings of death for every man.

The sleeping disciples had been suddenly awakened by the light surrounding the Saviour. They saw the angel bending over their prostrate Master. They saw him lift the Saviour's head upon his bosom, and point toward heaven. They heard his voice, like sweetest music, speaking words of comfort and hope. The disciples recalled the scene upon the mount of transfiguration. They remembered the glory that in the temple had encircled Jesus, and the voice of God that spoke from the cloud. Now that same glory was again revealed, and they had no further fear for their Master. He was under the care of God; a mighty angel had been sent to protect Him. Again the disciples in their weariness yield to the strange stupor that overpowers them. Again Jesus finds them sleeping.

Looking sorrowfully upon them He says, "Sleep on now, and take your rest: behold, the hour is at hand, and the Son of man is betrayed into the hands of sinners."

Even as He spoke these words, He heard the footsteps of the mob in search of Him, and said, "Rise, let us be going: behold, he is at hand that doth betray Me."

No traces of His recent agony were visible as Jesus stepped forth to meet His betrayer. Standing in advance of His disciples He said, "Whom seek ye?" They answered, "Jesus of Nazareth." Jesus replied, "I am He." As these words were spoken, the angel who had lately ministered to Jesus moved between Him and the mob. A divine light illuminated the Saviour's face, and a dovelike form overshadowed Him. In the presence of this divine glory, the murderous throng could not stand for a moment. They staggered back. Priests, elders, soldiers, and even Judas, fell as dead men to the ground.

The angel withdrew, and the light faded away. Jesus had opportunity to escape, but He remained, calm and self-possessed. As one glorified He stood in the midst of that hardened band, now prostrate and helpless at His feet. The disciples looked on, silent with wonder and awe.

But quickly the scene changed. The mob started up. The Roman soldiers, the priests and Judas, gathered about Christ. They seemed ashamed of their weakness, and fearful that He would yet escape. Again the question was asked by the Redeemer, "Whom seek ye?" They had had evidence that He who stood before them was the Son of God, but they would not be convinced. To the question, "Whom seek ye?" again they answered, "Jesus of Nazareth." The Saviour then said, "I have told you that I am He: if therefore ye seek Me, let these go their way"—pointing to the disciples. He knew how weak was their faith, and He sought to shield them from temptation and trial. For them He was ready to sacrifice Himself.

Judas the betrayer did not forget the part he was to act. When the mob entered the garden, he had led the way, closely followed by the high priest. To the pursuers of Jesus he had given a sign, saying, "Whomsoever I shall kiss, that same is He: hold Him fast." Matthew 26:48. Now he pretends to have no part with them. Coming close to Jesus, he takes His hand as a familiar friend. With the words, "Hail, Master," he kisses Him repeatedly, and appears to weep as if in sympathy with Him in His peril.

Jesus said to him, "Friend, wherefore art thou come?" His voice trembled with sorrow as He added, "Judas, betrayest thou the Son of man with a kiss?" This appeal should have aroused the conscience of the betrayer, and touched his stubborn heart; but honor, fidelity, and human tenderness had forsaken him. He stood bold and defiant, showing no disposition to relent. He had given himself up to Satan, and he had no power to resist him. Jesus did not refuse the traitor's kiss.

The mob grew bold as they saw Judas touch the person of Him who had so recently been glorified before their eyes. They now laid hold of Jesus, and proceeded to bind those precious hands that had ever been employed in doing good.

The disciples had thought that their Master would not suffer Himself to be taken. For the same power that had caused the mob to fall as dead men could keep them helpless, until Jesus and His companions should escape. They were disappointed and indignant as they saw the cords brought forward to bind the hands of Him whom they loved. Peter in his anger rashly drew his sword and tried to defend his Master, but he only cut off an ear of the high priest's servant. When Jesus saw what was done, He released His hands, though held firmly by the Roman soldiers, and saying, "Suffer ye thus far," He touched the wounded ear, and it was instantly made whole. He then said to Peter, "Put up again thy sword into his place: for all they that take the sword shall perish with the sword. Thinkest thou that I cannot now pray to My Father, and He shall presently give Me more than twelve legions of angels?"—a legion in place of each one of the disciples. Oh, why, the disciples thought, does He not save Himself and us? Answering their unspoken thought, He added, "But how then shall the scriptures be fulfilled, that thus it must be?" "The cup which My Father hath given Me, shall I not drink it?"

The official dignity of the Jewish leaders had not prevented them from joining in the pursuit of Jesus. His arrest was too important a matter to be trusted to subordinates; the wily priests and elders had joined the temple police and the rabble in following Judas to Gethsemane. What a company for those dignitaries to unite with—a mob that was eager for excitement, and armed with all kinds of implements, as if in pursuit of a wild beast!

Turning to the priests and elders, Christ fixed upon them His searching glance. The words He spoke they would never forget as long as life should last. They were as the sharp arrows of the Almighty. With dignity He said: You come out against Me with swords and staves as you would against a thief or a robber. Day by day I sat teaching in the temple. You had every opportunity of laying hands upon Me, and you did nothing. The night is better suited to your work. "This is your hour, and the power of darkness."

The disciples were terrified as they saw Jesus permit Himself to be taken and bound. They were offended that He should suffer this humiliation to Himself and them. They could not understand His conduct, and they blamed Him for submitting to the mob. In their indignation and fear, Peter proposed that they save themselves. Following this suggestion, "they all forsook Him, and fled." But Christ had foretold this desertion, "Behold," He had said, "the hour cometh, yea, is now come, that ye shall be scattered, every man to his own, and shall leave Me alone: and yet I am not alone, because the Father is with Me." John 16:32.

18

Before Annas and the Court of Caiaphas

This chapter is based on Matthew 26:57–75; 27:1; Mark 14:53–72; 15:1; Luke 22:54–71; John 18:13–27.

....

Over the brook Kedron, past gardens and olive groves, and through the hushed streets of the sleeping city, they hurried Jesus. It was past midnight, and the cries of the hooting mob that followed Him broke sharply upon the still air. The Saviour was bound and closely guarded, and He moved painfully. But in eager haste His captors made their way with Him to the palace of Annas, the ex-high priest.

Annas was the head of the officiating priestly family, and in deference to his age he was recognized by the people as high priest. His counsel was sought and carried out as the voice of God. He must first see Jesus a captive to priestly power. He must be present at the examination of the prisoner, for fear that the less-experienced Caiaphas might fail of securing the object for which they were working. His artifice, cunning, and subtlety must be used on this occasion; for, at all events, Christ's condemnation must be secured.

Christ was to be tried formally before the Sanhedrin; but before Annas He was subjected to a preliminary trial. Under the Roman rule the Sanhedrin could not execute the sentence of death. They could only examine a prisoner, and pass judgment, to be ratified by the Roman authorities. It was therefore necessary to bring against Christ charges that would be regarded as criminal by the Romans. An accusation must also be found which would condemn Him in the eyes of the Jews. Not a few among the priests and rulers had been convicted by Christ's teaching, and only fear of excommunication prevented them from confessing Him. The priests well remembered the question of Nicodemus, "Doth our law judge any man, before it hear him, and know what he doeth?" John 7:51. This question had for the time broken up the council, and thwarted their plans. Joseph of Arimathaea and Nicodemus were not now to be summoned, but there were others who might dare to speak in favor of justice. The trial must be so conducted as to unite the members of the Sanhedrin against Christ. There were two charges which the priests desired to maintain. If Jesus could be proved a blasphemer, He would be condemned by the Jews. If convicted of sedition, it would secure His condemnation by the Romans. The second charge Annas tried first to establish. He questioned Jesus concerning His disciples and His doctrines, hoping the prisoner would say something that would give him material upon which to work. He thought to draw out some statement to prove that He was seeking to establish a secret society, with the purpose of setting up a new kingdom. Then the priests could deliver Him to the Romans as a disturber of the peace and a creator of insurrection.

Christ read the priest's purpose as an open book. As if reading the inmost soul of His questioner, He denied that there was between Him and His followers any secret bond of union, or that He gathered them secretly and in the darkness to conceal His designs. He had no secrets in regard to His purposes or doctrines. "I spake openly to the world," He answered; "I ever taught in the synagogue, and in the temple, whither the Jews always resort; and in secret have I said nothing."

The Saviour contrasted His own manner of work with the methods of His accusers. For months they had hunted Him, striving to entrap Him and bring Him before a secret tribunal, where they might obtain by perjury what it was impossible to gain by fair means. Now they were carrying out their purpose. The midnight seizure by a mob, the mockery and abuse before He was condemned, or even accused, was their manner of work, not His. Their action was in violation of the law. Their own rules declared that every man should be treated as innocent until proved guilty. By their own rules the priests stood condemneTurning upon His questioner, Jesus said, "Why askest thou Me?" Had not the priests and rulers sent spies to watch His movements, and report His every word? Had not these been present at every gathering of the people, and carried to the priests information of all His sayings and doings? "Ask them which heard Me, what I have said unto them," replied Jesus; "behold, they know what I said."

Annas was silenced by the decision of the answer. Fearing that Christ would say something regarding his course of action that he would prefer to keep covered up, he said nothing more to Him at this time. One of his officers, filled with wrath as he saw Annas silenced, struck Jesus on the face, saying, "Answerest Thou the high priest so?"

Christ calmly replied, "If I have spoken evil, bear witness of the evil: but if well, why smitest thou Me?" He spoke no burning words of retaliation. His calm answer came from a heart sinless, patient, and gentle, that would not be provoked.

Christ suffered keenly under abuse and insult. At the hands of the beings whom He had created, and for whom He was making an infinite sacrifice, He received every indignity. And He suffered in proportion to the perfection of His holiness and His hatred of sin. His trial by men who acted as fiends was to Him a perpetual sacrifice. To be surrounded by human beings under the control of Satan was revolting to Him. And He knew that in a moment, by the flashing forth of His divine power, He could lay His cruel tormentors in the dust. This made the trial the harder to bear.

The Jews were looking for a Messiah to be revealed in outward show. They expected Him, by one flash of overmastering will, to change the current of men's thoughts, and force from them an acknowledgment of His supremacy. Thus, they believed, He was to secure His own exaltation, and gratify their ambitious hopes. Thus when Christ was treated with contempt, there came to Him a strong temptation to manifest His divine character. By a word, by a look, He could compel His persecutors to confess that He was Lord above kings and rulers, priests and temple. But it was His difficult task to keep to the position He had chosen as one with humanity.

The angels of heaven witnessed every movement made against their loved Commander. They longed to deliver Christ. Under God the angels are all-powerful. On one occasion, in obedience to the command of Christ, they slew of the Assyrian army in one night one hundred and eighty-five thousand men. How easily could the angels, beholding the shameful scene of the trial of Christ, have testified their indignation by consuming the adversaries of God! But they were not commanded to do this. He who could have doomed His enemies to death bore with their cruelty. His love for His Father, and His pledge, made from the foundation of the world, to become the Sin Bearer, led Him to endure uncomplainingly the coarse treatment of those He came to save. It was a part of His mission to bear, in His humanity, all the taunts and abuse that

Christ suffered keenly under abuse and insult. At the hands of the beings whom He had created, and for whom He was making an infinite sacrifice, He received every indignity.

men could heap upon Him. The only hope of humanity was in this submission of Christ to all that He could endure from the hands and hearts of men.

Christ had said nothing that could give His accusers an advantage; yet He was bound, to signify that He was condemned. There must, however, be a pretense of justice. It was necessary that there should be the form of a legal trial. This the authorities were determined to hasten. They knew the regard in which Jesus was held by the people, and feared that if the arrest were noised abroad, a rescue would be attempted. Again, if the trial and execution were not brought about at once, there would be a week's delay on account of the celebration of the Passover. This might defeat their plans. In securing the condemnation of Jesus they depended largely upon the clamor of the mob, many of them the rabble of Jerusalem. Should there be a week's delay, the excitement would abate, and a reaction would be likely to set in. The better part of the people would be aroused in Christ's favor; many would come forward with testimony in His vindication, bringing to light the mighty works He had done. This would excite popular indignation against the Sanhedrin. Their proceedings would be condemned, and Jesus would be set free, to receive new homage from the multitudes. The priests and rulers therefore determined that before their purpose could become known, Jesus should be delivered into the hands of the Romans.

But first of all, an accusation was to be found. They had gained nothing as yet. Annas ordered Jesus to be taken to Caiaphas. Caiaphas belonged to the Sadducees, some of whom were now the most desperate enemies of Jesus. He himself, though wanting in force of character, was fully as severe, heartless, and unscrupulous as was Annas. He would leave no means untried to destroy Jesus. It was now early morning, and very dark; by the light of torches and lanterns the armed band with their prisoner proceeded to the high priest's palace. Here, while the members of the Sanhedrin were coming together, Annas and Caiaphas again questioned Jesus, but without success.

When the council had assembled in the judgment hall, Caiaphas took his seat as presiding officer. On either side were the judges, and those specially interested in the trial. The Roman soldiers were stationed on the platform below the throne. At the foot of the throne stood Jesus. Upon Him the gaze of the whole multitude was fixed. The excitement was intense. Of all the throng He alone was calm and serene. The very atmosphere surrounding Him seemed pervaded by a holy influence.

Caiaphas had regarded Jesus as his rival. The eagerness of the people to hear the Saviour, and their apparent readiness to accept His teachings, had aroused the bitter jealousy of the high priest. But as Caiaphas now looked upon the prisoner, he was struck with admiration for His noble and dignified bearing. A conviction came over him that this Man was akin to God. The next instant he scornfully banished the thought. Immediately his voice was heard in sneering, haughty tones demanding that Jesus work one of His mighty miracles before them. But his words fell upon the Saviour's ears as though He heard them not. The people compared the excited and malignant deportment of Annas and Caiaphas with the calm, majestic bearing of Jesus. Even in the minds of that hardened multitude arose the question, Is this man of godlike presence to be condemned as a criminal?

Caiaphas, perceiving the influence that was obtaining, hastened the trial. The enemies of Jesus were in great perplexity. They were bent on securing His condemnation, but how to accomplish this they knew not. The members of the council were divided between the Pharisees and the Sadducees. There was bitter animosity and controversy between them; certain disputed points they dared not approach for fear of a quarrel. With a few words Jesus could have excited their prejudices against each other, and thus have averted their wrath from Himself. Caiaphas knew this, and he wished to avoid stirring up a contention. There were plenty of witnesses to prove that Christ had denounced the priests and scribes, that He had called them hypocrites and murderers; but this testimony it was not expedient to bring forward. The Sadducees in their sharp contentions with the Pharisees had used to them similar language. And such testimony would have no weight with the Romans, who were themselves disgusted with the pretensions of the Pharisees. There was abundant evidence that Jesus had disregarded the traditions of the Jews, and had spoken irreverently of many of their ordinances; but in regard to tradition the Pharisees and Sadducees were at swords' points; and this evidence also would have no weight with the Romans. Christ's enemies dared not accuse Him of Sabbathbreaking, lest an examination should reveal the character of His work. If His miracles of healing were brought to light, the very object of the priests would be defeated.

False witnesses had been bribed to accuse Jesus of inciting rebellion and seeking to establish a separate government. But their testimony proved to be vague and contradictory. Under examination they falsified their own statements.

Early in His ministry Christ had said, "Destroy this temple, and in three days I will raise it up." In the figurative language of prophecy, He had thus foretold His own death and resurrection. "He spake of the temple of His body." John 2:19, 21. These words the Jews had understood in a literal sense, as referring to the temple at Jerusalem. Of all that Christ had said, the priests could find nothing to use against Him save this. By misstating these words they hoped to gain an advantage. The Romans had engaged in rebuilding and embellishing the temple, and they took great pride in it; any contempt shown to it would be sure to excite their indignation. Here Romans and Jews, Pharisees and Sadducees, could meet; for all held the temple in great veneration. On this point two witnesses were found whose testimony was not so contradictory as that of the others had been. One of them, who had been bribed to accuse Jesus, declared, "This fellow said, I am able to destroy the temple of God, and to build it in three days." Thus Christ's words were misstated. If they had been reported exactly as He spoke them, they would not have secured His condemnation even by the Sanhedrin. Had Jesus been a mere man, as the Jews claimed, His declaration would only have indicated an unreasonable, boastful spirit, but could not have been construed into blasphemy. Even as misrepresented by the false witnesses, His words contained nothing which would be regarded by the Romans as a crime worthy of death.

Patiently Jesus listened to the conflicting testimonies. No word did He utter in self-defense. At last His accusers were entangled, confused, and maddened. The trial was making no headway; it seemed that their plottings were to fail. Caiaphas was desperate. One last resort remained; Christ must be forced to condemn Himself. The high priest started from the judgment seat, his face contorted with passion, his voice and demeanor plainly indicating that were it in his power he would strike down the prisoner before him. "Answerest Thou nothing?" he exclaimed; "what is it which these witness against Thee?"

Jesus held His peace. "He was oppressed, and He was afflicted, yet He opened not His mouth: He is brought as a lamb to the slaughter, and as a sheep before her shearers is dumb, so He openeth not His mouth." Isaiah 53:7.

At last, Caiaphas, raising his right hand toward heaven, addressed Jesus in the form of a solemn oath: "I adjure Thee by the living God, that Thou tell us whether Thou be the Christ, the Son of God."

To this appeal Christ could not remain silent. There was a time to be silent, and a time to speak. He had not spoken until directly questioned. He knew that to answer now would make His death certain. But the appeal was made by the highest acknowledged authority of the nation, and in the name of the Most High. Christ would not fail to show proper respect for the law. More than this, His own relation to the Father was called in question. He must plainly declare His character and mission.

Jesus had said to His disciples, "Whosoever therefore shall confess Me before men, him will I confess also before My Father which is in heaven." Matthew 10:32. Now by His own example He repeated the lesson.

Every ear was bent to listen, and every eye was fixed on His face as He answered, "Thou hast said." A heavenly light seemed to illuminate His pale countenance as He added, "Nevertheless I say unto you, Hereafter shall ye see the Son of man sitting on the right hand of power, and coming in the clouds of heaven."

For a moment the divinity of Christ flashed through His guise of humanity. The high priest quailed before the penetrating eyes of the Saviour. That look seemed to read his hidden thoughts, and burn into his heart. Never in afterlife did he forget that searching glance of the persecuted Son of God.

"Hereafter," said Jesus, "shall ye see the Son of man sitting on the right hand of power, and coming in the clouds of heaven." In these words Christ presented the reverse of the scene then taking place. He, the Lord of life and glory, would be seated at God's right hand. He would be the judge of all the earth, and from His decision there could be no appeal. Then every secret thing would be set in the light of God's countenance, and judgment be passed upon every man according to his deeds.

The words of Christ startled the high priest. The thought that there was to be a resurrection of the dead, when all would stand at the bar of God, to be rewarded according to their works, was a thought of terror to Caiaphas. He did not wish to believe that in future he would receive sentence according to his works. There rushed before his mind as a panorama the scenes of the final judgment. For a moment he saw the fearful spectacle of the graves giving up their dead, with the secrets he had hoped were forever hidden. For a moment he felt as if standing before the eternal Judge, whose eye, which sees all things, was reading his soul, bringing to light mysteries supposed to be hidden with the dead.

The scene passed from the priest's vision. Christ's words cut him, the Sadducee, to the quick. Caiaphas had denied the doctrine of the resurrection, the judgment, and a future life. Now he was maddened by satanic fury. Was this man, a prisoner before him, to assail his most cherished theories? Rending his robe, that the people might see his pretended horror, he demanded that without further preliminaries the prisoner be condemned for blasphemy. "What further need have we of witnesses?" he said; "behold, now ye have heard His blasphemy. What think ye?" And they all condemned Him.

Conviction mingled with passion led Caiaphas to do as he did. He was furious with himself for believing Christ's words, and instead of rending his heart under a deep sense of truth, and confessing that Jesus was the Messiah, he rent his priestly robes in determined resistance. This act was deeply significant. Little did Caiaphas realize its meaning. In this act, done to influence the judges and secure Christ's condemnation, the high priest had condemned himself. By the law of God he was disqualified for the priesthood. He had pronounced upon himself the death sentence.

A high priest was not to rend his garments. By the Levitical law, this was prohibited under sentence of death. Under no circumstances, on no occasion, was the priest to rend his robe. It was the custom among the Jews for the garments to be rent at the death of friends, but this custom the priests were not to observe. Express command had been given by Christ to Moses concerning this (Leviticus 10:6).

Everything worn by the priest was to be whole and without blemish. By those beautiful official garments was represented the character of the great antitype, Jesus Christ. Nothing but perfection, in dress and attitude, in word and spirit, could be acceptable to God. He is holy, and His glory and perfection must be represented by the earthly service. Nothing but perfection could properly represent the sacredness of the heavenly service. Finite man might rend his own heart by showing a contrite and humble spirit. This God would discern. But no rent must be made in the priestly robes, for this would mar the representation of heavenly things. The high priest who dared to appear in holy office, and engage in the service of the sanctuary, with a rent robe, was looked upon as having severed himself from God. By rending his garment he cut himself off from being a representative character. He was no longer accepted by God as an officiating priest. This course of action, as exhibited by Caiaphas, showed human passion, human imperfection.

By rending his garments, Caiaphas made of no effect the law of God, to follow the tradition of men. A man-made law provided that in case of blasphemy a priest might rend his garments in horror at the sin, and be guiltless. Thus the law of God was made void by the laws of men.

Each action of the high priest was watched with interest by the people; and Caiaphas thought for effect to display his piety. But in this act, designed as an accusation against Christ, he was reviling the One of whom God had said, "My name is in Him." Exodus 23:21. He himself was committing blasphemy. Standing under the condemnation of God, he pronounced sentence upon Christ as a blasphemer.

> *By rending his garments, Caiaphas made of no effect the law of God, to follow the tradition of men.*

When Caiaphas rent his garment, his act was significant of the place that the Jewish nation as a nation would thereafter occupy toward God. The once favored people of God were separating themselves from Him, and were fast becoming a people disowned by Jehovah. When Christ upon the cross cried out, "It is finished" (John 19:30), and the veil of the temple was rent in twain, the Holy Watcher declared that the Jewish people had rejected Him who was the antitype of all their types, the substance of all their shadows. Israel was divorced from God. Well might Caiaphas then rend his official robes, which signified that he claimed to be a representative of the great High Priest; for no longer had they any meaning for him or for the people. Well might the high priest rend his robes in horror for himself and for the nation.

The Sanhedrin had pronounced Jesus worthy of death; but it was contrary to the Jewish law to try a prisoner by night. In legal condemnation nothing could be done except in the light of day and before a full session of the council. Notwithstanding this, the Saviour was now treated as a condemned criminal, and given up to be abused by the lowest and vilest of humankind. The palace of the high priest surrounded an open court in which the soldiers and the multitude had gathered. Through this court, Jesus was taken to the guardroom, on every side meeting with mockery of His claim to be the Son of God. His own words, "sitting on the right hand of power," and, "coming in the clouds of heaven," were jeeringly repeated. While in the guardroom, awaiting His legal trial, He was not protected. The ignorant rabble had seen the cruelty with which He was treated before the council, and from this they took license to manifest all the satanic elements of their nature. Christ's very nobility and godlike bearing goaded them to madness. His meekness, His innocence, His majestic patience, filled them with hatred born of Satan. Mercy and justice were trampled upon. Never was criminal treated in so inhuman a manner as was the Son of God.

But a keener anguish rent the heart of Jesus; the blow that inflicted the deepest pain no enemy's hand could have dealt. While He was undergoing the mockery of an examination before Caiaphas, Christ had been denied by one of His own disciples.

After deserting their Master in the garden, two of the disciples had ventured to follow, at a distance, the mob that had Jesus in charge. These disciples were Peter and John. The priests recognized John as a well-known disciple of Jesus, and admitted him to the hall, hoping that as he witnessed the humiliation of his Leader, he would scorn the idea of such a one being the Son of God. John spoke in favor of Peter, and gained an entrance for him also.

In the court a fire had been kindled; for it was the coldest hour of the night, being just before the dawn. A company drew about the fire, and Peter presumptuously took his place with them. He did not wish to be recognized as a disciple of Jesus. By mingling carelessly with the crowd, he hoped to be taken for one of those who had brought Jesus to the hall.

But as the light flashed upon Peter's face, the woman who kept the door cast a searching glance upon him. She had noticed that he came in with John, she marked the look of dejection on his face, and thought that he might be a disciple of Jesus. She was one of the servants of Caiaphas' household, and was curious to know. She said to Peter, "Art not thou also one of this Man's disciples?" Peter was startled and confused; the eyes of the company instantly fastened upon him. He pretended not to understand her; but she was persistent, and said to those around her that this man was with Jesus. Peter felt compelled to answer, and said angrily, "Woman, I know Him not." This was the first denial, and immediately the cock crew. O Peter, so soon ashamed of thy Master! so soon to deny thy Lord!

The disciple John, upon entering the judgment hall, did not try to conceal the fact that he was a follower of Jesus. He did not mingle with the rough company who were reviling his Master. He was not questioned, for he did not assume a false character, and thus lay himself liable to suspicion. He sought a retired corner secure from the notice of the mob, but as near Jesus as it was possible for him to be. Here he could see and hear all that took place at the trial of his Lord.

Peter had not designed that his real character should be known. In assuming an air of indifference he had placed himself on the enemy's ground, and he became an easy prey to temptation. If he had been called to fight for his Master, he would have been a courageous soldier; but when the finger of scorn was pointed at him, he proved himself a coward. Many who do not shrink from active warfare for their Lord are driven by ridicule to deny their faith. By associating with those whom they should avoid, they place themselves in the way of temptation. They invite the enemy to tempt them, and are led to say

and do that of which under other circumstances they would never have been guilty. The disciple of Christ who in our day disguises his faith through dread of suffering or reproach denies his Lord as really as did Peter in the judgment hall.

Peter tried to show no interest in the trial of his Master, but his heart was wrung with sorrow as he heard the cruel taunts, and saw the abuse He was suffering. More than this, he was surprised and angry that Jesus should humiliate Himself and His followers by submitting to such treatment. In order to conceal his true feelings, he endeavored to join with the persecutors of Jesus in their untimely jests. But his appearance was unnatural. He was acting a lie, and while seeking to talk unconcernedly he could not restrain expressions of indignation at the abuse heaped upon his Master.

Attention was called to him the second time, and he was again charged with being a follower of Jesus. He now declared with an oath, "I do not know the Man." Still another opportunity was given him. An hour had passed, when one of the servants of the high priest, being a near kinsman of the man whose ear Peter had cut off, asked him, "Did not I see thee in the garden with Him?" "Surely thou art one of them: for thou art a Galilean, and thy speech agreeth thereto." At this Peter flew into a rage. The disciples of Jesus were noted for the purity of their language, and in order fully to deceive his questioners, and justify his assumed character, Peter now denied his Master with cursing and swearing. Again the cock crew. Peter heard it then, and he remembered the words of Jesus, "Before the cock crow twice, thou shalt deny Me thrice." Mark 14:30.

While the degrading oaths were fresh upon Peter's lips, and the shrill crowing of the cock was still ringing in his ears, the Saviour turned from the frowning judges, and looked full upon His poor disciple. At the same time Peter's eyes were drawn to his Master. In that gentle countenance he read deep pity and sorrow, but there was no anger there.

The sight of that pale, suffering face, those quivering lips, that look of compassion and forgiveness, pierced his heart like an arrow. Conscience was aroused. Memory was active. Peter called to mind his promise of a few short hours before that he would go with his Lord to prison and to death. He remembered his grief when the Saviour told him in the upper chamber that he would deny his Lord thrice that same night.

> *I t was in sleeping when Jesus bade him watch and pray that Peter had prepared the way for his great sin. All the disciples, by sleeping in that critical hour, sustained a great loss. Christ knew the fiery ordeal through which they were to pass.*

Peter had just declared that he knew not Jesus, but he now realized with bitter grief how well his Lord knew him, and how accurately He had read his heart, the falseness of which was unknown even to himself.

A tide of memories rushed over him. The Saviour's tender mercy, His kindness and long-suffering, His gentleness and patience toward His erring disciples—all was remembered.

The scene of a few hours before came vividly to his mind. The suffering face of his Lord, stained with bloody sweat and convulsed with anguish, rose before him. He remembered with bitter remorse that Jesus had wept and agonized in prayer alone, while those who should have united with Him in that trying hour were sleeping. He remembered His solemn charge, "Watch and pray, that ye enter not into temptation." Matthew 26:41. He

He recalled the caution, "Simon, behold, Satan hath desired to have you, that he may sift you as wheat: but I have prayed for thee, that thy faith fail not." Luke 22:31, 32. He reflected with horror upon his own ingratitude, his falsehood, his perjury. Once more he looked at his Master, and saw a sacrilegious hand raised to smite Him in the face. Unable longer to endure the scene, he rushed, heartbroken, from the hall.

He pressed on in solitude and darkness, he knew not and cared not whither. At last he found himself in Gethsemane.

witnessed again the scene in the judgment hall. It was torture to his bleeding heart to know that he had added the heaviest burden to the Saviour's humiliation and grief. On the very spot where Jesus had poured out His soul in agony to His Father, Peter fell upon his face, and wished that he might die.

It was in sleeping when Jesus bade him watch and pray that Peter had prepared the way for his great sin. All the disciples, by sleeping in that critical hour, sustained a great loss. Christ knew the fiery ordeal through which they were to pass. He knew how Satan would work to paralyze their senses that they might be unready for the trial. Therefore it was that He gave them warning. Had those hours in the garden been spent in watching and prayer, Peter would not have been left to depend upon his own feeble strength. He would not have denied his Lord. Had the disciples watched with Christ in His agony, they would have been prepared to behold His suffering upon the cross. They would have understood in some degree the nature of His overpowering anguish. They would have been able to recall His words that foretold His sufferings, His death, and His resurrection. Amid the gloom of the most trying hour, some rays of hope would have lighted up the darkness and sustained their faith.

As soon as it was day, the Sanhedrin again assembled, and again Jesus was brought into the council room. He had declared Himself the Son of God, and they had construed His words into a charge against Him. But they could not condemn Him on this, for many of them had not been present at the night session, and they had not heard His words. And they knew that the Roman tribunal would find in them nothing

Then came the third scene of abuse and mockery, worse even than that received from the ignorant rabble. In the very presence of the priests and rulers, and with their sanction, this took place. Every feeling of sympathy or humanity had gone out of their hearts. If their arguments were weak, and failed to silence His voice, they had other weapons, such as in all ages have been used to silence heretics—suffering, and violence, and death.

When the condemnation of Jesus was pronounced by the judges, a satanic fury took possession of the people. The roar of voices was like that of wild beasts. The crowd made a rush toward Jesus, crying, He is guilty, put Him to death! Had it not been for the Roman soldiers, Jesus would not have lived to be nailed to the cross of Calvary. He would have been torn in pieces before His judges, had not Roman authority interfered, and by force of arms restrained the violence of the mob.

Heathen men were angry at the brutal treatment of one against whom nothing had been proved. The Roman officers declared that the Jews in pronouncing condemnation upon Jesus were infringing upon the Roman power, and that it was

The angels of God faithfully recorded every insulting look, word, and act against their beloved Commander. One day the base men who scorned and spat upon the calm, pale face of Christ will look upon it in its glory, shining brighter than the sun.

worthy of death. But if from His own lips they could all hear those words repeated, their object might be gained. His claim to the Messiahship they might construe into a seditious political claim.

"Art Thou the Christ?" they said, "tell us." But Christ remained silent. They continued to ply Him with questions. At last in tones of mournful pathos He answered, "If I tell you, ye will not believe; and if I also ask you, ye will not answer Me, nor let Me go." But that they might be left without excuse He added the solemn warning, "Hereafter shall the Son of man sit on the right hand of the power of God."

"Art Thou then the Son of God?" they asked with one voice. He said unto them, "Ye say that I am." They cried out, "What need we any further witness? for we ourselves have heard of His own mouth."

And so by the third condemnation of the Jewish authorities, Jesus was to die. All that was now necessary, they thought, was for the Romans to ratify this condemnation, and deliver Him into their hands.

even against the Jewish law to condemn a man to death upon his own testimony. This intervention brought a momentary lull in the proceedings; but the Jewish leaders were dead alike to pity and to shame.

Priests and rulers forgot the dignity of their office, and abused the Son of God with foul epithets. They taunted Him with His parentage. They declared that His presumption in proclaiming Himself the Messiah made Him deserving of the most ignominious death. The most dissolute men engaged in infamous abuse of the Saviour. An old garment was thrown over His head, and His persecutors struck Him in the face, saying, "Prophesy unto us, Thou Christ, Who is he that smote Thee?" When the garment was removed, one poor wretch spat in His face.

The angels of God faithfully recorded every insulting look, word, and act against their beloved Commander. One day the base men who scorned and spat upon the calm, pale face of Christ will look upon it in its glory, shining brighter than the sun.

19

In Pilate's Judgment Hall

This chapter is based on Matthew 27:2, 11–31; Mark 15:1–20; Luke 23:1–25; John 18:28–40; 19:1–16.

. . . .

In the judgment hall of Pilate, the Roman governor, Christ stands bound as a prisoner. About Him are the guard of soldiers, and the hall is fast filling with spectators. Just outside the entrance are the judges of the Sanhedrin, priests, rulers, elders, and the mob.

After condemning Jesus, the council of the Sanhedrin had come to Pilate to have the sentence confirmed and executed. But these Jewish officials would not enter the Roman judgment hall. According to their ceremonial law they would be defiled thereby, and thus prevented from taking part in the feast of the Passover. In their blindness they did not see that murderous hatred had defiled their hearts. They did not see that Christ was the real Passover lamb, and that, since they had rejected Him, the great feast had for them lost its significance.

When the Saviour was brought into the judgment hall, Pilate looked upon Him with no friendly eyes. The Roman governor had been called from his bedchamber in haste, and he determined to do his work as quickly as possible. He was prepared to deal with the prisoner with magisterial severity. Assuming his severest expression, he turned to see what kind of man he had to examine, that he had been called from his repose at so early an hour. He knew that it must be someone whom the Jewish authorities were anxious to have tried and punished with haste.

Pilate looked at the men who had Jesus in charge, and then his gaze rested searchingly on Jesus. He had had to deal with all kinds of criminals; but never before had a man bearing marks of such goodness and nobility been brought before him. On His face he saw no sign of guilt, no expression of fear, no boldness or defiance. He saw a man of calm and dignified bearing, whose countenance bore not the marks of a criminal, but the signature of heaven.

Christ's appearance made a favorable impression upon Pilate. His better nature was roused. He had heard of Jesus and His works. His wife had told him something of the wonderful deeds performed by the Galilean prophet, who cured the sick and raised the dead. Now this revived as a dream in Pilate's mind. He recalled rumors that he had heard from several sources. He resolved to demand of the Jews their charges against the prisoner.

Who is this Man, and wherefore have ye brought Him? he said. What accusation bring ye against Him? The Jews were disconcerted. Knowing that they could not substantiate their charges against Christ, they did not desire a public examination. They answered that He was a deceiver called Jesus of Nazareth.

Again Pilate asked, "What accusation bring ye against this Man?" The priests did not answer his question, but in words that showed their irritation, they said, "If He were not a malefactor, we would not have delivered Him up unto thee." When those composing the Sanhedrin, the first men of the nation, bring to you a man they deem worthy of death, is there need to ask for an accusation against him? They hoped to impress Pilate with a sense of their importance, and thus lead him to accede to their request without going through many preliminaries. They were eager to have their sentence ratified; for they knew that the people who had witnessed Christ's marvelous works could tell a story very different from the fabrication they themselves were now rehearsing.

The priests thought that with the weak and vacillating Pilate they could carry through their plans without trouble. Before this he had signed the death warrant hastily, condemning to death men they knew were not worthy of death. In his estimation the life of a prisoner was of little account; whether he were innocent or guilty was of no special consequence. The priests hoped that Pilate would now inflict the death penalty on Jesus without giving Him a hearing. This they besought as a favor on the occasion of their great national festival.

But there was something in the prisoner that held Pilate back from this. He dared not do it. He read the purposes of the priests. He remembered how, not long before, Jesus had raised Lazarus, a man that had been dead four days; and he determined to know, before signing the sentence of condemnation, what were the charges against Him, and whether they could be proved.

If your judgment is sufficient, he said, why bring the prisoner to me? "Take ye Him, and judge Him according to your law." Thus pressed, the priests said that they had already passed sentence upon Him, but that they must have Pilate's sentence to render their condemnation valid. What is your sentence? Pilate asked. The death sentence, they answered; but it is not lawful for us to put any man to death. They asked Pilate to take their word as to Christ's guilt, and enforce their sentence. They would take the responsibility of the result.

Pilate was not a just or a conscientious judge; but weak though he was in moral power, he refused to grant this request. He would not condemn Jesus until a charge had been brought against Him.

The priests were in a dilemma. They saw that they must cloak their hypocrisy under the thickest conceal-ment. They must not allow it to appear that Christ had been arrested on religious grounds. Were this put forward as a reason, their proceedings would have no weight with Pilate. They must make it appear that Jesus was working against the common law; then He could be punished as a political offender. Tumults and insurrection against the Roman government were constantly arising among the Jews. With these revolts the Romans had dealt very rigor-ously, and they were constantly on the watch to repress everything that could lead to an outbreak.

Only a few days before this the Pharisees had tried to entrap Christ with the question, "Is it lawful for us to give tribute unto Caesar?" But Christ had unveiled their hypocrisy. The Romans who were present had seen the utter failure of the plotters, and their discomfiture at His answer, "Render there-fore unto Caesar the things which be Caesar's." Luke 20:22–25.

Now the priests thought to make it appear that on this occasion Christ had taught what they hoped He would teach. In their extremity they called false witnesses to their aid, "and they began to accuse Him, saying, We found this fellow per-verting the nation, and forbidding to give tribute to Caesar, saying that He Himself is Christ a King." Three charges, each without foundation. The priests knew this, but they were will-ing to commit perjury could they but secure their end.

Pilate saw through their purpose. He did not believe that the prisoner had plotted against the government. His meek and humble appearance was altogether out of har-mony with the charge. Pilate was convinced that a deep plot had been laid to destroy an innocent man who stood in the way of the Jewish dignitaries. Turning to Jesus he asked, "Art Thou the King of the Jews?" The Saviour answered, "Thou

sayest it." And as He spoke, His countenance lighted up as if a sunbeam were shining upon it.

When they heard His answer, Caiaphas and those that were with him called Pilate to witness that Jesus had admit-ted the crime with which He was charged. With noisy cries, priests, scribes, and rulers demanded that He be sentenced to death. The cries were taken up by the mob, and the uproar was deafening. Pilate was confused. Seeing that Jesus made no answer to His accusers, Pilate said to Him, "Answerest Thou nothing? behold how many things they witness against Thee. But Jesus yet answered nothing."

Standing behind Pilate, in view of all in the court, Christ heard the abuse; but to all the false charges against Him He answered not a word. His whole bearing gave evidence of conscious innocence. He stood unmoved by the fury of the waves that beat about Him. It was as if the heavy surges of wrath, rising higher and higher, like the waves of the bois-terous ocean, broke about Him, but did not touch Him. He stood silent, but His silence was eloquence. It was as a light shining from the inner to the outer man.

Pilate was astonished at His bearing. Does this Man dis-regard the proceedings because He does not care to save His life? he asked himself. As he looked at Jesus, bearing insult and mockery without retaliation, he felt that He could not be as unrighteous and unjust as were the clamoring priests. Hoping to gain the truth from Him and to escape the tumult of the crowd, Pilate took Jesus aside with him, and again ques-tioned, "Art Thou the King of the Jews?"

Jesus did not directly answer this question. He knew that the Holy Spirit was striving with Pilate, and He gave him opportunity to acknowledge his conviction. "Sayest thou this thing of thyself," He asked, "or did others tell it thee of Me?" That is, was it the accusations of the priests, or a desire to receive light from Christ, that prompted Pilate's question? Pilate understood Christ's meaning; but pride arose in his heart. He would not acknowledge the convic-tion that pressed upon him. "Am I a Jew?" he said. "Thine own nation and the chief priests have delivered Thee unto me: what hast Thou done?"

Pilate's golden opportunity had passed. Yet Jesus did not leave him without further light. While He did not directly answer Pilate's question, He plainly stated His own mission. He gave Pilate to understand that He was not seeking an earthly throne.

"My kingdom is not of this world," He said; "if My king-dom were of this world, then would My servants fight, that I should not be delivered to the Jews: but now is My kingdom not from hence. Pilate therefore said unto Him, Art Thou a king then? Jesus answered, Thou sayest that I am a king. To this end was I born, and for this cause came I into the world, that I should bear witness unto the truth. Everyone that is of the truth heareth My voice."

Christ affirmed that His word was in itself a key which would unlock the mystery to those who were prepared to receive it. It had a self-commending power, and this was the secret of the spread of His kingdom of truth. He desired Pilate to understand that only by receiving and appropriating truth could his ruined nature be reconstructed.

Pilate had a desire to know the truth. His mind was confused. He eagerly grasped the words of the Saviour, and his heart was stirred with a great longing to know what it really was, and how he could obtain it. "What is truth?" he inquired. But he did not wait for an answer. The tumult outside recalled him to the interests of the hour; for the priests were clamorous for immediate action. Going out to the Jews, he declared emphatically, "I find in Him no fault at all."

These words from a heathen judge were a scathing rebuke to the perfidy and falsehood of the rulers of Israel who were accusing the Saviour. As the priests and elders heard this from Pilate, their disappointment and rage knew no bounds. They had long plotted and waited for this opportunity. As they saw the prospect of the release of Jesus, they seemed ready to tear Him in pieces. They loudly denounced Pilate, and threatened him with the censure of the Roman government. They accused him of refusing to condemn Jesus, who, they affirmed, had set Himself up against Caesar.

Angry voices were now heard, declaring that the seditious influence of Jesus was well known throughout the country. The priests said, "He stirreth up the people, teaching throughout all Jewry, beginning from Galilee to this place."

Pilate at this time had no thought of condemning Jesus. He knew that the Jews had accused Him through hatred and prejudice. He knew what his duty was. Justice demanded that Christ should be immediately released. But Pilate dreaded the ill will of the people. Should he refuse to give Jesus into their hands, a tumult would be raised, and this he feared to meet. When he heard that Christ was from Galilee, he decided to send Him to Herod, the ruler of that province, who was then in Jerusalem. By this course, Pilate thought to shift the responsibility of the trial from himself to Herod. He also thought this a good opportunity to heal an old quarrel between himself and Herod. And so it proved. The two magistrates made friends over the trial of the Saviour.

Pilate delivered Jesus again to the soldiers, and amid the jeers and insults of the mob He was hurried to the judgment hall of Herod. "When Herod saw Jesus, he was exceeding glad." He had never before met the Saviour, but "he was desirous to see Him of a long season, because he had heard many things of Him; and he hoped to have seen some miracle done by Him." This Herod was he whose hands were stained with the blood of John the Baptist. When Herod first heard of Jesus, he was terror-stricken, and said, "It is John, whom I beheaded: he is risen from the dead;" "therefore mighty works do show forth themselves in him." Mark 6:16; Matthew 14:2. Yet Herod desired to see Jesus. Now there was opportunity to save the life of this prophet, and the king hoped to banish forever from his mind the memory of that bloody head brought to him in a charger. He also desired to have his curiosity gratified, and thought that if Christ were given any prospect of release, He would do anything that was asked of Him.

A large company of the priests and elders had accompanied Christ to Herod. And when the Saviour was brought in, these dignitaries, all speaking excitedly, urged their accusations against Him. But Herod paid little regard to their charges. He commanded silence, desiring an opportunity to question Christ. He ordered that the fetters of Christ should be unloosed, at the same time charging His enemies with roughly treating Him. Looking with compassion into the serene face of the world's Redeemer, he read in it only wisdom and purity. He as well as Pilate was satisfied that Christ had been accused through malice and envy.

Herod questioned Christ in many words, but throughout the Saviour maintained a profound silence. At the command of the king, the decrepit and maimed were then called in, and Christ was ordered to prove His claims by working a miracle. Men say that Thou canst heal the sick, said Herod. I am anxious to see that Thy widespread fame has not been belied. Jesus did not respond, and Herod still continued to urge: If Thou canst work miracles for others, work them now for Thine own good, and it will serve Thee a good purpose. Again he commanded, Show us a sign that Thou hast the power with which rumor hath accredited Thee. But Christ was as one who heard and saw not. The Son of God had taken upon Himself man's nature. He must do as man must do in

> *Christ affirmed that His word was in itself a key which would unlock the mystery to those who were prepared to receive it.*

In answer to Christ's prayer, the wife of Pilate had been visited by an angel from heaven, and in a dream she had beheld the Saviour and conversed with Him. Pilate's wife was not a Jew, but as she looked upon Jesus in her dream, she had no doubt of His character or mission. She knew Him to be the Prince of God.

like circumstances. Therefore He would not work a miracle to save Himself the pain and humiliation that man must endure when placed in a similar position.

Herod promised that if Christ would perform some miracle in his presence, He should be released. Christ's accusers had seen with their own eyes the mighty works wrought by His power. They had heard Him command the grave to give up its dead. They had seen the dead come forth obedient to His voice. Fear seized them lest He should now work a miracle. Of all things they most dreaded an exhibition of His power. Such a manifestation would prove a deathblow to their plans, and would perhaps cost them their lives. Again the priests and rulers, in great anxiety, urged their accusations against Him. Raising their voices, they declared, He is a traitor, a blasphemer. He works His miracles through the power given Him by Beelzebub, the prince of the devils. The hall became a scene of confusion, some crying one thing and some another.

Herod's conscience was now far less sensitive than when he had trembled with horror at the request of Herodias for the head of John the Baptist. For a time he had felt the keen stings of remorse for his terrible act; but his moral perceptions had become more and more degraded by his licentious life. Now his heart had become so hardened that he could even boast of the punishment he had inflicted upon John for daring to reprove him. And he now threatened Jesus, declaring repeatedly that he had power to release or to condemn Him. But no sign from Jesus gave evidence that He heard a word.

Herod was irritated by this silence. It seemed to indicate utter indifference to his authority. To the vain and pompous king, open rebuke would have been less offensive than to be thus ignored. Again he angrily threatened Jesus, who still remained unmoved and silent.

The mission of Christ in this world was not to gratify idle curiosity. He came to heal the brokenhearted. Could He have spoken any word to heal the bruises of sin-sick souls, He would not have kept silent. But He had no words for those who would but trample the truth under their unholy feet.

Christ might have spoken words to Herod that would have pierced the ears of the hardened king. He might have stricken him with fear and trembling by laying before him the full iniquity of his life, and the horror of his approaching doom. But Christ's silence was the severest rebuke that He could have given. Herod had rejected the truth spoken to him by the greatest of the prophets, and no other message was he to receive. Not a word had the Majesty of heaven for him. That ear that had ever been open to human woe, had no room for Herod's commands. Those eyes that had ever rested upon the penitent sinner in pitying, forgiving love had no look to bestow upon Herod. Those lips that had uttered the most impressive truth, that in tones of tenderest entreaty had pleaded with the most sinful and the most degraded, were closed to the haughty king who felt no need of a Saviour.

Herod's face grew dark with passion. Turning to the multitude, he angrily denounced Jesus as an impostor. Then to Christ he said, If You will give no evidence of Your claim, I will deliver You up to the soldiers and the people. They may succeed in making You speak. If You are an impostor, death at their hands is only what You merit; if You are the Son of God, save Yourself by working a miracle.

No sooner were these words spoken than a rush was made for Christ. Like wild beasts, the crowd darted upon their prey. Jesus was dragged this way and that, Herod joining the mob in seeking to humiliate the Son of God. Had not the Roman soldiers interposed, and forced back the maddened throng, the Saviour would have been torn in pieces.

"Herod with his men of war set Him at nought, and mocked Him, and arrayed Him in a gorgeous robe." The Roman soldiers joined in this abuse. All that these wicked, corrupt soldiers, helped on by Herod and the Jewish dignitaries, could instigate was heaped upon the Saviour. Yet His divine patience failed not.

Christ's persecutors had tried to measure His character by their own; they had represented Him as vile as themselves. But back of all the present appearance another scene intruded itself—a scene which they will one day see in all its glory. There were some who trembled in Christ's presence. While the rude throng were bowing in mockery before Him, some who came forward for that purpose turned back, afraid and silenced. Herod was convicted. The last rays of merciful light were shining upon his sin-hardened heart. He felt that this was no common man; for divinity had flashed through humanity. At the very time when Christ was encompassed by mockers, adulterers, and murderers, Herod felt that he was beholding a God upon His throne.

Hardened as he was, Herod dared not ratify the condemnation of Christ. He wished to relieve himself of the terrible responsibility, and he sent Jesus back to the Roman judgment hall.

Pilate was disappointed and much displeased. When the Jews returned with their prisoner, he asked impatiently what they would have him do. He reminded them that he had already examined Jesus, and found no fault in Him; he told them that they had brought complaints against Him, but they had not been able to prove a single charge. He had sent Jesus to Herod, the tetrarch of Galilee, and one of their own nation, but he also had found in Him nothing worthy of death. "I will therefore chastise Him," Pilate said, "and release Him."

Here Pilate showed his weakness. He had declared that Jesus was innocent, yet he was willing for Him to be scourged to pacify His accusers. He would sacrifice justice and principle in order to compromise with the mob. This placed him at a disadvantage. The crowd presumed upon his indecision, and clamored the more for the life of the prisoner. If at the first Pilate had stood firm, refusing to condemn a man whom he found guiltless, he would have broken the fatal chain that was to bind him in remorse and guilt as long as he lived. Had he carried out his convictions of right, the Jews would not have presumed to dictate to him. Christ would have been put to death, but the guilt would not have rested upon Pilate. But Pilate had taken step after step in the violation of his conscience. He had excused himself from judging with justice and equity, and he now found himself almost helpless in the hands of the priests and rulers. His wavering and indecision proved his ruin.

Even now Pilate was not left to act blindly. A message from God warned him from the deed he was about to commit. In answer to Christ's prayer, the wife of Pilate had been visited by an angel from heaven, and in a dream she had beheld the Saviour and conversed with Him. Pilate's wife was not a Jew, but as she looked upon Jesus in her dream, she had no doubt of His character or mission. She knew Him to be the Prince of God. She saw Him on trial in the judgment hall. She saw the hands tightly bound as the hands of a criminal. She saw Herod and his soldiers doing their dreadful work. She heard the priests and rulers, filled with envy and malice, madly accusing. She heard the words, "We have a law, and by our law He ought to die." She saw Pilate give Jesus to the scourging, after he had declared, "I find no fault in Him." She heard the condemnation pronounced by Pilate, and saw him give Christ up to His murderers. She saw the cross uplifted on Calvary. She saw the earth wrapped in darkness, and heard the mysterious cry, "It is finished." Still another scene met her gaze. She saw Christ seated upon the great white cloud, while the earth reeled in space, and His murderers fled from the presence of His glory. With a cry of horror she awoke, and at once wrote to Pilate words of warning.

While Pilate was hesitating as to what he should do, a messenger pressed through the crowd, and handed him the letter from his wife, which read:

"Have thou nothing to do with that just Man: for I have suffered many things this day in a dream because of Him."

Pilate's face grew pale. He was confused by his own conflicting emotions. But while he had been delaying to act, the priests and rulers were still further inflaming the minds of the people. Pilate was forced to action. He now bethought himself of a custom which might serve to secure Christ's release. It was customary at this feast to release some one prisoner whom the people might choose. This custom was of pagan invention; there was not a shadow of justice in it, but it was greatly prized by the Jews. The Roman authorities at this time held a prisoner named Barabbas, who was under sentence of death. This man had claimed to be the Messiah. He claimed authority to establish a different order of things, to set the world right. Under satanic delusion he claimed that whatever he could obtain by theft and robbery was his own. He had done wonderful things through satanic agencies, he had gained a following among the people, and had excited sedition against the Roman government. Under cover of religious enthusiasm he was a hardened and desperate villain, bent on rebellion and cruelty. By giving the people a choice between this man and the innocent Saviour, Pilate thought to arouse them to a sense of justice. He hoped to gain their sympathy for Jesus in opposition to the priests and rulers. So, turning to the crowd, he said with great earnestness, "Whom will ye that I release unto you? Barabbas, or Jesus which is called Christ?"

Like the bellowing of wild beasts came the answer of the mob, "Release unto us Barabbas!" Louder and louder swelled the cry, Barabbas! Barabbas! Thinking that the people had not understood his question, Pilate asked, "Will ye that I release unto you the King of the Jews?" But they cried out again, "Away with this Man, and release unto us Barabbas"! "What shall I do then with Jesus which is called Christ?" Pilate asked. Again the surging multitude roared like demons. Demons themselves, in human form, were in the crowd, and what could be expected but the answer, "Let Him be crucified"?

Pilate was troubled. He had not thought it would come to that. He shrank from delivering an innocent man to the most ignominious and cruel death that could be inflicted. After the roar of voices had ceased, he turned to the people, saying, "Why, what evil hath He done?" But the case had gone too far for argument. It was not evidence of Christ's innocence that they wanted, but His condemnation.

Still Pilate endeavored to save Him. "He said unto them the third time, Why, what evil hath He done? I have found no cause of death in Him: I will therefore chastise Him, and let Him go." But the very mention of His release stirred the people to a tenfold frenzy. "Crucify Him, crucify Him," they cried. Louder and louder swelled the storm that Pilate's indecision had called forth.

Jesus was taken, faint with weariness and covered with wounds, and scourged in the sight of the multitude. "And the soldiers led Him away into the hall, called Praetorium, and they call together the whole band. And they clothed Him with purple, and platted a crown of thorns, and put it about His head, and began to salute Him, Hail, King of the Jews! And they … did spit upon Him, and bowing their knees worshiped Him." Occasionally some wicked hand snatched the reed that had been placed in His hand, and struck the crown upon His brow, forcing the thorns into His temples, and sending the blood trickling down His face and beard.

Wonder, O heavens! and be astonished, O earth! Behold the oppressor and the oppressed. A maddened throng enclose the Saviour of the world. Mocking and jeering are mingled with the coarse oaths of blasphemy. His lowly birth and humble life are commented upon by the unfeeling mob. His claim to be the Son of God is ridiculed, and the vulgar jest and insulting sneer are passed from lip to lip.

Satan led the cruel mob in its abuse of the Saviour. It was his purpose to provoke Him to retaliation if possible, or to drive Him to perform a miracle to release Himself, and thus break up the plan of salvation. One stain upon His human life, one failure of His humanity to endure the terrible test, and the Lamb of God would have been an imperfect offering, and the redemption of man a failure. But He who by a command could bring the heavenly host to His aid—He who could have driven that mob in terror from His sight by the flashing forth of His divine majesty—submitted with perfect calmness to the coarsest insult and outrage.

Christ's enemies had demanded a miracle as evidence of His divinity. They had evidence far greater than any they had sought. As their cruelty degraded His torturers below humanity into the likeness of Satan, so did His meekness and patience exalt Jesus above humanity, and prove His kinship to God. His abasement was the pledge of His exaltation. The blood drops of agony that from His wounded temples flowed down His face and beard were the pledge of His anointing with "the oil of gladness" (Hebrews 1:9) as our great high priest.

Satan's rage was great as he saw that all the abuse inflicted upon the Saviour had not forced the least murmur from His lips. Although He had taken upon Him the nature of man, He was sustained by a godlike fortitude, and departed in no particular from the will of His Father.

When Pilate gave Jesus up to be scourged and mocked, he thought to excite the pity of the multitude. He hoped they would decide that this was sufficient punishment. Even the malice of the priests, he thought, would now be satisfied. But with keen perception the Jews saw the weakness of thus punishing a man who had been declared innocent. They knew that Pilate was trying to save the life of the prisoner, and they were determined that Jesus should not be released. To please and satisfy us, Pilate has scourged Him, they thought, and if we press the matter to a decided issue, we shall surely gain our end.

Pilate now sent for Barabbas to be brought into the court. He then presented the two prisoners side by side, and pointing to the Saviour he said in a voice of solemn entreaty, "Behold the Man!" "I bring Him forth to you, that ye may know that I find no fault in Him."

There stood the Son of God, wearing the robe of mockery and the crown of thorns. Stripped to the waist, His back showed the long, cruel stripes, from which the blood flowed freely. His face was stained with blood, and bore the marks of exhaustion and pain; but never had it appeared more beautiful than now. The Saviour's visage was not marred before His enemies. Every feature expressed gentleness and resignation and the tenderest pity for His cruel foes. In His manner there was no cowardly weakness, but the strength and dignity of long-suffering. In striking contrast was the prisoner at His side. Every line of the countenance of Barabbas proclaimed him the hardened ruffian that he was. The contrast spoke to every beholder. Some of the spectators were weeping. As they looked upon Jesus, their hearts were full of sympathy. Even the priests and rulers were convicted that He was all that He claimed to be.

The Roman soldiers that surrounded Christ were not all hardened; some were looking earnestly into His face for one evidence that He was a criminal or dangerous character. From time to time they would turn and cast a look of contempt upon Barabbas. It needed no deep insight to read him through and through. Again they would turn to the One upon trial. They looked at the divine sufferer with feelings of deep pity. The silent submission of Christ stamped upon their minds the scene, never to be effaced until they either acknowledged Him as the Christ, or by rejecting Him decided their own destiny.

Pilate was filled with amazement at the uncomplaining patience of the Saviour. He did not doubt that the sight of this Man, in contrast with Barabbas, would move the Jews to sympathy. But he did not understand the fanatical hatred of the priests for Him, who, as the Light of the world, had made manifest their darkness and error. They had moved the mob to a mad fury, and again priests, rulers, and people raised that awful cry, "Crucify Him, crucify Him." At last, losing all patience with their unreasoning cruelty, Pilate cried out despairingly, "Take ye Him, and crucify Him: for I find no fault in Him."

The Roman governor, though familiar with cruel scenes, was moved with sympathy for the suffering prisoner, who, condemned and scourged, with bleeding brow and lacerated back, still had the bearing of a king upon his throne. But the priests declared, "We have a law, and by our law He ought to die, because He made Himself the Son of God."

Pilate was startled. He had no correct idea of Christ and His mission; but he had an indistinct faith in God and in beings superior to humanity. A thought that had once before passed through his mind now took more definite shape. He questioned whether it might not be a divine being that stood before him, clad in the purple robe of mockery, and crowned with thorns.

Again he went into the judgment hall, and said to Jesus, "Whence art Thou?" But Jesus gave him no answer. The Saviour had spoken freely to Pilate, explaining His own mission as a witness to the truth. Pilate had disregarded the light. He had abused the high office of judge by yielding his principles and authority to the demands of the mob. Jesus had no further light for him. Vexed at His silence, Pilate said haughtily:

"Speakest Thou not unto me? knowest Thou not that I have power to crucify Thee, and have power to release Thee?"

Jesus answered, "Thou couldest have no power at all against Me, except it were given thee from above: therefore he that delivered Me unto thee hath the greater sin." Thus

> *The Saviour's visage was not marred before His enemies. Every feature expressed gentleness and resignation and the tenderest pity for His cruel foes. In His manner there was no cowardly weakness, but the strength and dignity of long-suffering.*

the pitying Saviour, in the midst of His intense suffering and grief, excused as far as possible the act of the Roman governor who gave Him up to be crucified. What a scene was this to hand down to the world for all time! What a light it sheds upon the character of Him who is the Judge of all the earth!

"He that delivered Me unto thee," said Jesus, "hath the greater sin." By this Christ meant Caiaphas, who, as high priest, represented the Jewish nation. They knew the principles that controlled the Roman authorities. They had had light in the prophecies that testified of Christ, and in His own teachings and miracles. The Jewish judges had received unmistakable evidence of the divinity of Him whom they condemned to death. And according to their light would they be judged.

The greatest guilt and heaviest responsibility belonged to those who stood in the highest places in the nation, the depositaries of sacred trusts that they were basely betraying. Pilate, Herod, and the Roman soldiers were comparatively ignorant of Jesus. They thought to please the priests and rulers by abusing Him. They had not the light which the Jewish nation had so abundantly received. Had the light been given to the soldiers, they would not have treated Christ as cruelly as they did.

Again Pilate proposed to release the Saviour. "But the Jews cried out, saying, If thou let this man go, thou art not Caesar's friend." Thus these hypocrites pretended to be jealous for the authority of Caesar. Of all the opponents of the Roman rule, the Jews were most bitter. When it was safe for them to do so, they were most tyrannical in enforcing their own national and religious requirements; but when they desired to bring about some purpose of cruelty, they exalted the power of Caesar. To accomplish the destruction of Christ, they would profess loyalty to the foreign rule which they hated.

"Whosoever maketh himself a king," they continued, "speaketh against Caesar." This was touching Pilate in a weak point. He was under suspicion by the Roman government, and he knew that such a report would be ruin to him. He knew that if the Jews were thwarted, their rage would be turned against him. They would leave nothing undone to accomplish their revenge. He had before him an example of the persistence with which they sought the life of One whom they hated without reason.

Pilate then took his place on the judgment seat, and again presented Jesus to the people, saying, "Behold your King!" Again the mad cry was heard, "Away with Him, crucify Him." In a voice that was heard far and near, Pilate asked, "Shall I crucify your King?" But from profane, blasphemous lips went forth the words, "We have no king but Caesar."

Thus by choosing a heathen ruler, the Jewish nation had withdrawn from the theocracy. They had rejected God as their king. Henceforth they had no deliverer. They had no king but Caesar. To this the priests and teachers had led the people. For this, with the fearful results that followed, they were responsible. A nation's sin and a nation's ruin were due to the religious leaders.

"When Pilate saw that he could prevail nothing, but that rather a tumult was made, he took water, and washed his hands before the multitude, saying, I am innocent of the blood of this just Person: see ye to it." In fear and self-condemnation Pilate looked upon the Saviour. In the vast sea of upturned faces, His alone was peaceful. About His head a soft light seemed to shine. Pilate said in his heart, He is a God. Turning to the multitude he declared, I am clear of His blood. Take ye Him, and crucify Him. But mark ye, priests and rulers, I pronounce Him a just man. May He whom He claims as His Father judge you and not me for this day's work. Then to Jesus he said, Forgive me for this act; I cannot save You. And when he had again scourged Jesus, he delivered Him to be crucified.

Pilate longed to deliver Jesus. But he saw that he could not do this, and yet retain his own position and honor. Rather than lose his worldly power, he chose to sacrifice an innocent life. How many, to escape loss or suffering, in like manner sacrifice principle. Conscience and duty point one way, and self-interest points another. The current sets strongly in the wrong direction, and he who compromises with evil is swept away into the thick darkness of guilt.

Pilate yielded to the demands of the mob. Rather than risk losing his position, he delivered Jesus up to be crucified. But in spite of his precautions, the very thing he dreaded afterward came upon him. His honors were stripped from him, he was cast down from his high office, and, stung by remorse and wounded pride, not long after the crucifixion he ended his own life. So all who compromise with sin will gain only sorrow and ruin. "There is a way which seemeth right unto a man, but the end thereof are the ways of death." Proverbs 14:12.

When Pilate declared himself innocent of the blood of Christ, Caiaphas answered defiantly, "His blood be on us, and on our children." The awful words were taken up by the priests and rulers, and echoed by the crowd in an inhuman roar of voices. The whole multitude answered and said, "His blood be on us, and on our children."

The people of Israel had made their choice. Pointing to Jesus they had said, "Not this man, but Barabbas." Barabbas, the robber and murderer, was the representative of Satan. Christ was the representative of God. Christ had been rejected; Barabbas had been chosen. Barabbas they were to have. In making this choice they accepted him who from the beginning was a liar and a murderer. Satan was their leader. As a nation they would act out his dictation. His works they would do. His rule they must endure. That people who chose Barabbas in the place of Christ were to feel the cruelty of Barabbas as long as time should last.

Looking upon the smitten Lamb of God, the Jews had cried, "His blood be on us, and on our children." That awful cry ascended to the throne of God. That sentence, pronounced upon themselves, was written in heaven. That prayer was heard. The blood of the Son of God was upon their children and their children's children, a perpetual curse.

Terribly was it realized in the destruction of Jerusalem. Terribly has it been manifested in the condition of the Jewish nation for eighteen hundred years—a branch severed from the vine, a dead, fruitless branch, to be gathered up and burned. From land to land throughout the world, from century to century, dead, dead in trespasses and sins!

Terribly will that prayer be fulfilled in the great judgment day. When Christ shall come to the earth again, not as a prisoner surrounded by a rabble will men see Him. They will see Him then as heaven's King. Christ will come in His own glory, in the glory of His Father, and the glory of the holy angels. Ten thousand times ten thousand, and thousands of thousands of angels, the beautiful and triumphant sons of God, possessing surpassing loveliness and glory, will escort Him on His way. Then shall He sit upon the throne of His glory, and before Him shall be gathered all nations. Then every eye shall see Him, and they also that pierced Him. In the place of a crown of thorns, He will wear a crown of glory—a crown within a crown. In place of that old purple kingly robe, He will be clothed in raiment of whitest white, "so as no fuller on earth can white them." Mark 9:3. And on His vesture and on His thigh a name will be written, "King of kings, and Lord of lords." Revelation 19:16. Those who mocked and smote Him will be there. The priests and rulers will behold again the scene in the judgment hall. Every circumstance will appear before them, as if written in letters of fire. Then those who prayed, "His blood be on us, and on our children," will receive the answer to their prayer. Then the whole world will know and understand. They will realize who and what they, poor, feeble, finite beings, have been warring against. In awful agony and horror they will cry to the mountains and rocks, "Fall on us, and hide us from the face of Him that sitteth on the throne, and from the wrath of the Lamb: for the great day of His wrath is come; and who shall be able to stand?" Revelation 6:16, 17.

Pilate yielded to the demands of the mob. Rather than risk losing his position, he delivered Jesus up to be crucified. But in spite of his precautions, the very thing he dreaded afterward came upon him.

20

Calvary

This chapter is based on Matthew 27:31–53; Mark 15:20–38; Luke 23:26–46; John 19:16–30.

．．．．．．．．．．．．

"And when they were come to the place, which is called Calvary, there they crucified Him."

"That He might sanctify the people with His own blood," Christ "suffered without the gate." Hebrews 13:12. For transgression of the law of God, Adam and Eve were banished from Eden. Christ, our substitute, was to suffer without the boundaries of Jerusalem. He died outside the gate, where felons and murderers were executed. Full of significance are the words, "Christ hath redeemed us from the curse of the law, being made a curse for us." Galatians 3:13.

A vast multitude followed Jesus from the judgment hall to Calvary. The news of His condemnation had spread throughout Jerusalem, and people of all classes and all ranks flocked toward the place of crucifixion. The priests and rulers had been bound by a promise not to molest Christ's followers if He Himself were delivered to them, and the disciples and believers from the city and the surrounding region joined the throng that followed the Saviour.

As Jesus passed the gate of Pilate's court, the cross which had been prepared for Barabbas was laid upon His bruised and bleeding shoulders. Two companions of Barabbas were to suffer death at the same time with Jesus, and upon them also crosses were placed. The Saviour's burden was too heavy for Him in His weak and suffering condition. Since the Passover supper with His disciples, He had taken neither food nor drink. He had agonized in the garden of Gethsemane in conflict with satanic agencies. He had endured the anguish of the betrayal, and had seen His disciples forsake Him and flee. He had been taken to Annas, then to Caiaphas, and then to Pilate. From Pilate He had been sent to Herod, then sent again to Pilate. From insult to renewed insult, from mockery to mockery, twice tortured by the scourge—all that night there had been scene after scene of a character to try the soul of man to the uttermost. Christ had not failed. He had spoken no word but that tended to glorify God. All through the disgraceful farce of a trial He had borne Himself with firmness and dignity. But when after the second scourging the cross was laid upon Him, human nature could bear no more. He fell fainting beneath the burden.

The crowd that followed the Saviour saw His weak and staggering steps, but they manifested no compassion. They taunted and reviled Him because He could not carry the heavy cross. Again the burden was laid upon Him, and again He fell fainting to the ground. His persecutors saw that it was impossible for Him to carry His burden farther. They were puzzled to find anyone who would bear the humiliating load. The Jews themselves could not do this, because the defilement would prevent them from keeping the Passover. None even of the mob that followed Him would stoop to bear the cross.

At this time a stranger, Simon a Cyrenian, coming in from the country, meets the throng. He hears the taunts and ribaldry of the crowd; he hears the words contemptuously repeated, Make way for the King of the Jews! He stops in astonishment at the scene; and as he expresses his compassion, they seize him and place the cross upon his shoulders.

Simon had heard of Jesus. His sons were believers in the Saviour, but he himself was not a disciple. The bearing of the cross to Calvary was a blessing to Simon, and he was ever after grateful for this providence. It led him to take upon himself the cross of Christ from choice, and ever cheerfully stand beneath its burden.

Not a few women are in the crowd that follow the Uncondemned to His cruel death. Their attention is fixed upon Jesus. Some of them have seen Him before. Some have carried to Him their sick and suffering ones. Some have themselves been healed. The story of the scenes that have taken place is related. They wonder at the hatred of the crowd toward Him for whom their own hearts are melting and ready to break.

And notwithstanding the action of the maddened throng, and the angry words of the priests and rulers, these women give expression to their sympathy. As Jesus falls fainting beneath the cross, they break forth into mournful wailing.

This was the only thing that attracted Christ's attention. Although full of suffering, while bearing the sins of the world, He was not indifferent to the expression of grief. He looked upon these women with tender compassion. They were not believers in Him; He knew that they were not lamenting Him as one sent from God, but were moved by feelings of human pity. He did not despise their sympathy, but it awakened in His heart a deeper sympathy for them. "Daughters of Jerusalem," He said, "weep not for Me, but weep for yourselves, and for your children." From the scene before Him, Christ looked forward to the time of Jerusalem's destruction. In that terrible scene, many of those who were now weeping for Him were to perish with their children.

From the fall of Jerusalem the thoughts of Jesus passed to a wider judgment. In the destruction of the impenitent city He saw a symbol of the final destruction to come upon the world. He said, "Then shall they begin to say to the mountains, Fall on us; and to the hills, Cover us. For if they do these things in a green tree, what shall be done in the dry?" By the green tree, Jesus represented Himself, the innocent Redeemer. God suffered His wrath against transgression to fall on His beloved Son. Jesus was to be crucified for the sins of men. What suffering, then, would the sinner bear who continued in sin? All the impenitent and unbelieving would know a sorrow and misery that language would fail to express.

Of the multitude that followed the Saviour to Calvary, many had attended Him with joyful hosannas and the waving of palm branches as He rode triumphantly into Jerusalem. But not a few who had then shouted His praise, because it was popular to do so, now swelled the cry of "Crucify Him, crucify Him." When Christ rode into Jerusalem, the hopes of the disciples had been raised to the highest pitch. They had pressed close about their Master, feeling that it was a high honor to be connected with Him. Now in His humiliation they followed Him at a distance. They were filled with grief, and bowed down with disappointed hopes. How were the words of Jesus verified: "All ye shall be offended because of Me this night: for it is written, I will smite the shepherd, and the sheep of the flock shall be scattered abroad." Matthew 26:31.

Arriving at the place of execution, the prisoners were bound to the instruments of torture. The two thieves wrestled in the hands of those who placed them on the cross; but Jesus made no resistance. The mother of Jesus, supported by John the beloved disciple, had followed the steps of her Son to Calvary. She had seen Him fainting under the burden of the cross, and had longed to place a supporting hand beneath His wounded head, and to bathe that brow which had once been pillowed upon her bosom. But she was not permitted this mournful privilege. With the disciples she still cherished the hope that Jesus would manifest His power, and deliver Himself from His enemies. Again her heart would sink as she recalled the words in which He had foretold the very scenes that were then taking place. As the thieves were bound to the cross, she looked on with agonizing suspense. Would He who had given life to the dead suffer Himself to be crucified? Would the Son of God suffer Himself to be thus cruelly slain? Must she give up her faith that Jesus was the Messiah? Must she witness His shame and sorrow, without even the privilege of ministering to Him in His distress? She saw His hands stretched upon the cross; the hammer and the nails were brought, and as the spikes were driven through the tender flesh, the heart-stricken disciples bore away from the cruel scene the fainting form of the mother of Jesus.

The Saviour made no murmur of complaint. His face remained calm and serene, but great drops of sweat stood upon His brow. There was no pitying hand to wipe the death

> *God suffered His wrath against transgression to fall on His beloved Son. Jesus was to be crucified for the sins of men.*

dew from His face, nor words of sympathy and unchanging fidelity to stay His human heart. While the soldiers were doing their fearful work, Jesus prayed for His enemies, "Father, forgive them; for they know not what they do." His mind passed from His own suffering to the sin of His persecutors, and the terrible retribution that would be theirs. No curses were called down upon the soldiers who were handling Him so roughly. No vengeance was invoked upon the priests and rulers, who were gloating over the accomplishment of their purpose. Christ pitied them in their ignorance and guilt. He breathed only a plea for their forgiveness—"for they know not what they do."

Had they known that they were putting to torture One who had come to save the sinful race from eternal ruin, they would have been seized with remorse and horror. But their ignorance did not remove their guilt; for it was their privilege to know and accept Jesus as their Saviour. Some of them would yet see their sin, and repent, and be converted. Some by their impenitence would make it an impossibility for the prayer of Christ to be answered for them. Yet, just the same, God's purpose was reaching its fulfillment. Jesus was earning the right to become the advocate of men in the Father's presence.

That prayer of Christ for His enemies embraced the world. It took in every sinner that had lived or should live, from the beginning of the world to the end of time. Upon all rests the guilt of crucifying the Son of God. To all, forgiveness is freely offered. "Whosoever will" may have peace with God, and inherit eternal life.

As soon as Jesus was nailed to the cross, it was lifted by strong men, and with great violence thrust into the place prepared for it. This caused the most intense agony to the Son of God. Pilate then wrote an inscription in Hebrew, Greek, and Latin, and placed it upon the cross, above the head of Jesus. It read, "Jesus of Nazareth the King of the Jews." This inscription irritated the Jews. In Pilate's court they had cried, "Crucify Him." "We have no king but Caesar." John 19:15. They had declared that whoever should acknowledge any other king was a traitor. Pilate wrote out the sentiment they had expressed. No offense was mentioned, except that Jesus was the King of the Jews. The inscription was a virtual acknowledgment of the allegiance of the Jews to the Roman power. It declared that whoever might claim to be the King of Israel would be judged by them worthy of death. The priests had overreached themselves. When they were plotting the death of Christ, Caiaphas had declared it expedient that one man should die to save the nation. Now their hypocrisy was revealed. In order to destroy Christ, they had been ready to sacrifice even their national existence.

The priests saw what they had done, and asked Pilate to change the inscription. They said, "Write not, The King of the Jews; but that He said, I am King of the Jews." But Pilate was angry with himself because of his former weakness, and he thoroughly despised the jealous and artful priests and rulers. He replied coldly, "What I have written I have written."

A higher power than Pilate or the Jews had directed the placing of that inscription above the head of Jesus. In the providence of God it was to awaken thought, and investigation of the Scriptures. The place where Christ was crucified was near to the city. Thousands of people from all lands were then at Jerusalem, and the inscription declaring Jesus of Nazareth the Messiah would come to their notice. It was a living truth, transcribed by a hand that God had guided.

In the sufferings of Christ upon the cross prophecy was fulfilled. Centuries before the crucifixion, the Saviour had foretold the treatment He was to receive. He said, "Dogs have compassed Me: the assembly of the wicked have enclosed Me: they pierced My hands and My feet. I may tell all My bones: they look and stare upon Me. They part My garments among them, and cast lots upon My vesture." Psalm 22:16–18. The prophecy concerning His garments was carried out without counsel or interference from the friends or the enemies of the Crucified One. To the soldiers who had placed Him upon the cross, His clothing was given. Christ heard the men's contention as they parted the garments among them. His tunic was woven throughout without seam, and they said, "Let us not rend it, but cast lots for it, whose it shall be."

In another prophecy the Saviour declared, "Reproach hath broken My heart; and I am full of heaviness: and I looked for some to take pity, but there was none; and for comforters, but I found none. They gave Me also gall for My meat; and in My thirst they gave Me vinegar to drink." Psalm 69:20, 21. To those who suffered death by the cross, it was permitted to give a stupefying potion, to deaden the sense of pain. This was offered to Jesus; but when He had tasted it, He refused it. He would receive nothing that could becloud His mind. His faith must keep fast hold upon God. This was His only strength. To becloud His senses would give Satan an advantage.

The enemies of Jesus vented their rage upon Him as He hung upon the cross. Priests, rulers, and scribes joined with the mob in mocking the dying Saviour. At the baptism and at the transfiguration the voice of God had been heard proclaiming Christ as His Son. Again, just before Christ's betrayal, the Father had spoken, witnessing to His divinity. But now the voice from heaven was silent. No testimony in Christ's favor was heard. Alone He suffered abuse and mockery from wicked men.

"If Thou be the Son of God," they said, "come down

from the cross." "Let Him save Himself, if He be Christ, the chosen of God." In the wilderness of temptation Satan had declared, "If Thou be the Son of God, command that these stones be made bread." "If Thou be the Son of God, cast Thyself down" from the pinnacle of the temple. Matthew 4:3, 6. And Satan with his angels, in human form, was present at the cross. The archfiend and his hosts were co-operating with the priests and rulers. The teachers of the people had stimulated the ignorant mob to pronounce judgment against One

this occasion. Yet in their blindness they did not see that they were fulfilling the prophecy. Those who in derision uttered the words, "He trusted in God; let Him deliver Him now, if He will have Him: for He said, I am the Son of God," little thought that their testimony would sound down the ages. But although spoken in mockery, these words led men to search the Scriptures as they had never done before. Wise men heard, searched, pondered, and prayed. There were those who never rested until, by comparing scripture with scripture, they saw

That prayer of Christ for His enemies embraced the world. It took in every sinner that had lived or should live, from the beginning of the world to the end of time. Upon all rests the guilt of crucifying the Son of God. To all, forgiveness is freely offered. "Whosoever will" may have peace with God, and inherit eternal life.

upon whom many of them had never looked, until urged to bear testimony against Him. Priests, rulers, Pharisees, and the hardened rabble were confederated together in a satanic frenzy. Religious rulers united with Satan and his angels. They were doing his bidding.

Jesus, suffering and dying, heard every word as the priests declared, "He saved others; Himself He cannot save. Let Christ the King of Israel descend now from the cross, that we may see and believe." Christ could have come down from the cross. But it is because He would not save Himself that the sinner has hope of pardon and favor with God.

In their mockery of the Saviour, the men who professed to be the expounders of prophecy were repeating the very words which Inspiration had foretold they would utter upon

the meaning of Christ's mission. Never before was there such a general knowledge of Jesus as when He hung upon the cross. Into the hearts of many who beheld the crucifixion scene, and who heard Christ's words, the light of truth was shining.

To Jesus in His agony on the cross there came one gleam of comfort. It was the prayer of the penitent thief. Both the men who were crucified with Jesus had at first railed upon Him; and one under his suffering only became more desperate and defiant. But not so with his companion. This man was not a hardened criminal; he had been led astray by evil associations, but he was less guilty than many of those who stood beside the cross reviling the Saviour. He had seen and heard Jesus, and had been convicted by His teaching, but he had been turned away from Him by the priests and rulers.

Seeking to stifle conviction, he had plunged deeper and deeper into sin, until he was arrested, tried as a criminal, and condemned to die on the cross. In the judgment hall and on the way to Calvary he had been in company with Jesus. He had heard Pilate declare, "I find no fault in Him." John 19:4. He had marked His godlike bearing, and His pitying forgiveness of His tormentors. On the cross he sees the many great religionists shoot out the tongue with scorn, and ridicule the Lord Jesus. He sees the wagging heads. He hears the upbraiding speeches taken up by his companion in guilt: "If Thou be Christ, save Thyself and us." Among the passers-by he hears many defending Jesus. He hears them repeat His words, and tell of His works. The conviction comes back to him that this is the Christ. Turning to his fellow criminal he says, "Dost not thou fear God, seeing thou art in the same condemnation?" The dying thieves have no longer anything to fear from man. But upon one of them presses the conviction that there is a God to fear, a future to cause him to tremble. And now, all sin-polluted as it is, his life history is about to close. "And we indeed justly," he moans; "for we receive the due reward of our deeds: but this Man hath done nothing amiss."

There is no question now. There are no doubts, no reproaches. When condemned for his crime, the thief had become hopeless and despairing; but strange, tender thoughts now spring up. He calls to mind all he has heard of Jesus, how He has healed the sick and pardoned sin. He has heard the words of those who believed in Jesus and followed Him weeping. He has seen and read the title above the Saviour's head. He has heard the passers-by repeat it, some with grieved, quivering lips, others with jesting and mockery. The Holy Spirit illuminates his mind, and little by little the chain of evidence is joined together. In Jesus, bruised, mocked, and hanging upon the cross, he sees the Lamb of God, that taketh away the sin of the world. Hope is mingled with anguish in his voice as the helpless, dying soul casts himself upon a dying Saviour. "Lord, remember me," he cries, "when Thou comest into Thy kingdom."

Quickly the answer came. Soft and melodious the tone, full of love, compassion, and power the words: Verily I say unto thee today, Thou shalt be with Me in paradise.

For long hours of agony, reviling and mockery have fallen upon the ears of Jesus. As He hangs upon the cross, there floats up to Him still the sound of jeers and curses. With longing heart He has listened for some expression of faith from His disciples. He has heard only the mournful words, "We trusted that it had been He which should have redeemed Israel." How grateful then to the Saviour was the utterance of faith and love from the dying thief! While the leading Jews deny Him, and even the disciples doubt His divinity, the poor thief, upon the brink of eternity, calls Jesus Lord. Many were ready to call Him Lord when He wrought miracles, and after He had risen from the grave; but none acknowledged Him as He hung dying upon the cross save the penitent thief who was saved at the eleventh hour.

The bystanders caught the words as the thief called Jesus Lord. The tone of the repentant man arrested their attention. Those who at the foot of the cross had been quarreling over Christ's garments, and casting lots upon His vesture, stopped to listen. Their angry tones were hushed. With bated breath they looked upon Christ, and waited for the response from those dying lips.

As He spoke the words of promise, the dark cloud that seemed to enshroud the cross was pierced by a bright and living light. To the penitent thief came the perfect peace of acceptance with God. Christ in His humiliation was glorified. He who in all other eyes appeared to be conquered was a Conqueror. He was acknowledged as the Sin Bearer. Men may exercise power over His human body. They may pierce the holy temples with the crown of thorns. They may strip from Him His raiment, and quarrel over its division. But they cannot rob Him of His power to forgive sins. In dying He bears testimony to His own divinity and to the glory of the Father. His ear is not heavy that it cannot hear, neither His arm shortened that it cannot save. It is His royal right to save unto the uttermost all who come unto God by Him.

I say unto thee today, Thou shalt be with Me in Paradise. Christ did not promise that the thief should be with Him in Paradise that day. He Himself did not go that day to Paradise. He slept in the tomb, and on the morning of the resurrection He said, "I am not yet ascended to My Father." John 20:17. But on the day of the crucifixion, the day of apparent defeat and darkness, the promise was given. "Today" while dying upon the cross as a malefactor, Christ assures the poor sinner, Thou shalt be with Me in Paradise.

The thieves crucified with Jesus were placed "on either side one, and Jesus in the midst." This was done by the direction of the priests and rulers. Christ's position between the thieves was to indicate that He was the greatest criminal of the three. Thus was fulfilled the scripture, "He was numbered with the transgressors." Isaiah 53:12. But the full meaning of their act the priests did not see. As Jesus, crucified with the thieves, was placed "in the midst," so His cross was placed in the midst of a world lying in sin. And the words of pardon spoken to the penitent thief kindled a light that will shine to the earth's remotest bounds.

With amazement the angels beheld the infinite love of

Jesus, who, suffering the most intense agony of mind and body, thought only of others, and encouraged the penitent soul to believe. In His humiliation He as a prophet had addressed the daughters of Jerusalem; as priest and advocate He had pleaded with the Father to forgive His murderers; as a loving Saviour He had forgiven the sins of the penitent thief.

As the eyes of Jesus wandered over the multitude about Him, one figure arrested His attention. At the foot of the cross stood His mother, supported by the disciple John. She could not endure to remain away from her Son; and John, knowing that the end was near, had brought her again to the cross. In His dying hour, Christ remembered His mother. Looking into her grief-stricken face and then upon John, He said to her, "Woman, behold thy son!" then to John, "Behold thy mother!" John understood Christ's words, and accepted the trust. He at once took Mary to his home, and from that hour cared for her tenderly. O pitiful, loving Saviour; amid all His physical pain and mental anguish, He had a thoughtful care for His mother! He had no money with which to provide for her comfort; but He was enshrined in the heart of John, and He gave His mother to him as a precious legacy. Thus He provided for her that which she most needed—the tender sympathy of one who loved her because she loved Jesus. And in receiving her as a sacred trust, John was receiving a great blessing. She was a constant reminder of his beloved Master.

The perfect example of Christ's filial love shines forth with undimmed luster from the mist of ages. For nearly thirty years Jesus by His daily toil had helped bear the burdens of the home. And now, even in His last agony, He remembers to provide for His sorrowing, widowed mother. The same spirit will be seen in every disciple of our Lord. Those who follow Christ will feel that it is a part of their religion to respect and provide for their parents. From the heart where His love is cherished, father and mother will never fail of receiving thoughtful care and tender sympathy.

And now the Lord of glory was dying, a ransom for the race. In yielding up His precious life, Christ was not upheld by triumphant joy. All was oppressive gloom. It was not the dread of death that weighed upon Him. It was not the pain and ignominy of the cross that caused His inexpressible agony.

Christ felt the anguish which the sinner will feel when mercy shall no longer plead for the guilty race. It was the sense of sin, bringing the Father's wrath upon Him as man's substitute, that made the cup He drank so bitter, and broke the heart of the Son of God.

Christ was the prince of sufferers; but His suffering was from a sense of the malignity of sin, a knowledge that through familiarity with evil, man had become blinded to its enormity. Christ saw how deep is the hold of sin upon the human heart, how few would be willing to break from its power. He knew that without help from God, humanity must perish, and He saw multitudes perishing within reach of abundant help.

Upon Christ as our substitute and surety was laid the iniquity of us all. He was counted a transgressor, that He might redeem us from the condemnation of the law. The guilt of every descendant of Adam was pressing upon His heart. The wrath of God against sin, the terrible manifestation of His displeasure because of iniquity, filled the soul of His Son with consternation. All His life Christ had been publishing to a fallen world the good news of the Father's mercy and pardoning love. Salvation for the chief of sinners was His theme. But now with the terrible weight of guilt He bears, He cannot see the Father's reconciling face. The withdrawal of the divine countenance from the Saviour in this hour of supreme anguish pierced His heart with a sorrow that can never be fully understood by man. So great was this agony that His physical pain was hardly felt.

Satan with his fierce temptations wrung the heart of Jesus. The Saviour could not see through the portals of the tomb. Hope did not present to Him His coming forth from the grave a conqueror, or tell Him of the Father's acceptance of the sacrifice. He feared that sin was so offensive to God that Their separation was to be eternal. Christ felt the anguish which the sinner will feel when mercy shall no longer plead for the guilty race. It was the sense of sin, bringing the Father's wrath upon Him as man's substitute, that made the cup He drank so bitter, and broke the heart of the Son of God.

With amazement angels witnessed the Saviour's despairing agony. The hosts of heaven veiled their faces from the fearful sight. Inanimate nature expressed sympathy with its insulted and dying Author. The sun refused to look upon the awful scene. Its full, bright rays were illuminating the earth at midday, when suddenly it seemed to be blotted out. Complete darkness, like a funeral pall, enveloped the cross. "There was darkness over all the land unto the ninth hour." There was no eclipse or other natural cause for this darkness, which was as

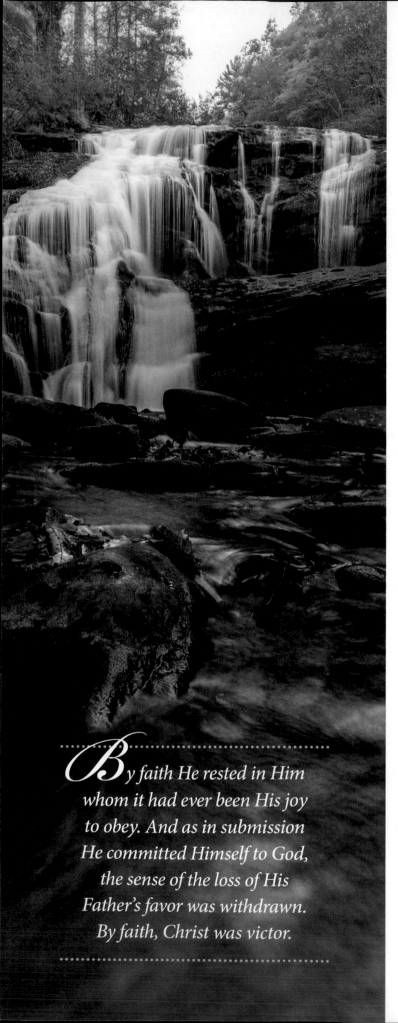

By faith He rested in Him whom it had ever been His joy to obey. And as in submission He committed Himself to God, the sense of the loss of His Father's favor was withdrawn. By faith, Christ was victor.

deep as midnight without moon or stars. It was a miraculous testimony given by God that the faith of after generations might be confirmed.

In that thick darkness God's presence was hidden. He makes darkness His pavilion, and conceals His glory from human eyes. God and His holy angels were beside the cross. The Father was with His Son. Yet His presence was not revealed. Had His glory flashed forth from the cloud, every human beholder would have been destroyed. And in that dreadful hour Christ was not to be comforted with the Father's presence. He trod the wine press alone, and of the people there was none with Him.

In the thick darkness, God veiled the last human agony of His Son. All who had seen Christ in His suffering had been convicted of His divinity. That face, once beheld by humanity, was never forgotten. As the face of Cain expressed his guilt as a murderer, so the face of Christ revealed innocence, serenity, benevolence—the image of God. But His accusers would not give heed to the signet of heaven. Through long hours of agony Christ had been gazed upon by the jeering multitude. Now He was mercifully hidden by the mantle of God.

The silence of the grave seemed to have fallen upon Calvary. A nameless terror held the throng that was gathered about the cross. The cursing and reviling ceased in the midst of half-uttered sentences. Men, women, and children fell prostrate upon the earth. Vivid lightnings occasionally flashed forth from the cloud, and revealed the cross and the crucified Redeemer. Priests, rulers, scribes, executioners, and the mob, all thought that their time of retribution had come. After a while some whispered that Jesus would now come down from the cross. Some attempted to grope their way back to the city, beating their breasts and wailing in fear.

At the ninth hour the darkness lifted from the people, but still enveloped the Saviour. It was a symbol of the agony and horror that weighed upon His heart. No eye could pierce the gloom that surrounded the cross, and none could penetrate the deeper gloom that enshrouded the suffering soul of Christ. The angry lightnings seemed to be hurled at Him as He hung upon the cross. Then "Jesus cried with a loud voice, saying, Eloi, Eloi, lama sabachthani?" "My God, My God, why hast Thou forsaken Me?" As the outer gloom settled about the Saviour, many voices exclaimed: The vengeance of heaven is upon Him. The bolts of God's wrath are hurled at Him, because He claimed to be the Son of God. Many who believed on Him heard His despairing cry. Hope left them. If God had forsaken Jesus, in what could His followers trust?

When the darkness lifted from the oppressed spirit of Christ, He revived to a sense of physical suffering, and said,

"I thirst." One of the Roman soldiers, touched with pity as he looked at the parched lips, took a sponge on a stalk of hyssop, and dipping it in a vessel of vinegar, offered it to Jesus. But the priests mocked at His agony. When darkness covered the earth, they had been filled with fear; as their terror abated, the dread returned that Jesus would yet escape them. His words, "Eloi, Eloi, lama sabachthani?" they had misinterpreted. With bitter contempt and scorn they said, "This man calleth for Elias." The last opportunity to relieve His sufferings they refused. "Let be," they said, "let us see whether Elias will come to save Him."

The spotless Son of God hung upon the cross, His flesh lacerated with stripes; those hands so often reached out in blessing, nailed to the wooden bars; those feet so tireless on ministries of love, spiked to the tree; that royal head pierced by the crown of thorns; those quivering lips shaped to the cry of woe. And all that He endured—the blood drops that flowed from His head, His hands, His feet, the agony that racked His frame, and the unutterable anguish that filled His soul at the hiding of His Father's face—speaks to each child of humanity, declaring, It is for thee that the Son of God consents to bear this burden of guilt; for thee He spoils the domain of death, and opens the gates of Paradise. He who stilled the angry waves and walked the foam-capped billows, who made devils tremble and disease flee, who opened blind eyes and called forth the dead to life—offers Himself upon the cross as a sacrifice, and this from love to thee.

He, the Sin Bearer, endures the wrath of divine justice, and for thy sake becomes sin itself.

In silence the beholders watched for the end of the fearful scene. The sun shone forth; but the cross was still enveloped in darkness. Priests and rulers looked toward Jerusalem; and lo, the dense cloud had settled over the city and the plains of Judea. The Sun of Righteousness, the Light of the world, was withdrawing His beams from the once favored city of Jerusalem. The fierce lightnings of God's wrath were directed against the fated city.

Suddenly the gloom lifted from the cross, and in clear, trumpetlike tones, that seemed to resound throughout creation, Jesus cried, "It is finished." "Father, into Thy hands I commend My spirit." A light encircled the cross, and the face of the Saviour shone with a glory like the sun. He then bowed His head upon His breast, and died.

Amid the awful darkness, apparently forsaken of God, Christ had drained the last dregs in the cup of human woe. In those dreadful hours He had relied upon the evidence of His Father's acceptance heretofore given Him. He was acquainted with the character of His Father; He understood His justice, His mercy, and His great love. By faith He rested in Him whom it had ever been His joy to obey. And as in submission He committed Himself to God, the sense of the loss of His Father's favor was withdrawn. By faith, Christ was victor.

Never before had the earth witnessed such a scene. The multitude stood paralyzed, and with bated breath gazed upon the Saviour. Again darkness settled upon the earth, and a hoarse rumbling, like heavy thunder, was heard. There was a violent earthquake. The people were shaken together in heaps. The wildest confusion and consternation ensued. In the surrounding mountains, rocks were rent asunder, and went crashing down into the plains. Sepulchers were broken open, and the dead were cast out of their tombs. Creation seemed to be shivering to atoms. Priests, rulers, soldiers, executioners, and people, mute with terror, lay prostrate upon the ground.

When the loud cry, "It is finished," came from the lips of Christ, the priests were officiating in the temple. It was the hour of the evening sacrifice. The lamb representing Christ had been brought to be slain. Clothed in his significant and beautiful dress, the priest stood with lifted knife, as did Abraham when he was about to slay his son. With intense interest the people were looking on. But the earth trembles and quakes; for the Lord Himself draws near. With a rending noise the inner veil of the temple is torn from top to bottom by an unseen hand, throwing open to the gaze of the multitude a place once filled with the presence of God. In this place the Shekinah had dwelt. Here God had manifested His glory above the mercy seat. No one but the high priest ever lifted the veil separating this apartment from the rest of the temple. He entered in once a year to make an atonement for the sins of the people. But lo, this veil is rent in twain. The most holy place of the earthly sanctuary is no longer sacred.

All is terror and confusion. The priest is about to slay the victim; but the knife drops from his nerveless hand, and the lamb escapes. Type has met antitype in the death of God's Son. The great sacrifice has been made. The way into the holiest is laid open. A new and living way is prepared for all. No longer need sinful, sorrowing humanity await the coming of the high priest. Henceforth the Saviour was to officiate as priest and advocate in the heaven of heavens. It was as if a living voice had spoken to the worshipers: There is now an end to all sacrifices and offerings for sin. The Son of God is come according to His word, "Lo, I come (in the volume of the Book it is written of Me,) to do Thy will, O God." "By His own blood" He entereth "in once into the holy place, having obtained eternal redemption for us." Hebrews 10:7; 9:12.

When Anna and Susan Warner published the words to "Jesus Loves Me," the sisters had no idea they were bringing a Christian classic to life. In 1860, Susan was writing a Christian novel called *Say and Seal*. Anna penned the simple poem as comforting words for a a dying child in her sister's story. Little did she know that the sweet message would soon comfort millions of people around the globe.

Jesus loves me—this I know,
For the Bible tells me so;
Little ones to him belong,—
They are weak, but he is strong.
Jesus loves me,—he who died
Heaven's gates to open wide;
He will wash away my sin,
Let his little child come in.
Jesus loves me—loves me still,
Though I'm very weak and ill;
From his shining throne on high
Comes to watch me where I lie.
Jesus loves me,—he will stay
Close beside me all the way.
Then his little child will take
Up to heaven for his dear sake.

In 1861, William Batchelder Bradbury, well-known Christian music composer, set the poem to music and added the chorus:

Yes, Jesus loves me!
Yes, Jesus loves me!
Yes, Jesus loves me!
The Bible tells me so.

What else do we know about the sisters who brought this classic to life? Susan was born in 1819 and Anna in 1827 to Henry and Anna Warner, both descendants from prominent Puritan and Pilgrim families. Susan and Anna were raised mostly by their aunt Fanny, who moved in with them after their mother died. During the summers the family would visit Henry's brother, Reverend Thomas Warner, who served as the chaplain at West Point Military Academy. The sisters went on to teach Bible classes for the West Point cadets for over 40 years. They were so well-respected that both sisters were eventually buried in the West Point cemetery. Susan died in 1885 at age 66. Anna lived for 30 more years, and continued to teach the Bible classes until she died at age 88 in 1915.

It Is Finished

············

Christ did not yield up His life till He had accomplished the work which He came to do, and with His parting breath He exclaimed, "It is finished." John 19:30. The battle had been won. His right hand and His holy arm had gotten Him the victory. As a Conqueror He planted His banner on the eternal heights. Was there not joy among the angels? All heaven triumphed in the Saviour's victory. Satan was defeated, and knew that his kingdom was lost.

To the angels and the unfallen worlds the cry, "It is finished," had a deep significance. It was for them as well as for us that the great work of redemption had been accomplished. They with us share the fruits of Christ's victory.

Not until the death of Christ was the character of Satan clearly revealed to the angels or to the unfallen worlds. The archapostate had so clothed himself with deception that even holy beings had not understood his principles. They had not clearly seen the nature of his rebellion.

It was a being of wonderful power and glory that had set himself against God. Of Lucifer the Lord says, "Thou sealest up the sum, full of wisdom, and perfect in beauty." Ezekiel 28:12. Lucifer had been the covering cherub. He had stood in the light of God's presence. He had been the highest of all created beings, and had been foremost in revealing God's purposes to the universe. After he had sinned, his power to deceive was the more deceptive, and the unveiling of his character was the more difficult, because of the exalted position he had held with the Father.

God could have destroyed Satan and his sympathizers as easily as one can cast a pebble to the earth; but He did not do this. Rebellion was not to be overcome by force. Compelling power is found only under Satan's government. The Lord's principles are not of this order. His authority rests upon goodness, mercy, and love; and the presentation of these principles is the means to be used. God's government is moral, and truth and love are to be the prevailing power.

It was God's purpose to place things on an eternal basis of security, and in the councils of heaven it was decided that time must be given for Satan to develop the principles which were the foundation of his system of government. He had claimed that these were superior to God's principles. Time was given for the working of Satan's principles, that they might be seen by the heavenly universe.

Satan led men into sin, and the plan of redemption was put in operation. For four thousand years, Christ was working for man's uplifting, and Satan for his ruin and degradation. And the heavenly universe beheld it all.

When Jesus came into the world, Satan's power was turned against Him. From the time when He appeared as a babe in Bethlehem, the usurper worked to bring about His destruction. In every possible way he sought to prevent Jesus from developing a perfect childhood, a faultless manhood, a holy ministry, and an unblemished sacrifice. But he was defeated. He could not lead Jesus into sin. He could not discourage Him, or drive Him from a work He had come on earth to do. From the desert to Calvary, the storm of Satan's wrath beat upon Him, but the more mercilessly it fell, the more firmly did the Son of God cling to the hand of His Father, and press on in the bloodstained path. All the efforts of Satan to oppress and overcome Him only brought out in a purer light His spotless character.

All heaven and the unfallen worlds had been witnesses to the controversy. With what intense interest did they follow the closing scenes of the conflict. They beheld the Saviour enter the garden of Gethsemane, His soul bowed down with the horror of a great darkness. They heard His bitter cry, "Father, if it be possible, let this cup pass from Me." Matthew 26:39. As the Father's presence was withdrawn, they saw Him sorrowful with a bitterness of sorrow exceeding that of the last great struggle with death. The bloody sweat was forced from His pores, and fell in drops upon the ground. Thrice the prayer for deliverance was wrung from His lips. Heaven could no longer endure the sight, and a messenger of comfort was sent to the Son of God.

Heaven beheld the Victim betrayed into the hands of the murderous mob, and with mockery and violence hurried from one tribunal to another. It heard the sneers of His persecutors because of His lowly birth. It heard the denial with cursing and swearing by one of His best-loved disciples. It saw the frenzied work of Satan, and his power over the hearts of men. Oh, fearful scene! the Saviour seized at midnight in Gethsemane, dragged to and fro from palace to judgment hall, arraigned twice before the priests, twice before the Sanhedrin, twice before Pilate, and once before Herod, mocked, scourged, condemned, and led out to be crucified, bearing the heavy burden of the cross, amid the wailing of the daughters of Jerusalem and the jeering of the rabble.

Heaven viewed with grief and amazement Christ hanging upon the cross, blood flowing from His wounded temples, and sweat tinged with blood standing upon His brow. From His hands and feet the blood fell, drop by drop, upon the rock drilled for the foot of the cross. The wounds made by the nails gaped as the weight of His body dragged upon His hands. His labored breath grew quick and deep, as His soul panted under

Could one sin have been found in Christ, had He in one particular yielded to Satan to escape the terrible torture, the enemy of God and man would have triumphed. Christ bowed His head and died, but He held fast His faith and His submission to God. "And I heard a loud voice saying in heaven, Now is come salvation, and strength, and the kingdom of our God, and the power of His Christ: for the accuser of our brethren is cast down, which accused them before our God day and night." Revelation 12:10.

Satan saw that his disguise was torn away. His administration was laid open before the unfallen angels and before the heavenly universe. He had revealed himself as a murderer. By shedding the blood of the Son of God, he had uprooted himself from the sympathies of the heavenly beings. Henceforth his work was restricted. Whatever attitude he might assume, he could no longer await the angels as they came from the heavenly courts, and before them accuse Christ's brethren of being clothed with the garments of blackness and the defile-

Could one sin have been found in Christ, had He in one particular yielded to Satan to escape the terrible torture, the enemy of God and man would have triumphed. Christ bowed His head and died, but He held fast His faith and His submission to God.

the burden of the sins of the world. All heaven was filled with wonder when the prayer of Christ was offered in the midst of His terrible suffering—"Father, forgive them; for they know not what they do." Luke 23:34. Yet there stood men, formed in the image of God, joining to crush out the life of His only-begotten Son. What a sight for the heavenly universe!

The principalities and powers of darkness were assembled around the cross, casting the hellish shadow of unbelief into the hearts of men. When the Lord created these beings to stand before His throne, they were beautiful and glorious. Their loveliness and holiness were in accordance with their exalted station. They were enriched with the wisdom of God, and girded with the panoply of heaven. They were Jehovah's ministers. But who could recognize in the fallen angels the glorious seraphim that once ministered in the heavenly courts?

Satanic agencies confederated with evil men in leading the people to believe Christ the chief of sinners, and to make Him the object of detestation. Those who mocked Christ as He hung upon the cross were imbued with the spirit of the first great rebel. He filled them with vile and loathsome speeches. He inspired their taunts. But by all this he gained nothing.

ment of sin. The last link of sympathy between Satan and the heavenly world was broken.

Yet Satan was not then destroyed. The angels did not even then understand all that was involved in the great controversy. The principles at stake were to be more fully revealed. And for the sake of man, Satan's existence must be continued. Man as well as angels must see the contrast between the Prince of light and the prince of darkness. He must choose whom he will serve.

In the opening of the great controversy, Satan had declared that the law of God could not be obeyed, that justice was inconsistent with mercy, and that, should the law be broken, it would be impossible for the sinner to be pardoned. Every sin must meet its punishment, urged Satan; and if God should remit the punishment of sin, He would not be a God of truth and justice. When men broke the law of God, and defied His will, Satan exulted. It was proved, he declared, that the law could not be obeyed; man could not be forgiven. Because he, after his rebellion, had been banished from heaven, Satan claimed that the human race must be forever shut out from God's favor. God could not be just, he urged, and yet show mercy to the sinner.

But even as a sinner, man was in a different position from that of Satan. Lucifer in heaven had sinned in the light of God's glory. To him as to no other created being was given a revelation of God's love.

Understanding the character of God, knowing His goodness, Satan chose to follow his own selfish, independent will. This choice was final. There was no more that God could do to save him. But man was deceived; his mind was darkened by Satan's sophistry. The height and depth of the love of God he did not know. For him there was hope in a knowledge of God's love. By beholding His character he might be drawn back to God.

Through Jesus, God's mercy was manifested to men; but mercy does not set aside justice. The law reveals the attributes

The law reveals the attributes of God's character, and not a jot or tittle of it could be changed to meet man in his fallen condition. God did not change His law, but He sacrificed Himself, in Christ, for man's redemption.

of God's character, and not a jot or tittle of it could be changed to meet man in his fallen condition. God did not change His law, but He sacrificed Himself, in Christ, for man's redemption. "God was in Christ, reconciling the world unto Himself." 2 Corinthians 5:19.

The law requires righteousness—a righteous life, a perfect character; and this man has not to give. He cannot meet the claims of God's holy law. But Christ, coming to the earth as man, lived a holy life, and developed a perfect character. These He offers as a free gift to all who will receive them. His life stands for the life of men. Thus they have remission of sins that are past, through the forbearance of God. More than this, Christ imbues men with the attributes of God. He builds up the human character after the similitude of the divine character, a goodly fabric of spiritual strength and beauty. Thus the very righteousness of the law is fulfilled in the believer in Christ. God can "be just, and the justifier of him which believeth in Jesus." Romams 3:26.

God's love has been expressed in His justice no less than in His mercy. Justice is the foundation of His throne, and the fruit of His love. It had been Satan's purpose to divorce mercy from truth and justice. He sought to prove that the righteousness of

God's law is an enemy to peace. But Christ shows that in God's plan they are indissolubly joined together; the one cannot exist without the other. "Mercy and truth are met together; righteousness and peace have kissed each other." Psalm 85:10.

By His life and His death, Christ proved that God's justice did not destroy His mercy, but that sin could be forgiven, and that the law is righteous, and can be perfectly obeyed. Satan's charges were refuted. God had given man unmistakable evidence of His love.

Another deception was now to be brought forward. Satan declared that mercy destroyed justice, that the death of Christ abrogated the Father's law. Had it been possible for the law to be changed or abrogated, then Christ need not have died. But to abrogate the law would be to immortalize transgression, and place the world under Satan's control. It was because the law was changeless, because man could be saved only through obedience to its precepts, that Jesus was lifted up on the cross. Yet the very means by which Christ established the law Satan represented as destroying it. Here will come the last conflict of the great controversy between Christ and Satan.

That the law which was spoken by God's own voice is faulty, that some specification has been set aside, is the claim which Satan now puts forward. It is the last great deception that he will bring upon the world. He needs not to assail the whole law; if he can lead men to disregard one precept, his purpose is gained. For "whosoever shall keep the whole law, and yet offend in one point, he is guilty of all." James 2:10. By consenting to break one precept, men are brought under Satan's power. By substituting human law for God's law, Satan will seek to control the world. This work is foretold in prophecy. Of the great apostate power which is the representative of Satan, it is declared, "He shall speak great words against the Most High, and shall wear out the saints of the Most High, and think to change times and laws: and they shall be given into his hand." Daniel 7:25.

Men will surely set up their laws to counterwork the laws of God. They will seek to compel the consciences of others, and in their zeal to enforce these laws they will oppress their fellow men.

The warfare against God's law, which was begun in heaven, will be continued until the end of time. Every man will be tested. Obedience or disobedience is the question to be decided by the whole world. All will be called to choose between the law of God and the laws of men. Here the dividing line will be drawn. There will be but two classes. Every character will be fully developed; and all will show whether they have chosen the side of loyalty or that of rebellion.

The warfare against God's law, which was begun in heaven, will be continued until the end of time. Every man will be tested. Obedience or disobedience is the question to be decided by the whole world.

Then the end will come. God will vindicate His law and deliver His people. Satan and all who have joined him in rebellion will be cut off. Sin and sinners will perish, root and branch (Malachi 4:1)—Satan the root, and his followers the branches. The word will be fulfilled to the prince of evil, "Because thou hast set thine heart as the heart of God: ... I will destroy thee, O covering cherub, from the midst of the stones of fire. ... Thou shalt be a terror, and never shalt thou be any more." Then "the wicked shall not be: yea, thou shalt diligently consider his place, and it shall not be;" "they shall be as though they had not been." Ezekiel 28:6–19; Psalm 37:10; Obadiah 16.

This is not an act of arbitrary power on the part of God. The rejecters of His mercy reap that which they have sown. God is the fountain of life; and when one chooses the service of sin, he separates from God, and thus cuts himself off from life. He is "alienated from the life of God." Christ says, "All they that hate Me love death." Ephesians 4:18; Proverbs 8:36. God gives them existence for a time that they may develop their character and reveal their principles. This accomplished, they receive the results of their own choice. By a life of rebellion, Satan and all who unite with him place themselves so out of harmony with God that His very presence is to them a consuming fire. The glory of Him who is love will destroy them.

At the beginning of the great controversy, the angels did not understand this. Had Satan and his host then been left to reap the full result of their sin, they would have perished; but it would not have been apparent to heavenly beings that this was the inevitable result of sin. A doubt of God's goodness would have remained in their minds as evil seed, to produce its deadly fruit of sin and woe.

But not so when the great controversy shall be ended. Then, the plan of redemption having been completed, the character of God is revealed to all created intelligences. The precepts of His law are seen to be perfect and immutable. Then sin has made manifest its nature, Satan his character. Then the extermination of sin will vindicate God's love and establish His honor before a universe of beings who delight to do His will, and in whose heart is His law.

Well, then, might the angels rejoice as they looked upon the Saviour's cross; for though they did not then understand all, they knew that the destruction of sin and Satan was forever made certain, that the redemption of man was assured, and that the universe was made eternally secure. Christ Himself fully comprehended the results of the sacrifice made upon Calvary. To all these He looked forward when upon the cross He cried out, "It is finished."

In Joseph's Tomb

. . . .

At last Jesus was at rest. The long day of shame and torture was ended. As the last rays of the setting sun ushered in the Sabbath, the Son of God lay in quietude in Joseph's tomb. His work completed, His hands folded in peace, He rested through the sacred hours of the Sabbath day.

In the beginning the Father and the Son had rested upon the Sabbath after Their work of creation. When "the heavens and the earth were finished, and all the host of them" (Genesis 2:1), the Creator and all heavenly beings rejoiced in contemplation of the glorious scene. "The morning stars sang together, and all the sons of God shouted for joy." Job 38:7. Now Jesus rested from the work of redemption; and though there was grief among those who loved Him on earth, yet there was joy in heaven. Glorious to the eyes of heavenly beings was the promise of the future. A restored creation, a redeemed race, that having conquered sin could never fall—this, the result to flow from Christ's completed work, God and angels saw. With this scene the day upon which Jesus rested is forever linked. For "His work is perfect;" and "whatsoever God doeth, it shall be forever." Deuteronomy 32:4; Ecclesiastes 3:14. When there shall be a "restitution of all things, which God hath spoken by the mouth of all His holy prophets since the world began" (Acts 3:21), the creation Sabbath, the day on which Jesus lay at rest in Joseph's tomb, will still be a day of rest and rejoicing. Heaven and earth will unite in praise, as "from one Sabbath to another" (Isaiah 66:23) the nations of the saved shall bow in joyful worship to God and the Lamb.

In the closing events of the crucifixion day, fresh evidence was given of the fulfillment of prophecy, and new witness borne to Christ's divinity. When the darkness had lifted from the cross, and the Saviour's dying cry had been uttered, immediately another voice was heard, saying, "Truly this was the Son of God." Matthew 27:54.

These words were said in no whispered tones. All eyes were turned to see whence they came. Who had spoken? It was the centurion, the Roman soldier. The divine patience of the Saviour, and His sudden death, with the cry of victory upon His lips, had impressed this heathen. In the bruised, broken body hanging upon the cross, the centurion recognized the form of the Son of God. He could not refrain from confessing his faith. Thus again evidence was given that our Redeemer was to see of the travail of His soul. Upon the very day of His death, three men, differing widely from one another, had declared their faith—he who commanded the Roman guard, he who bore the cross of the Saviour, and he who died upon the cross at His side.

As evening drew on, an unearthly stillness hung over Calvary. The crowd dispersed, and many returned to Jerusalem greatly changed in spirit from what they had been in the morning. Many had flocked to the crucifixion from curiosity, and not from hatred toward Christ. Still they believed the accusations of the priests, and looked upon Christ as a malefactor. Under an unnatural excitement they had united with the mob in railing against Him. But when the earth was wrapped in blackness, and they stood accused by their own consciences, they felt guilty of a great wrong. No jest or mocking laughter was heard in the midst of that fearful gloom; and when it was lifted, they made their way to their homes in solemn silence. They were convinced that the charges of the priests were false, that Jesus was no pretender; and a few weeks later, when Peter preached upon the day of Pentecost, they were among the thousands who became converts to Christ.

But the Jewish leaders were unchanged by the events they had witnessed. Their hatred of Jesus had not abated. The darkness that had mantled the earth at the crucifixion was not more dense than that which still enveloped the minds of the priests and rulers. At His birth the star had known Christ, and had guided the wise men to the manger where He lay. The heavenly hosts had known Him, and had sung His praise over the plains of Bethlehem. The sea had known His voice, and had obeyed His command. Disease and death had recognized His authority, and had yielded to Him their prey. The sun had known Him, and at the sight of His dying anguish, had hidden its face of light. The rocks had known Him, and had shivered into

They dreaded the dead Christ more, far more, than they had ever feared the living Christ. They dreaded to have the attention of the people directed any further to the events attending His crucifixion. They feared the results of that day's work. Not on any account would they have had His body remain on the cross during the Sabbath. The Sabbath was now drawing on, and it would be a violation of its sanctity for the bodies to hang upon the cross. So, using this as a pretext, the leading Jews requested Pilate that the death of the victims might be hastened, and their bodies be removed before the setting of the sun.

Pilate was as unwilling as they for the body of Jesus to remain upon the cross. His consent having been obtained, the legs of the two thieves were broken to hasten their death; but Jesus was found to be already dead. The rude soldiers had been softened by what they had heard and seen of Christ, and they were restrained from breaking His limbs. Thus in the offering of the Lamb of God was fulfilled the law of the Passover, "They shall leave none of it unto the morning, nor break any bone of it: according to all the ordinances of the Passover they shall keep it." Numbers 9:12.

The priests and rulers were amazed to find that Christ was dead. Death by the cross was a lingering process; it was difficult to determine when life had ceased. It was an unheard-of thing for one to die within six hours of crucifixion. The priests wished to make sure of the death of Jesus, and at their suggestion a soldier thrust a spear

That cry, uttered "with a loud voice" … at the moment of death, the stream of blood and water that flowed from His side, declared that He died of a broken heart.

fragments at His cry. Inanimate nature had known Christ, and had borne witness to His divinity. But the priests and rulers of Israel knew not the Son of God.

Yet the priests and rulers were not at rest. They had carried out their purpose in putting Christ to death; but they did not feel the sense of victory they had expected. Even in the hour of their apparent triumph, they were harassed with doubts as to what would next take place. They had heard the cry, "It is finished." "Father, into Thy hands I commend My spirit." John 19:30; Luke 23:46. They had seen the rocks rent, and had felt the mighty earthquake, and they were restless and uneasy.

They had been jealous of Christ's influence with the people when living; they were jealous of Him even in death.

into the Saviour's side. From the wound thus made, there flowed two copious and distinct streams, one of blood, the other of water. This was noted by all the beholders, and John states the occurrence very definitely. He says, "One of the soldiers with a spear pierced His side, and forthwith came there out blood and water. And he that saw it bare record, and his record is true: and he knoweth that he saith true, that ye might believe. For these things were done, that the scripture should be fulfilled, A bone of Him shall not be broken. And again another scripture saith, They shall look on Him whom they pierced." John 19:34–37.

After the resurrection the priests and rulers circulated the report that Christ did not die upon the cross, that He merely fainted, and was afterward revived. Another report affirmed that it was not a real body of flesh and bone, but the likeness of a body, that was laid in the tomb. The action of the Roman soldiers disproves these falsehoods. They broke not His legs, because He was already dead. To satisfy the priests, they pierced His side. Had not life been already extinct, this wound would have caused instant death.

But it was not the spear thrust, it was not the pain of the cross, that caused the death of Jesus. That cry, uttered "with a loud voice" (Matthew 27:50; Luke 23:46), at the moment of death, the stream of blood and water that flowed from His side, declared that He died of a broken heart. His heart was broken by mental anguish. He was slain by the sin of the world.

With the death of Christ the hopes of His disciples perished. They looked upon His closed eyelids and drooping head, His hair matted with blood, His pierced hands and feet, and their anguish was indescribable. Until the last they had not believed that He would die; they could hardly believe that He was really dead. Overwhelmed with sorrow, they did not recall His words foretelling this very scene. Nothing that He had said now gave them comfort. They saw only the cross and its bleeding Victim. The future seemed dark with despair. Their faith in Jesus had perished; but never had they loved their Lord as now. Never before had they so felt His worth, and their need of His presence.

Even in death, Christ's body was very precious to His disciples. They longed to give Him an honored burial, but knew not how to accomplish this. Treason against the Roman government was the crime for which Jesus was condemned, and persons put to death for this offense were consigned to a burial ground especially provided for such criminals. The disciple John with the women from Galilee had remained at the cross. They could not leave the body of their Lord to be handled by the unfeeling soldiers, and buried in a dishonored grave. Yet they could not prevent it. They could obtain no favors from the Jewish authorities, and they had no influence with Pilate.

In this emergency, Joseph of Arimathaea and Nicodemus came to the help of the disciples. Both these men were members of the Sanhedrin, and were acquainted with Pilate. Both were men of wealth and influence. They were determined that the body of Jesus should have an honorable burial.

Joseph went boldly to Pilate, and begged from him the body of Jesus. For the first time, Pilate learned that Jesus was really dead. Conflicting reports had reached him in regard to the events attending the crucifixion, but the knowledge of Christ's death had been purposely kept from him. Pilate had been warned by the priests and rulers against deception by Christ's disciples in regard to His body. Upon hearing Joseph's request, he therefore sent for the centurion who had charge at the cross, and learned for a certainty of the death of Jesus. He also drew from him an account of the scenes of Calvary, confirming the testimony of Joseph.

The request of Joseph was granted. While John was troubled about the burial of his Master, Joseph returned with Pilate's order for the body of Christ; and Nicodemus came bringing a costly mixture of myrrh and aloes, of about a hundred pounds' weight, for His embalming. The most honored in all Jerusalem could not have been shown more respect in death. The disciples were astonished to see these wealthy rulers as much interested as they themselves in the burial of their Lord.

Neither Joseph nor Nicodemus had openly accepted the Saviour while He was living. They knew that such a step would exclude them from the Sanhedrin, and they hoped to protect Him by their influence in its councils. For a time they had seemed to succeed; but the wily priests, seeing their favor to Christ, had thwarted their plans. In their absence Jesus had been condemned and delivered to be crucified. Now that He was dead, they no longer concealed their attachment to Him. While the disciples feared to show themselves openly as His followers, Joseph and Nicodemus came boldly to their aid. The help of these rich and honored men was greatly needed at this time. They could do for their dead Master what it was impossible for the poor disciples to do; and their wealth and influence protected them, in a great measure, from the malice of the priests and rulers.

Gently and reverently they removed with their own hands the body of Jesus from the cross. Their tears of sympathy fell fast as they looked upon His bruised and lacerated form. Joseph owned a new tomb, hewn in a rock. This he was reserving for himself; but it was near Calvary, and he now prepared it for Jesus. The body, together with the spices brought by Nicodemus, was carefully wrapped in a linen sheet, and the Redeemer was borne to the tomb. There the three disciples straightened the mangled limbs, and folded the bruised hands upon the pulseless breast. The Galilean women came to see that all had been done that could be done for the lifeless form of their beloved Teacher. Then they saw the heavy stone rolled against the entrance of the tomb, and the Saviour was left at rest. The women were last at the cross, and last at the tomb of Christ. While the evening shades were gathering, Mary Magdalene and the other Marys lingered about the resting place of their Lord, shedding tears of sorrow over the fate of Him whom they loved. "And they returned, … and rested the Sabbath day according to the commandment." Luke 23:56.

That was a never-to-be-forgotten Sabbath to the sorrowing disciples, and also to the priests, rulers, scribes, and people. At the setting of the sun on the evening of the preparation day the trumpets sounded, signifying that the Sabbath had begun. The Passover was observed as it had been for centuries, while He to whom it pointed had been slain by wicked hands, and lay in Joseph's tomb. On the Sabbath the courts of the temple were filled with worship-

One after another inquired about a strange event that had taken place. Hitherto the most holy place had been sacredly guarded from intrusion. But now it was open to all eyes. The heavy veil of tapestry, made of pure linen, and beautifully wrought with gold, scarlet, and purple, was rent from top to bottom. The place where Jehovah had met with the high priest, to communicate His glory, the place that had been God's sacred audience chamber, lay open to every eye—a place no longer recognized by the Lord. With gloomy presentiments the priests ministered before the altar. The uncovering of the sacred mystery of the most holy place filled them with dread of coming calamity.

Many minds were busy with thoughts started by the

The Passover was observed as it had been for centuries, while He to whom it pointed had been slain by wicked hands, and lay in Joseph's tomb.

ers. The high priest from Golgotha was there, splendidly robed in his sacerdotal garments. White-turbaned priests, full of activity, performed their duties. But some present were not at rest as the blood of bulls and goats was offered for sin. They were not conscious that type had met antitype, that an infinite sacrifice had been made for the sins of the world. They knew not that there was no further value in the performance of the ritual service. But never before had that service been witnessed with such conflicting feelings. The trumpets and musical instruments and the voices of the singers were as loud and clear as usual. But a sense of strangeness pervaded everything.

scenes of Calvary. From the crucifixion to the resurrection many sleepless eyes were constantly searching the prophecies, some to learn the full meaning of the feast they were then celebrating, some to find evidence that Jesus was not what He claimed to be; and others with sorrowful hearts were searching for proofs that He was the true Messiah. Though searching with different objects in view, all were convicted of the same truth—that prophecy had been fulfilled in the events of the past few days, and that the Crucified One was the world's Redeemer. Many who at that time united in the service never again took part in the paschal rites. Many even of the priests were convicted of the true character of Jesus. Their searching of the prophecies had not been in vain, and after His resurrection they acknowledged Him as the Son of God.

Nicodemus, when he saw Jesus lifted up on the cross, remembered His words spoken by night in the Mount of Olives: "As Moses lifted up the serpent in the wilderness, even so must the Son of man be lifted up: that whosoever believeth in Him should not perish, but have eternal life." John 3:14, 15. On that Sabbath, when Christ lay in the grave, Nicodemus had opportunity for reflection. A clearer light now illuminated his mind, and the words which Jesus had spoken to him were no longer mysterious. He felt that he had lost much by not connecting himself with the Saviour during His life. Now he recalled the events of Calvary. The prayer of Christ for His murderers and His answer to the petition of the dying thief spoke to the heart of the learned councilor. Again he looked upon the Saviour in His agony; again he heard that last cry, "It is finished," spoken like the words of a conqueror. Again he beheld the reeling earth, the darkened heavens, the rent veil, the shivered rocks, and his faith was forever established. The very event that destroyed the hopes of the disciples convinced Joseph and Nicodemus of the divinity of Jesus. Their fears were overcome by the courage of a firm and unwavering faith.

Never had Christ attracted the attention of the multitude as now that He was laid in the tomb. According to their practice, the people brought their sick and suffering ones to the temple courts, inquiring, Who can tell us of Jesus of Nazareth? Many had come from far to find Him who had healed the sick and raised the dead. On every side was heard the cry, We want Christ the Healer! Upon this occasion those who were thought to show indications of the leprosy were examined by the priests. Many were forced to hear their husbands, wives, or children pronounced leprous, and doomed to go forth from the shelter of their homes and the care of their friends, to warn off the stranger with the mournful cry, "Unclean, unclean!" The friendly hands of Jesus of Nazareth, that never refused to touch with healing the loathsome leper, were folded on His breast. The lips that had answered his petition with the comforting words, "I will; be thou clean" (Matthew 8:3), were now silent. Many appealed to the chief priests and rulers for sympathy and relief, but in vain. Apparently they were determined to have the living Christ among them again. With persistent earnestness they asked for Him. They would not be turned away. But they were driven from the temple courts, and soldiers were stationed at the gates to keep back the multitude that came with their sick and dying, demanding entrance.

The sufferers who had come to be healed by the Saviour sank under their disappointment. The streets were filled with mourning. The sick were dying for want of the healing touch of Jesus. Physicians were consulted in vain; there was no skill like that of Him who lay in Joseph's tomb.

The mourning cries of the suffering ones brought home to thousands of minds the conviction that a great

The very efforts made to prevent Christ's resurrection are the most convincing arguments in its proof. The greater the number of soldiers placed around the tomb, the stronger would be the testimony that He had risen.

light had gone out of the world. Without Christ, the earth was blackness and darkness. Many whose voices had swelled the cry of "Crucify Him, crucify Him," now realized the calamity that had fallen upon them, and would as eagerly have cried, Give us Jesus! had He still been alive.

When the people learned that Jesus had been put to death by the priests, inquiries were made regarding His death. The particulars of His trial were kept as private as possible; but during the time when He was in the grave, His name was on thousands of lips, and reports of His mock trial, and of the inhumanity of the priests and rulers, were circulated everywhere. By men of intellect these priests and rulers were called upon to explain the prophecies of the Old Testament concerning the Messiah, and while trying to frame some falsehood in reply, they became like men insane. The prophecies that pointed to Christ's sufferings and death they could not explain, and many inquirers were convinced that the Scriptures had been fulfilled.

The revenge which the priests had thought would be so sweet was already bitterness to them. They knew that they were meeting the severe censure of the people; they knew that the very ones whom they had influenced against Jesus were now horrified by their own shameful work. These priests had tried to believe Jesus a deceiver; but it was in vain. Some of them had stood by the grave of Lazarus, and had seen the dead brought back to life. They trembled for fear that Christ would Himself rise from the dead, and again appear before them. They had heard Him declare that He had power to lay down His life and to take it again. They remembered that He had said, "Destroy this temple, and in three days I will raise it up." John 2:19. Judas had told them the words spoken by Jesus to the disciples while on the last journey to Jerusalem: "Behold, we go up to Jerusalem; and the Son of man shall be betrayed unto the chief priests and unto the scribes, and they shall condemn Him to death, and shall deliver Him to the Gentiles to mock, and to scourge, and to crucify Him: and the third day He shall rise again." Matthew 20:18, 19. When they heard these words, they had mocked and ridiculed. But now they remembered that Christ's predictions had so far been fulfilled. He had said that He would rise again the third day, and who could say that this also would not come to pass? They longed to shut out these thoughts, but they could not. Like their father, the devil, they believed and trembled.

Now that the frenzy of excitement was past, the image of Christ would intrude upon their minds. They beheld Him as He stood serene and uncomplaining before His enemies, suffering without a murmur their taunts and abuse. All the events of His trial and crucifixion came back to them with an overpowering conviction that He was the Son of God. They felt that He might at any time stand before them, the accused to become the accuser, the condemned to condemn, the slain to demand justice in the death of His murderers.

They could rest little upon the Sabbath. Though they would not step over a Gentile's threshold for fear of defilement, yet they held a council concerning the body of Christ. Death and the grave must hold Him whom they had crucified. "The chief priests and Pharisees came together unto Pilate, saying, Sir, we remember that that deceiver said, while He was yet alive, After three days I will rise again. Command therefore that the sepulcher be made sure until the third day, lest His disciples come by night, and steal Him away, and say unto the people, He is risen from the dead: so the last error shall be worse than the first. Pilate said unto them, Ye have a watch: go your way, make it as sure as ye can." Matthew 27:62–65.

The priests gave directions for securing the sepulcher. A great stone had been placed before the opening. Across this stone they placed cords, securing the ends to the solid rock, and sealing them with the Roman seal. The stone could not be moved without breaking the seal. A guard of one hundred soldiers was then stationed around the sepulcher to prevent it from being tampered with. The priests did all they could to keep Christ's body where it had been laid. He was sealed as securely in His tomb as if He were to remain there through all time.

So weak men counseled and planned. Little did these murderers realize the uselessness of their efforts. But by their action God was glorified. The very efforts made to prevent Christ's resurrection are the most convincing arguments in its proof. The greater the number of soldiers placed around the tomb, the stronger would be the testimony that He had risen. Hundreds of years before the death of Christ, the Holy Spirit had declared through the psalmist, "Why do the heathen rage, and the people imagine a vain thing? The kings of the earth set themselves, and the rulers take counsel together, against the Lord, and against His anointed. … He that sitteth in the heavens shall laugh: the Lord shall have them in derision." Psalm 2:1–4. Roman guards and Roman arms were powerless to confine the Lord of life within the tomb. The hour of His release was near.

The Lord Is Risen

This chapter is based on Matthew 28:2–4, 11–15.

....

The night of the first day of the week had worn slowly away. The darkest hour, just before daybreak, had come. Christ was still a prisoner in His narrow tomb. The great stone was in its place; the Roman seal was unbroken; the Roman guards were keeping their watch. And there were unseen watchers. Hosts of evil angels were gathered about the place. Had it been possible, the prince of darkness with his apostate army would have kept forever sealed the tomb that held the Son of God. But a heavenly host surrounded the sepulcher. Angels that excel in strength were guarding the tomb, and waiting to welcome the Prince of life.

"And, behold, there was a great earthquake: for the angel of the Lord descended from heaven." Clothed with the panoply of God, this angel left the heavenly courts. The bright beams of God's glory went before him, and illuminated his pathway. "His countenance was like lightning, and his raiment white as snow: and for fear of him the keepers did shake, and became as dead men."

Now, priests and rulers, where is the power of your guard? Brave soldiers that have never been afraid of human power are now as captives taken without sword or spear. The face they look upon is not the face of mortal warrior; it is the face of the mightiest of the Lord's host. This messenger is he who fills the position from which Satan fell. It is he who on the hills of Bethlehem proclaimed Christ's birth. The earth trembles at his approach, the hosts of darkness flee, and as he rolls away the stone, heaven seems to come down to the earth. The soldiers see him removing the stone as he would a pebble, and hear him cry, Son of God, come forth; Thy Father calls Thee. They see Jesus come forth from the grave, and hear Him proclaim over the rent sepulcher, "I am the resurrection, and the life." As He comes forth in majesty and glory, the angel host bow low in adoration before the Redeemer, and welcome Him with songs of praise.

An earthquake marked the hour when Christ laid down His life, and another earthquake witnessed the moment when He took it up in triumph. He who had vanquished death and the grave came forth from the tomb with the tread of a conqueror, amid the reeling of the earth, the flashing of lightning, and the roaring of thunder. When He shall come to the earth again, He will shake "not the earth only, but also heaven." "The earth shall reel to and fro like a drunkard, and shall be removed like a cottage." "The heavens shall be rolled together as a scroll;" "the elements shall melt with fervent heat, the earth also and the works that are therein shall be burned up." But "the Lord will be the hope of His people, and the strength of the children of Israel." Hebrews 12:26; Isaiah 24:20; 34:4; 2 Peter 3:10; Joel 3:16.

At the death of Jesus the soldiers had beheld the earth wrapped in darkness at midday; but at the resurrection they saw the brightness of the angels illuminate the night, and heard the inhabitants of heaven singing with great joy and triumph: Thou hast vanquished Satan and the powers of darkness; Thou hast swallowed up death in victory!

Christ came forth from the tomb glorified, and the Roman guard beheld Him. Their eyes were riveted upon the face of Him whom they had so recently mocked and derided. In this glorified Being they beheld the prisoner whom they had seen in the judgment hall, the one for whom they had plaited a crown of thorns. This was the One who had stood unresisting before Pilate and Herod, His form lacerated by the cruel scourge. This was He who had been nailed to the cross, at whom the priests and rulers, full of self-satisfaction, had wagged their heads, saying, "He saved others; Himself He cannot save." Matthew 27:42. This was He who had been laid in Joseph's new tomb. The decree of heaven had loosed the captive. Mountains piled upon mountains over His sepulcher could not have prevented Him from coming forth.

At sight of the angels and the glorified Saviour the Roman guard had fainted and become as dead men. When the heavenly train was hidden from their view, they arose to their feet, and as quickly as their trembling limbs could carry them, made their way to the gate of the garden. Staggering like drunken men, they hurried on to the city, telling those whom they met the wonderful news. They were making their way to Pilate, but their report had been carried to the Jewish authorities, and the chief priests and rulers sent for them to be brought first into their presence. A strange appearance those soldiers presented. Trembling with fear, their faces colorless, they bore testimony to the resurrection of Christ. The soldiers told all, just as they had seen it; they had not had time to think or speak anything but the truth. With painful utterance they said, It was the Son of God who was crucified; we have heard an angel proclaiming Him as the Majesty of heaven, the King of glory.

The faces of the priests were as those of the dead. Caiaphas tried to speak. His lips moved, but they uttered no sound. The soldiers were about to leave the council room, when a voice stayed them. Caiaphas had at last found speech. Wait, wait, he said. Tell no one the things you have seen.

> *He who had vanquished death and the grave came forth from the tomb with the tread of a conqueror, amid the reeling of the earth, the flashing of lightning, and the roaring of thunder.*

A lying report was then given to the soldiers. "Say ye," said the priests, "His disciples came by night, and stole Him away while we slept." Here the priests overreached themselves. How could the soldiers say that the disciples had stolen the body while they slept? If they were asleep, how could they know? And if the disciples had been proved guilty of stealing Christ's body, would not the priests have been first to condemn them? Or if the sentinels had slept at the tomb, would not the priests have been foremost in accusing them to Pilate?

The soldiers were horrified at the thought of bringing upon themselves the charge of sleeping at their post. This was an offense punishable with death. Should they bear false witness, deceiving the people, and placing their own lives in peril? Had they not kept their weary watch with sleepless vigilance? How could they stand the trial, even for the sake of money, if they perjured themselves?

In order to silence the testimony they feared, the priests promised to secure the safety of the guard, saying that Pilate would not desire to have such a report circulated any more than they did. The Roman soldiers sold their integrity to the Jews for money. They came in before the priests burdened with a most startling message of truth; they went out with a burden of money, and on their tongues a lying report which had been framed for them by the priests.

Meanwhile the report of Christ's resurrection had been carried to Pilate. Though Pilate was responsible for having given Christ up to die, he had been comparatively unconcerned. While he had condemned the Saviour unwillingly, and with a feeling of pity, he had felt no real compunction until now. In terror he now shut himself within his house, determined to see no one. But the priests made their way into his presence, told the story which they had invented, and urged him to overlook the sentinels' neglect of duty. Before consenting to this, he himself privately questioned the guard. They, fearing for their own safety, dared not conceal anything, and Pilate drew from them an account of all that had taken place. He did not prosecute the matter further, but from that time there was no peace for him.

When Jesus was laid in the grave, Satan triumphed. He dared to hope that the Saviour would not take up His life again. He claimed the Lord's body, and set his guard about the tomb, seeking to hold Christ a prisoner. He was bitterly angry when his angels fled at the approach of the heavenly messenger. When he saw Christ come forth in triumph, he knew that his kingdom would have an end, and that he must finally die.

The priests, in putting Christ to death, had made themselves the tools of Satan. Now they were entirely in his power. They were entangled in a snare from which they saw no escape but in continuing their warfare against Christ. When they heard the report of His resurrection, they feared the wrath of the people. They felt that their own lives were in danger. The only hope for them was to prove Christ an impostor by denying that He had risen. They bribed the soldiers, and secured Pilate's silence. They spread their lying reports far and near. But there were witnesses whom they could not silence. Many had heard of the soldiers' testimony to Christ's resurrection. And certain of the dead who came forth with Christ appeared to many, and declared that He had risen. Reports were brought to the priests of persons who had seen these risen ones, and heard their testimony. The priests and rulers were in continual dread, lest in walking the streets, or within the privacy of their own homes, they should come face to face with Christ. They felt that there was no safety for them. Bolts and bars were but poor protection against the

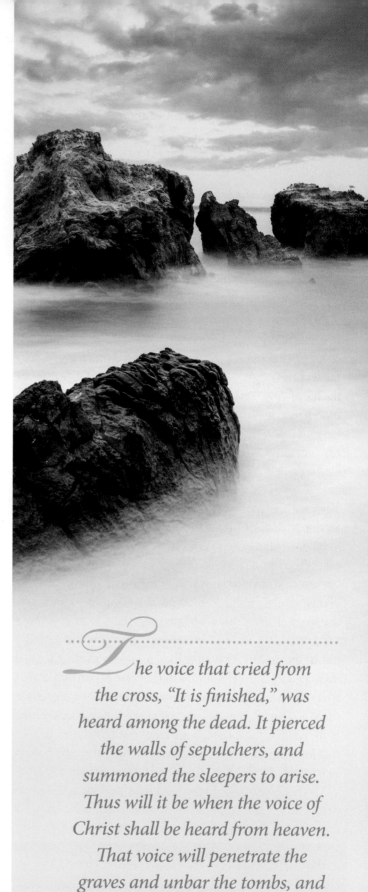

The voice that cried from the cross, "It is finished," was heard among the dead. It pierced the walls of sepulchers, and summoned the sleepers to arise. Thus will it be when the voice of Christ shall be heard from heaven. That voice will penetrate the graves and unbar the tombs, and the dead in Christ shall arise.

Son of God. By day and by night that awful scene in the judgment hall, when they had cried, "His blood be on us, and on our children," was before them. Matthew 27:25. Nevermore would the memory of that scene fade from their minds. Nevermore would peaceful sleep come to their pillows.

When the voice of the mighty angel was heard at Christ's tomb, saying, Thy Father calls Thee, the Saviour came forth from the grave by the life that was in Himself. Now was proved the truth of His words, "I lay down My life, that I might take it again. … I have power to lay it down, and I have power to take it again." Now was fulfilled the prophecy He had spoken to the priests and rulers, "Destroy this temple, and in three days I will raise it up." John 10:17, 18; 2:19.

Over the rent sepulcher of Joseph, Christ had proclaimed in triumph, "I am the resurrection, and the life." These words could be spoken only by the Deity. All created beings live by the will and power of God. They are dependent recipients of the life of God. From the highest seraph to the humblest animate being, all are replenished from the Source of life. Only He who is one with God could say, I have power to lay down My life, and I have power to take it again. In His divinity, Christ possessed the power to break the bonds of death.

Christ arose from the dead as the first fruits of those that slept. He was the antitype of the wave sheaf, and His resurrection took place on the very day when the wave sheaf was to be presented before the Lord. For more than a thousand years this symbolic ceremony had been performed. From the harvest fields the first heads of ripened grain were gathered, and when the people went up to Jerusalem to the Passover, the sheaf of first fruits was waved as a thank offering before the Lord. Not until this was presented could the sickle be put to the grain, and it be gathered into sheaves. The sheaf dedicated to God represented the harvest. So Christ the first fruits represented the great spiritual harvest to be gathered for the kingdom of God. His resurrection is the type and pledge of the resurrection of all the righteous dead. "For if we believe that Jesus died and rose again, even so them also which sleep in Jesus will God bring with Him." 1 Thessalonians 4:14.

As Christ arose, He brought from the grave a multitude of captives. The earthquake at His death had rent open their graves, and when He arose, they came forth with Him. They were those who had been co-laborers with God, and who at the cost of their lives had borne testimony to the truth. Now they were to be witnesses for Him who had raised them from the dead.

During His ministry, Jesus had raised the dead to life. He had raised the son of the widow of Nain, and the ruler's daughter and Lazarus. But these were not clothed with immortality. After they were raised, they were still subject to death. But those who came forth from the grave at Christ's resurrection were raised to everlasting life. They ascended with Him as trophies of His victory over death and the grave. These, said Christ, are no longer the captives of Satan; I have redeemed them. I have brought them from the grave as the first fruits of My power, to be with Me where I am, nevermore to see death or experience sorrow.

These went into the city, and appeared unto many, declaring, Christ has risen from the dead, and we be risen with Him. Thus was immortalized the sacred truth of the resurrection. The risen saints bore witness to the truth of the words, "Thy dead men shall live, together with My dead body shall they arise." Their resurrection was an illustration of the fulfillment of the prophecy, "Awake and sing, ye that dwell in dust: for thy dew is as the dew of herbs, and the earth shall cast out the dead." Isaiah 26:19.

To the believer, Christ is the resurrection and the life. In our Saviour the life that was lost through sin is restored; for He has life in Himself to quicken whom He will. He is invested with the right to give immortality. The life that He laid down in humanity, He takes up again, and gives to humanity. "I am come," He said, "that they might have life, and that they might have it more abundantly." "Whosoever drinketh of the water that I shall give him shall never thirst; but the water that I shall give him shall be in him a well of water springing up into everlasting life." "Whoso eateth My flesh, and drinketh My blood, hath eternal life; and I will raise him up at the last day." John 10:10; 4:14; 6:54.

To the believer, death is but a small matter. Christ speaks of it as if it were of little moment. "If a man keep My saying, he shall never see death," "he shall never taste of death." To the Christian, death is but a sleep, a moment of silence and darkness. The life is hid with Christ in God, and "when Christ, who is our life, shall appear, then shall ye also appear with Him in glory." John 8:51, 52; Colossians 3:4.

The voice that cried from the cross, "It is finished," was heard among the dead. It pierced the walls of sepulchers, and summoned the sleepers to arise. Thus will it be when the voice of Christ shall be heard from heaven. That voice will penetrate the graves and unbar the tombs, and the dead in Christ shall arise. At the Saviour's resurrection a few graves were opened, but at His second coming all the precious dead shall hear His voice, and shall come forth to glorious, immortal life. The same power that raised Christ from the dead will raise His church, and glorify it with Him, above all principalities, above all powers, above every name that is named, not only in this world, but also in the world to come.

Right on Time!

He wrote no music, yet famous composers like Haydn and Handel, Beethoven and Bach wrote their greatest symphonies about Him. He wrote no poetry, yet He inspired Dante, Milton, and scores of others. He created no art, yet Raphael, Michelangelo, and many others made Him the center of their masterpieces. He was no architect, yet some of the greatest architectural wonders of the world were built in His name. Who was this man?

Jesus.

THE CLAIM

While Jesus may not have been a musician, poet, or architect, He did claim to be the Son of God (Luke 22:70, John 10:33). He claimed to have power to forgive sins (Luke 5:20), and said He was the Savior of the world (John 3:16). Was Jesus the man He claimed to be?

One of the strongest evidences of Jesus' claim is a prophecy written in the book of Daniel. Written in 538 B.C., this prophecy pointed to a Messiah who would be the Savior of the world. The prophecy foretold the very year the Messiah would be anointed and the very year He would die. Did Jesus fulfill this prophecy?

THE COMMAND

The prophetic timeline begins with the commandment to restore and rebuild Jerusalem. The angel Gabriel tells Daniel that from the "going forth of the command to restore and build Jerusalem" until the Messiah came, there would be exactly 69 weeks (Daniel 9:25). To discover if Jesus fits the prophecy, we must answer two important questions. First, during what year in history was this command given? Second, did Jesus really appear as the Messiah or "Anointed One" 69 weeks later? Let's consider the first.

While there were several different commands to rebuild the temple at Jerusalem, only one command included the city of Jerusalem in the rebuilding. Ezra 7:7–13 tells the story, including that this command was given in the 7th year of King Artaxerxes' reign. History places that year as 457 B.C.

THE COMING

Now, the second question needs an answer. Did the Messiah show up 69 weeks after the 457 B.C. date? If these weeks are literal, 7-day weeks, the answer is no. No Messiah appeared a year and a half later. However, the Bible tells us that a day equals a year in Bible prophecy (Ezekiel 4:6; Numbers 14:34). 69 weeks is 483 days. If we apply the Biblical principle of a day equalling a year, the result is 483 years. The Messiah should appear 483 years after the command to restore Jerusalem in 457 B.C. With no zero year between B.C. and A.D. dates, the math brings us to 27 A.D. Did Jesus show up in 27 A.D.?

The gospel of Luke tells us that Jesus was baptized by John the Baptist in the 15th year of Tiberius Caesars' reign (Luke 3:1–22). When Jesus emerged from the water, "the Holy Spirit descended in bodily form like a dove upon Him." In the book of Acts, Luke clarifies that "God anointed Jesus of Nazareth with the Holy Spirit" (Acts 10:37–38). Since Messiah simply means "Anointed One," this anointing of the Holy Spirit at Jesus' baptism was God's way of announcing the Messiah's arrival! But what year did this anointing occur? Was it on time according to Daniel's prophecy? History informs us that Tiberius Caesar's reign began in 12 A.D., which makes the 15th year of his reign 27 A.D. Yes, Jesus came exactly on time!

But there's more. Daniel also prophesies that this same Messiah would be "cut off" just 3 ½ years later (Daniel 9:26–27). Sure enough, Jesus died exactly 3 ½ years after His baptism, in the year 31 A.D. Sadly, the Bible says, "He came to His own, and His own did not receive Him" (John 1:11). The very ones He came to save rejected Him. The words of Daniel came to pass as predicted. Jesus began His ministry on time, and He ended His ministry on time. Jesus is the Messiah of prophecy!

THE CALL

Jesus' legacy changed the world! No other person has made as great an impact as He did. Yet while Jesus may have impacted musicians, poets, artists, and even architects, the most important question is this: Has Jesus impacted your life? Have you allowed Him to be your Savior? Will you invite the Prince of Peace into your heart, right now?

To My Father, and Your Father

This chapter is based on Luke 24:50–53; Acts 1:9–12.

. . . .

The time had come for Christ to ascend to His Father's throne. As a divine conqueror He was about to return with the trophies of victory to the heavenly courts. Before His death He had declared to His Father, "I have finished the work which Thou gavest Me to do." John 17:4. After His resurrection He tarried on earth for a season, that His disciples might become familiar with Him in His risen and glorified body. Now He was ready for the leave-taking. He had authenticated the fact that He was a living Saviour. His disciples need no longer associate Him with the tomb. They could think of Him as glorified before the heavenly universe.

As the place of His ascension, Jesus chose the spot so often hallowed by His presence while He dwelt among men. Not Mount Zion, the place of David's city, not Mount Moriah, the temple site, was to be thus honored. There Christ had been mocked and rejected. There the waves of mercy, still returning in a stronger tide of love, had been beaten back by hearts as hard as rock. Thence Jesus, weary and heart-burdened, had gone forth to find rest in the Mount of Olives. The holy Shekinah, in departing from the first temple, had stood upon the eastern mountain, as if loath to forsake the chosen city; so Christ stood upon Olivet, with yearning heart overlooking Jerusalem. The groves and glens of the mountain had been consecrated by His prayers and tears. Its steeps had echoed the triumphant shouts of the multitude that proclaimed Him king. On its sloping descent He had found a home with Lazarus at Bethany. In the garden of Gethsemane at its foot He had prayed and agonized alone. From this mountain He was to ascend to heaven. Upon its summit His feet will rest when He shall come again. Not as a man of sorrows, but as a glorious and triumphant king He will stand upon Olivet, while Hebrew hallelujahs mingle with Gentile hosannas, and the voices of the redeemed as a mighty host shall swell the acclamation, "Crown Him Lord of all!"

Now with the eleven disciples Jesus made His way toward the mountain. As they passed through the gate of Jerusalem, many wondering eyes looked upon the little company, led by One whom a few weeks before the rulers had condemned and crucified. The disciples knew not that this was to be their last interview with their Master. Jesus spent the time in conversation with them, repeating His former instruction. As they approached Gethsemane, He paused, that they might call to mind the lessons He had given them on the night of His great agony. Again He looked upon the vine by which He had then represented the union of His church with Himself and His Father; again He repeated the truths He had then unfolded. All around Him were reminders of His unrequited love. Even the disciples who were so dear to His heart, had, in the hour of His humiliation, reproached and forsaken Him.

Christ had sojourned in the world for thirty-three years; He had endured its scorn, insult, and mockery; He had been rejected and crucified. Now, when about to ascend to His throne of glory—as He reviews the ingratitude of the people He came to save—will He not withdraw from them His sympathy and love? Will not His affections be centered upon that realm where He is appreciated, and where sinless angels wait to do His bidding? No; His promise to those loved ones whom He leaves on earth is, "I am with you alway, even unto the end of the world." Matthew 28:20.

Upon reaching the Mount of Olives, Jesus led the way across the summit, to the vicinity of Bethany. Here He paused, and the disciples gathered about Him. Beams of light seemed to radiate from His countenance as He looked lovingly upon them. He upbraided them not for their faults and failures; words of the deepest tenderness were the last that fell upon their ears from the lips of their Lord. With hands outstretched in blessing, and as if in assurance of His protecting care, He slowly ascended from among them, drawn heavenward by a power stronger than any earthly attraction. As He passed upward, the awe-stricken disciples looked with straining eyes for the last glimpse of their ascending Lord. A cloud of glory hid Him from their sight; and the words came back to them as the cloudy chariot of angels received Him,

From this mountain He was to ascend to heaven. Upon its summit His feet will rest when He shall come again. Not as a man of sorrows, but as a glorious and triumphant king He will stand upon Olivet, while Hebrew hallelujahs mingle with Gentile hosannas, and the voices of the redeemed as a mighty host shall swell the acclamation, "Crown Him Lord of all!"

"Lo, I am with you alway, even unto the end of the world." At the same time there floated down to them the sweetest and most joyous music from the angel choir.

While the disciples were still gazing upward, voices addressed them which sounded like richest music. They turned, and saw two angels in the form of men, who spoke to them, saying, "Ye men of Galilee, why stand ye gazing up into heaven? this same Jesus, which is taken up from you into heaven, shall so come in like manner as ye have seen Him go into heaven."

These angels were of the company that had been waiting in a shining cloud to escort Jesus to His heavenly home. The most exalted of the angel throng, they were the two who had come to the tomb at Christ's resurrection, and they had been with Him throughout His life on earth. With eager desire all heaven had waited for the end of His tarrying in a world

and the dead in Christ shall rise." "The Son of man shall come in His glory, and all the holy angels with Him, then shall He sit upon the throne of His glory." Revelation 1:7; 1 Thessalonians 4:16; Matthew 25:31. Thus will be fulfilled the Lord's own promise to His disciples: "If I go and prepare a place for you, I will come again, and receive you unto Myself; that where I am, there ye may be also." John 14:3. Well might the disciples rejoice in the hope of their Lord's return.

When the disciples went back to Jerusalem, the people looked upon them with amazement. After the trial and crucifixion of Christ, it had been thought that they would appear downcast and ashamed. Their enemies expected to see upon their faces an expression of sorrow and defeat. Instead of this there was only gladness and triumph. Their faces were aglow with a happiness not born of earth. They did not mourn over disappointed hopes, but were full of praise and thanksgiv-

Before the foundations of the earth were laid, the Father and the Son had united in a covenant to redeem man if he should be overcome by Satan. They had clasped Their hands in a solemn pledge that Christ should become the surety for the human race. This pledge Christ has fulfilled. … Now He declares: Father, it is finished. I have done Thy will, O My God. I have completed the work of redemption. If Thy justice is satisfied, "I will that they also, whom Thou hast given Me, be with Me where I am."

marred by the curse of sin. The time had now come for the heavenly universe to receive their King. Did not the two angels long to join the throng that welcomed Jesus? But in sympathy and love for those whom He had left, they waited to give them comfort. "Are they not all ministering spirits, sent forth to minister for them who shall be heirs of salvation?" Hebrews 1:14.

Christ had ascended to heaven in the form of humanity. The disciples had beheld the cloud receive Him. The same Jesus who had walked and talked and prayed with them; who had broken bread with them; who had been with them in their boats on the lake; and who had that very day toiled with them up the ascent of Olivet—the same Jesus had now gone to share His Father's throne. And the angels had assured them that the very One whom they had seen go up into heaven, would come again even as He had ascended. He will come "with clouds; and every eye shall see Him." "The Lord Himself shall descend from heaven with a shout, with the voice of the Archangel, and with the trump of God:

ing to God. With rejoicing they told the wonderful story of Christ's resurrection and His ascension to heaven, and their testimony was received by many.

The disciples no longer had any distrust of the future. They knew that Jesus was in heaven, and that His sympathies were with them still. They knew that they had a friend at the throne of God, and they were eager to present their requests to the Father in the name of Jesus. In solemn awe they bowed in prayer, repeating the assurance, "Whatsoever ye shall ask the Father in My name, He will give it you. Hitherto have ye asked nothing in My name: ask, and ye shall receive, that your joy may be full." John 16:23, 24. They extended the hand of faith higher and higher, with the mighty argument, "It is Christ that died, yea rather, that is risen again, who is even at the right hand of God, who also maketh intercession for us." Romans 8:34. And Pentecost brought them fullness of joy in the presence of the Comforter, even as Christ had promised.

All heaven was waiting to welcome the Saviour to the celestial courts. As He ascended, He led the way, and the multitude of captives set free at His resurrection followed. The heavenly host, with shouts and acclamations of praise and celestial song, attended the joyous train.

As they drew near to the city of God, the challenge is given by the escorting angels—

"Lift up your heads, O ye gates;
And be ye lift up, ye everlasting doors;
And the King of glory shall come in."

Joyfully the waiting sentinels respond—

"Who is this King of glory?"

This they say, not because they know not who He is, but because they would hear the answer of exalted praise—

"The Lord strong and mighty,
The Lord mighty in battle!
Lift up your heads, O ye gates;
Even lift them up, ye everlasting doors;
And the King of glory shall come in."

Again is heard the challenge, "Who is this King of glory?" for the angels never weary of hearing His name exalted. The escorting angels make reply—

"The Lord of hosts;
He is the King of glory." Psalm 24:7–10.

Then the portals of the city of God are opened wide, and the angelic throng sweep through the gates amid a burst of rapturous music.

There is the throne, and around it the rainbow of promise. There are cherubim and seraphim. The commanders of the angel hosts, the sons of God, the representatives of the unfallen worlds, are assembled. The heavenly council before which Lucifer had accused God and His Son, the representatives of those sinless realms over which Satan had thought to establish his dominion—all are there to welcome the Redeemer. They are eager to celebrate His triumph and to glorify their King.

But He waves them back. Not yet; He cannot now receive the coronet of glory and the royal robe. He enters into the presence of His Father. He points to His wounded head, the pierced side, the marred feet; He lifts His hands, bearing the print of nails. He points to the tokens of His triumph; He presents to God the wave sheaf, those raised with Him as representatives of that great multitude who shall come forth from the grave at His second coming. He approaches the Father, with whom there is joy over one sinner that repents; who rejoices over one with singing. Before the foundations of the earth were laid, the Father and the Son had united in a covenant to redeem man if he should be overcome by Satan. They had clasped Their hands in a solemn pledge that Christ should become the surety for the human race. This pledge Christ has fulfilled. When upon the cross He cried out, "It is finished," He addressed the Father. The compact had been fully carried out. Now He declares: Father, it is finished. I have done Thy will, O My God. I have completed the work of redemption. If Thy justice is satisfied, "I will that they also, whom Thou hast given Me, be with Me where I am." John 19:30; 17:24.

The voice of God is heard proclaiming that justice is satisfied. Satan is vanquished. Christ's toiling, struggling ones on earth are "accepted in the Beloved." Ephesians 1:6. Before the heavenly angels and the representatives of unfallen worlds, they are declared justified. Where He is, there His church shall be. "Mercy and truth are met together; righteousness and peace have kissed each other." Psalm 85:10. The Father's arms encircle His Son, and the word is given, "Let all the angels of God worship Him." Hebrews 1:6.

With joy unutterable, rulers and principalities and powers acknowledge the supremacy of the Prince of life. The angel host prostrate themselves before Him, while the glad shout fills all the courts of heaven, "Worthy is the Lamb that was slain to receive power, and riches, and wisdom, and strength, and honor, and glory, and blessing." Revelation 5:12.

Songs of triumph mingle with the music from angel harps, till heaven seems to overflow with joy and praise. Love has conquered. The lost is found. Heaven rings with voices in lofty strains proclaiming, "Blessing, and honor, and glory, and power, be unto Him that sitteth upon the throne, and unto the Lamb forever and ever." Revelation 5:13.

From that scene of heavenly joy, there comes back to us on earth the echo of Christ's own wonderful words, "I ascend unto My Father, and your Father; and to My God, and your God." John 20:17. The family of heaven and the family of earth are one. For us our Lord ascended, and for us He lives. "Wherefore He is able also to save them to the uttermost that come unto God by Him, seeing He ever liveth to make intercession for them." Hebrews 7:25.